THE PHILOSOPHY
OF LUDWIG FEUERBACH

EUGENE KAMENKA

The Philosophy of
Ludwig Feuerbach

PRAEGER PUBLISHERS

New York · Washington

BOOKS THAT MATTER

Published in the United States of America in 1970
by Praeger Publishers Inc.
111 Fourth Avenue, New York, N.Y. 10003

© *1969, in London, England, by Eugene Kamenka*

Library of Congress Catalog Card Number: 79-97183

Printed in Great Britain

CONTENTS

Preface and Acknowledgments   vii
Bibliographical Note   xiii

PART I: THE TIMES, THE MAN AND THE WORK

1   The Promethean background   3
2   The man and his work   15

PART II: THE CRITICAL PHILOSOPHY

3   Ludwig Feuerbach's critique of religion   35
4   Ludwig Feuerbach's critique of philosophy   69

PART III: THE 'PHILOSOPHY OF THE FUTURE'

5   Feuerbach's 'Transformation of Philosophy'   83
6   Feuerbach's method   92
7   Feuerbach's theory of knowledge and his 'materialism'   98
8   Feuerbach's concept of man   114
9   Feuerbach's ethics   124

POSTSCRIPT

10   In place of a conclusion   149

Notes   153
Bibliography   176
Index   184

PREFACE AND ACKNOWLEDGMENTS

A little more than 120 years ago, Ludwig Feuerbach was the talk of Europe. To the young radicals of Germany, including Karl Marx and Friedrich Engels, he was the man who had overcome the Hegelian system, who had restored man's alienated essence to man, who had pointed the way to true social and political liberation through the doctrine that man was the highest being for man. In St Petersburg, the members of the Petrashevskii circle excitedly discussed his (forbidden) ideas; in London, in the early 1850s, Mary Ann Evans (George Eliot) translated the second edition of his *Essence of Christianity*: in France, a decade later, the French Feuerbachian Eduard Vaillant was urging the elderly Proudhon to read the new French translation of the *Essence of Christianity* by Joseph Roy.

Acclaimed as the foremost radical thinker of his generation in the Germany of the 1840s, Feuerbach was virtually forgotten in the Germany of the 1850s and 1860s. The Hegelianism that he attacked from within was no longer the public philosophy; the revolution that he heralded had ended in the shameful indecisions of the National Assembly of 1848; the liberation of man that was the point of Feuerbach's philosophy, therefore, would not be achieved by criticism alone, and certainly not by the criticism of religion. 'Feuerbach', Marx and Engels had written in the *German Ideology* in 1845–6, 'goes as far as a theoretician can go without ceasing to be a theoretician and a philosopher' – i.e., without turning to human *praxis*, to history and economics and the study of society as opposed to the critique of religion and philosophy. Feuerbach, indeed, *had* proclaimed that the philosophy of the future would be natural science and politics; yet he himself had remained on philosophical soil, seriously pursuing neither science nor politics. With the failure of the revolutions of 1848 and the growing impact of the industrial revolution, the climate changed. Science replaced philosophy as the paradigm of knowledge and criticism; the careful investigator and the specialized expert dethroned the 'free spirit' and the philosophical system-builder from their commanding positions in intellectual life; the ever-increasing division of labour led to a significant shift in standards and attitudes in philosophical as well as scientific discussion. Industrial production, as Feuerbach himself had predicted, became infinitely more important than religion for the understanding of social development and social life. Feuerbach's naturalism and empiricism were absorbed in and replaced by the medical materialism of Moleschott and Büchner, not to speak of Darwin, J. S. Mill and Spencer; Feuerbach's critique of religion gave way to Renan's; Feuerbach's concern with political liberation as a philosophical (and political) act had to bow to Lassalle's 'iron law of wages' and to the economic, historical and revolutionary concerns of the Marxian system. For over fifty years, indeed, the name 'Ludwig Feuerbach' was best and most widely known as the short title of a work by Engels; Feuerbach's reputation, during this period, rested almost entirely on his relationship to Marx; his memory was kept alive (rather one-sidedly) almost solely by Marxists. The professional philosophers of the period 1860–1920, especially the Hegelian historians of philosophy and the neo-Kantian epistemologists, had little sympathy with Feuerbach's penchant for aphorisms, his perfunctory and unsystematic treatment of fundamental philosophical problems and his failure to work out and expound a clear logic and method. The few disciples who tried to propagandize the Feuerbachian philosophy only de-radicalized his thought and compromised his reputation by their well-meaning enthusiasm and their lack of philosophical incisiveness. It was largely outside formal philosophy, indeed, in the work of such diverse figures as Karl Marx, Søren Kierkegaard, Friedrich Nietzsche and Sigmund Freud, that the perceptive reader could find evidence of the fertility and importance of Feuerbach's ideas.

Since the 1920s, there has been a marked revival of interest in Feuerbach which has steadily moved towards restoring him to his place in the history of ideas, and which has further extended the range of his influence. The Hegelian revival in Germany in the 1920s and the rise of existentialist philosophy and theology have given Feuerbach a new contemporary significance. Max Scheler, in 1925, wrote of Feuerbach's significance for a psychology of drives: Berdyaev, Heidegger, Buber and Sartre have fastened on to his concept of man and his doctrine of the I–Thou; Karl Barth, insisting that Feuerbach represents the most consistent and significant development of the radical subjectivism in nineteenth-century theology, consciously developed his own theological views as a direct reply to the Feuerbachian view of religion. The

publication of Marx's early philosophical writings in the late
1920s and early 1930s, culminating in the new 'philosophical' and
'humanist' interpretations of Marx, has shown that a detailed
understanding of Feuerbach is crucial to an appreciation of the
intellectual origin and content of Marxian thought. It has thus
brought Feuerbach back into the centre of any serious consideration of Marx's philosophy.

All this has led to a renewed spate of discussion. Since the
early 1950s, especially, there has been an ever-increasing volume
of publication and re-publication, both of Feuerbach's own works
and of critical studies devoted to him, especially in Germany and
France. The English reader, however, is still badly served. When
I began work on this book, only the *Essence of Christianity*, so far
as I know, had been fully translated into English;[1] three more of
Feuerbach's works have become available in English in the last
three years.[2] There is, in the English language, still no serious
full-length study of Feuerbach: W. Chamberlain's *Heaven Wasn't
His Destination*, though in some ways more earnest than its title
suggests, can hardly be called a serious study. The present volume
attempts to fill this lack, to provide an introduction to the various
aspects of Feuerbach's thought that will balance exposition and
criticism, taking into account the unavailability in English of the
major bulk of Feuerbach's writings as well as the results of
Continental discussion and scholarship. Where the tendency of
Continental writers, on the whole, has been to metaphysicalize
Feuerbach, this book seeks rather to remain true to the Feuerbachian empiricism, to present him as a man struggling through
the morass of Hegelian terminology towards a naturalistic philosophy and a positivist conception of man.

Feuerbach saw pure (speculative) philosophy as a form of
alienation, of vicious abstraction, analogous to theology. It had no
real, concrete subject; it studied Thought instead of studying men
thinking; it tore human functions out of their natural context and
dealt with them as lifeless abstractions. In doing so, he believed,
it both falsified the nature of thinking and made impossible the
passage from thought to reality, from logic to nature. The transformation of philosophy for which Feuerbach called was the fusion
of philosophy with the positive science of man as a concrete,
natural and historical being, shaped in intercourse with others and
with the natural world around him. It is not surprising, therefore,

that Feuerbach's thought leads us, if anything, away from the concerns of the pure philosopher towards anthropology, psychology, sociology and physiology, while presenting us with a radical critique of the very basis of theology and of the idealist tradition in philosophy. In writing this book, I have assumed that it will be of interest to people in various fields, who may seek in it what is of special concern to them. Feuerbach was not a systematic philosopher; to summarize his thought in a systematic way, leaving out his illustrations, his suggestive but imprecise aphorisms, his unconnected flashes of insight, would be to present Feuerbach at his weakest. Feuerbach's reputation has suffered enough from well-meaning efforts of such disciples as Starke, Bolin and Jodl, who attempted to systematize his thought under such headings as 'Naturalism', 'Sensualism', etc., and put on his writing a load it simply would not bear. On the whole, Feuerbach's contemporaries were right in seeing him as an exciting and illuminating *critic*, whose analysis of religion carried with it interesting implications in a variety of fields which Feuerbach saw but did not explore further in any serious fashion. I have therefore begun the detailed exposition of Feuerbach's work with his critique of religion, even though most of his critique of idealism was historically earlier. It is the most important thread running through his work. A great deal of the time, I have allowed Feuerbach to speak for himself: this seemed especially appropriate when dealing with a thinker whose writing is often most suggestive when it is least to the immediate point and when addressing a reader who must still go to a foreign language to read even a representative selection of Feuerbach for himself. In trying to cover the whole range of Feuerbach's writing, I leave it to the reader to connect this with his own interests and concerns. Feuerbach's thought displayed a number of strains or tendencies, but it hardly formed even a pretended pattern or template for doing philosophy or dealing with reality. I have therefore been less concerned to bring out his confusions and inadequacies (which will be evident enough for the modern reader) than to present what is interesting and suggestive in his thought, either for the student of the history of ideas or for the specialist in particular fields.

The writing of this book has been stretched, with interruptions for other work, over a number of years and a number of countries. Throughout that period I have been a member of the History of

Ideas Unit in the Institute of Advanced Studies in the Australian National University, benefiting from its generous conditions for research. In the academic year 1965–6 I was able to work in the Philosophy Faculty in Moscow State University under an exchange agreement with the Australian National University. In the summer of 1968, while I was engaged in a final revision of the manuscript, and in other writing for the Research Institute on Communist Affairs of Columbia University, New York, the Philosophy Department in the London School of Economics and Political Science graciously offered me hospitality in its rooms. I owe a considerable debt of gratitude to the Secretary of the Australian National University, Mr R. A. Hohnen, who made my visit to the Soviet Union possible, and to Professor Sir Karl Popper, Professor J. N. Watkins and Dr I. Lakatos who made room for me in a crowded department in London. The International Division of the Rectorate of Moscow State University and the University's Department of the History of Philosophy of the Peoples of the U.S.S.R. did their best, within their lights, to help a visitor who could not have been wholly congenial to them. Mr Yu. N. Boronenkov of that department was kind enough to prepare a bibliography of (Russian and Marxist) writings on Feuerbach for me; my friend Professor A. S. Bogomolov of the Department of the History of Foreign Philosophy did much to make my stay in Moscow as pleasant and fruitful as he could make it. Mrs J. Di Fronzo, then research assistant in the Department of Philosophy in the Institute of Advanced Studies in the A.N.U., and her successor, Mrs E. Y. Short, have helped me considerably with bibliographical references and the checking of translations; Dr H. Jakuszew and Mrs M. Freiberg of the History of Ideas Unit in the A.N.U. have read the proofs and checked part of the Index; for the errors that remain I am responsible.

EUGENE KAMENKA   *Canberra, March 1969*

BIBLIOGRAPHICAL NOTE

The bibliography of Feuerbach's work contains thirty-four items published between 1828 and 1846, from his university dissertation *De ratione, una, universali, infinita* to his *Essence of Religion,* published in Leipzig in 1846. Between 1846 and 1866 Feuerbach published, in ten volumes, his collected works. In these volumes he reprinted, often with substantial revisions, books, and articles published before 1846, and included such new works from his pen as the *Lectures on the Essence of Religion,* which appeared as volume 8 of the *Sämtliche Werke* in 1851, and his *Theogony,* which appeared as volume 9 in 1857. Apart from the material that went into the collected works, Feuerbach published only four essays in the period 1846–66. However, he left behind a set of unfinished writings on ethics, dating from the 1860s, published posthumously by Karl Grün, as well as a fair body of correspondence. The collected works published in Feuerbach's lifetime, then, are incomplete and to some extent misleading in so far as they do not indicate clearly the extent to which Feuerbach revised what purports to be early work. There has, however, been no *scholarly* edition of Feuerbach's collected works since. The East German Academy of Sciences has announced that it will be issuing, in honour of the centenary of Feuerbach's death, a sixteen-volume Academy edition of his complete works, to be completed by 1975. At the time of writing, the first two volumes (Volume 4 and Volume 6, containing *Pierre Bayle* and the *Lectures on the Essence of Religion* respectively) have appeared; four more are promised before the end of 1969. The volumes to hand have been edited by Wolfgang Harich under the supervision of the general editor Werner Schuffenhauer, a serious but pedestrian Feuerbach-scholar working from an orthodox Marxist viewpoint under the conditions of censorship still obtaining in East Germany. The volumes published so far contain no critical commentary and only the barest bones of an introduction, but in Volume 4 (where variants are involved) the editors have followed the scholarly practice of printing the text of the original edition of 1838 and of indicating in footnotes all significant alterations introduced into the corrected reprint of 1844 and the revised edition of 1848. If this practice is followed consistently, it is extremely likely that the

East German edition will become a standard edition that can be used by Feuerbach-scholars.

In the meantime, the scholar must use, with some care, the only comparatively complete and convenient edition of Feuerbach's work and correspondence now available – the edition issued by Feuerbach's disciples Wilhelm Bolin and Friedrich Jodl in Stuttgart between 1903 and 1911 in ten volumes and supplemented by Bolin's two-volume collection of Feuerbach's letters, with a biographical introduction, published by him in 1904. The Bolin and Jodl edition, issued as a popular edition, prints Feuerbach's works in their revised form without indicating the exact nature or extent of these revisions; it often lists these works under the date of original publication, thus giving a misleading impression of Feuerbach's intellectual development. (This is especially true of the writings which Bolin and Jodl put in their Volume 1 under the heading 'Todesgedanken 1830', which consist primarily of the very heavily revised 1846 version of Feuerbach's *Thoughts on Death and Immortality*, concerned to eliminate the much greater Hegelianism of the 1830 version, and of other writings. Further, Bolin and Jodl, in their anxiety to make Feuerbach accessible, took frequent – if minor – liberties with his text, altering sentences and eliminating or translating (rather freely) foreign phrases in order to promote clarity. Their very free and abridged German translation of Feuerbach's doctoral dissertation, published in Latin, on a number of occasions misses the point and misrepresents Feuerbach's view. Nevertheless, Feuerbach was not a sufficiently careful, rigorous and systematic thinker for these deviations to be as important as they might be if one were considering the work of Kant. The reader interested in Feuerbach's general position, rather than in the details of his intellectual development, can use the Bolin and Jodl edition provided he keeps its limitations in mind. The edition has in fact been considerably improved in the photographic reprint issued from Stuttgart-Bad Cannstatt between 1960 and 1964, where the ten volumes of the first Bolin and Jodl edition have been supplemented by three more volumes, containing reprints of Bolin's selection of Feuerbach's correspondence with additional letters not included by Bolin, the Latin original of Feuerbach's university dissertation and the 1830 text of his *Thoughts on Death and Immortality*. I have therefore used this reprint edition as the basic source for all Feuerbach citations; only in a few isolated and unimportant cases have I found it necessary to go outside it. Translations from it and from other foreign-language sources are my own. For the *Essence of Christianity*, however, I have mostly kept to George Eliot's magnificent translation, which is more accurate than its verve and readability would have made one expect, and which is likely to remain the standard translation.

The reader will find the following abbreviations used in the text:

W Ludwig Feuerbach, *Sämtliche Werke*, in XIII volumes, Stuggart-Bad Cannstatt, 1960–4, being a photographic reprint of the Bolin and Jodl edition of 1903–10, with additional material selected and arranged by Hans-Martin Sass. (Roman and Arabic numerals after the W indicate volume and page number respectively.)

GW Ludwig Feuerbach, *Gesammelte Werke*, (projected) in sixteen volumes, (East) Berlin 1967–. Two volumes, volumes 4 and 6 under the general editorship of Werner Schuffenhauer, bearing the date 1967, became available in 1968; the remaining volumes are to be published at intervals until the whole series is completed in 1975. (Roman and Arabic numerals after the GW indicate volume and page number; they have been inserted, where possible, after the W reference to aid readers who are acquiring the East German edition.)

EC Ludwig Feuerbach, *The Essence of Christianity*, translated from the second, revised German edition by Marian Evans (George Eliot), first published in London in 1854. (Arabic numerals after EC indicate the page number.)

In the body of the work, all citations give only the author or editor, the title of the book and the page number; the publication details of the edition used are indicated in the bibliography of works mentioned and cited, at the end of this book. Citations from the (English translation of the second German edition of the) *Essence of Christianity* are followed by the page references to the Bolin and Jodl reprint of the (3rd) German edition to facilitate comparison with the German.

PART ONE

The Times, the Man
and the Work

1. The Promethean background

As the scientific rationality of Western civilization began to
bear its full fruit, it became increasingly conscious of its
psychical implications. The ego which undertook the rational
transformation of the human and natural environment
revealed itself as an essentially aggressive, offensive subject,
whose thoughts and action were designed for mastering
objects. It was a subject *against* an object. This *a priori*
antagonistic experience defined the *ego cogitans* as well as the
ego agens. Nature (its own as well as the external world)
was 'given' to the ego as something that had to be fought,
conquered, and even violated.[1]

The conception of the Great Chain of Being, with man as its
middle link, led, in the earlier part of the eighteenth century, to
what A. O. Lovejoy has rightly called an ethic of prudent medio-
crity.[2] Man's duty was to take his place in the order of creation,
to cultivate within himself that specific human excellence which is
as distinct from the excellence of the angels and of God as it is
from the nature of the beasts. As Pope put it,

> The bliss of man (could pride that blessing find)
> Is not to act or think beyond mankind:
> No pow'rs of body or of soul to share
> But what his nature and his state can bear.[3]

Even to the growing number of Deists and sceptics, increasingly
influential as the century grew older, man's essential limitations
were quite clear. David Hume hoped, as the *Abstract* confirms for
us, to substitute the science of man for the metaphysics of the
schools; but if Hume denied God it was not for the sake of
ascribing God's omnipotence to man. The *Grande Encyclopédie*
published by Diderot between 1751 and 1765 informed the reader,
under the heading 'Religion', that natural religion teaches us, on

the basis of reason alone, to render homage to God and not to abuse his creatures – wherefore natural religion may also be called moral philosophy or ethics, 'because it is immediately concerned with the conduct and duties of men toward each other and themselves considered as creatures of the Supreme Being'. Voltaire, remarking on Pascal's *Pensées*, saw no reason why Pascal should consider man a mystery:

> Man appears to hold his due place in the scale of beings, superior to brutes . . . but inferior to other beings. . . . Man is like everything else we see around us; a composition in which good and evil, pleasures and pains, are found. . . . If man were perfect, he would be God; and those contrarieties which you call contradictions are so many necessary ingredients to the composition of man, who is like everything else in nature, just what he ought to be.[4]

The Age of Reason, as it is sometimes called, ran its course between two revolutions – the English and the French. The balanced propriety of its sentiments could and did become as alien-seeming and 'unnatural' as the wigs that were the symbol of gentility. To those who classify their history into periods and put their movements into pigeon-holes, the Age of Reason is followed by the Romantic Revolt. The true position is, of course, more complex. There were themes raised and developed in the 'Age of Reason' that were still vigorous in the ensuing 'age'; there were men like Rousseau who pointed from one 'age' to the next; there were national distinctions and difficulties of chronology that make the whole conception of cultural and philosophical ages rather too definite, and often as misleading as it can be helpful. Suffice it to say here, that against balanced propriety and detached, critical Reason, some late eighteenth-century thinkers began to stress the creative, infinite mind implied but not developed in the Cartesian *cogito*. This mind not only knows but also strives, it is the centre of man's universe and therefore the centre of the universe itself. To these thinkers, knowledge was no longer passive, no longer mere receptivity, and man's character was no longer static and circumscribed by his place in 'the order of things'. As the rumblings of the French Revolution grew louder, the 'order of things' seemed no more eternal. To combine, into one metaphysical structure, Reason and Will, Philosophy and Romanticism, to put man into the centre of the universe, that became (as Marx saw) the *German*, i.e., philosophical-metaphysical, version of and response to the French Revolution.

The problems that occupied what Professor Frederick Hertz has called the 'German Public Mind' at the very end of the eighteenth century were set by Germany's greatest philosopher, Immanuel Kant. To later generations they may to some extent be exemplified by the tension that dominated the work of Germany's most famous writer, Johann Wolfgang von Goethe. The motto later enunciated by Feuerbach – 'erudition and philosophy are to me only the means by which I bring to light the treasure hid in man' – was, in one aspect of his thought, also the motto of Goethe, who had as little doubt of the illusory nature of the consolations of revealed religion as did Hume, Feuerbach, Schopenhauer and Nietzsche. In 1773 he had written the fragments of his drama 'Prometheus', in his play *Iphigenie auf Tauris* he had striven to show (as he put it in later years) that 'pure humanity atones for every human frailty'; in the first part of *Faust*, published in 1808, he gave Germany and the world the image of (Faustian) man – man proud, restless and insatiable, man driven by the inexorable thirst for knowledge, man seeking to attain the infinite through restless striving, to taste all experiences, to bring the world within himself.[5]

> If e'er upon my couch, stretched at my ease, I lie,
> Then may my life that instant cease!
> Canst thou with lying flattery rule me,
> Until self-pleased myself I see,
> Canst thou with rich enjoyment fool me,
> Let that day be the last for me.

Such is Faust's compact with the Devil: if he should find even the briefest interval of satisfaction and 'bid the fleeting moment stay', his soul shall be the Devil's; if man's restless striving can be stilled, then will Faust gladly go to hell.

Yet Goethe still stood with more than one foot in the climate of the Age of Reason.[6] Faust's striving and Faust's very compact are part of a divine plan or, at the least, of a divine amusement. In the long, 'philosophical' second part of the drama (completed in 1831), Faust learns to be wisely (and prudently) active, to limit his practical activity to ends that lie within his power, to follow Pope in preference to Prometheus. As he lies on his death-bed, Faust admits that he has found happiness and satisfaction in the service of mankind and now would bid the fleeting moment stay. The Devil, by rights, has triumphed – but God intervenes for what one must surmise to be reasons of policy. Angels bear upward the no-more Faustian soul, singing:

> Gerettet ist das edle Glied
> Der Geisterwelt vom Bösen:
> Wer immer strebend sich bemüht
> Den können wir erlösen.[7]

It is God with his angels, not man, who saves: 'my servant Faust', as God calls him with patronizing good nature in the Prologue, leaves the stage God's servant still. Faust, like Goethe, is not yet Promethean – not yet ready to burst the fetters of the Great Chain of Being and sit as Master in the house of God.[8]

Something of the same spirit of incomplete Prometheanism, of unconsummated rebellious humanism, seemed to young Germans of the decade after the French Revolution to have marred the brilliant work of Kant. In the *Critique of Pure Reason* he had shown, to their satisfaction, that the necessary structure of the phenomenal world was imposed upon it by the knowing mind, by the forms of 'intuition' or sensibility, and that the concept of God was merely one of the 'regulative ideas' of pure reason, making it seek a single principle of explanation and an ultimate unity in nature. In the *Critique of Practical Reason* he had argued, to their even greater satisfaction, that morality presupposes behind the phenomenal human being subject to the laws of nature and of reason a pure, rational will moving freely in the intelligible, noumenal world, bound only by the self-imposed rational law to treat humanity in every case as an end, and never as a means. Kant had proclaimed, in short (as they saw it), the autonomy of man as a free, self-determined being, subject only to the laws he sets himself. In the *Critique of Judgment*, further, Kant attempted to show that man is the measure of all things beautiful: aesthetic appreciation arises from the harmony between an object of cognition and the forms of cognition; it is therefore man who gives nature a supreme end or divine form so as to give the particular contents of nature meaning and significance. Viewed as a systematic whole, however, the Critical philosophy had left itself with an insupportable dualism of noumenal and phenomenal and with a radical discontinuity between its concept of man as a free moral agent and its concept of man as an *ego cogitans*. The shadowy noumenal world of things retains its ontological independence – for Kant it is a happy accident, in no way accounted for by his philosophy, that noumena are capable of being organized under the forms of sensibility and that reason seeks a principle of unity. The thing-in-itself, though in principle unknowable, stands co-ordinate with consciousness; its existence is assumed but never demonstrated. The special conditions under which we know, though on Kant's view necessary, are not by him deduced from the nature of consciousness itself. In the field of practical reason, of morality, the intelligible nature prescribes to itself its own laws; in the field of cognition such laws are simply found 'empirically', by the analysis of phenomena as they appear before us. For the generation that followed him, Kant had not been metaphysical enough: he had not succeeded in forging a system in which everything could be deduced from the initial premise; he had not established the unity of the *ego agens* and the *ego cogitans*; he had not robbed the world of all independence *vis-à-vis* the spirit of man. It is thus that Schelling speaks of himself as trying to find the premise for justifying the conclusions reached by Kant and that the young Fichte – claiming to be a more systematic Kantian than Kant – set about the task of showing in the early version of the *Wissenschaftlehre* produced in 1794 that all the necessary conditions of cognition recognized by Kant can be demonstrated from a single fundamental principle: the existence of consciousness.

True, *scientific* knowledge – Fichte argued – can commence only with the absolute self. Otherwise it retains some vestige of faith (i.e., of mere belief), for even the belief in the objectivity of what I see before me is a purely subjective belief. Scientifically, we cannot divide the universe into mind and nature. We can only report what we *know*: we know that in some of our mental processes we are conscious of acting freely, whereas in others (in our sensations) we are aware of *being obliged to have* certain things in our consciousness and of being obliged to experience certain feelings. We feel ourselves circumscribed and are thus led to imagine that an external reality exists. Actually, we merely objectify (project outside ourselves) the internal laws by which our activity is limited. These laws, projected outside the knowing mind, we call matter. Viewed historically – and here we have that Fichtean dialectic that was to grow into the far more brilliant and subtle structure of Hegel's *Phenomenology of Mind* – the development of our inner experience is this: The mind is first unconsciously active; it then finds that in this unconscious spontaneous activity it is limited by the laws of its being; it thus comes to objectify and project these limitations and call them an external world. (For this, for the mind's external projection and objectification of its own laws, Fichte coined the term *Entäusserung* – *alienation* – which came to play such an important rôle in the philosophy of Hegel and the Hegelians, right through to Feuerbach and Marx.) Only *after* the mind had posited such an external world could it come to the consciousness of itself as a mind, since it could only recognize *its* qualities by first contrasting itself with something it takes to be non-mind. (Here, again, is the Fichtean root of the German idealist conception that alienation, growing into estrangement, is *necessary* error, necessary for self-knowledge.) Thereafter, but only slowly, the mind comes to recognize that the experiences it has must be read as *its*, that the mind alone is the sphere of its operations, that it is at once subject and object, the sole and absolute starting point and the ultimate content of all knowledge which can claim to be scientific (i.e., of all knowledge not based on postulates of faith, on mere belief, as opposed to certain and immediate knowledge).

The true ground of the historical dialectic, however, Fichte (like Hegel) finds in a logical dialectic. Philosophy, for Fichte, must begin with the analysis of the beliefs that seem to us *certain*, carried through until we find the primary proposition that is axiomatically true. Take the concept of 'mind'. The clearest notion we have is that this concept represents the power of thinking, while the concept of 'consciousness' is that of a point or focus in which all our thoughts unite and from which they appear to emanate. If we then turn to look for some act of mind which is in every way axiomatically true, we find it in the affirmation of the principle of identity (*Satz der Identität*) on which Schelling, too, was to base an entire philosophy. 'A = A' is axiomatically true when treated as a hypothetical proposition, as 'if there be any A, then it is A'. But we cannot yet make it a categorical proposition, because we do not know that 'A' exists. Here Fichte calls on Descartes. In asserting even a hypothetical truth, I think and thus I affirm myself. The principle of identity therefore becomes an axiomatically true categorical proposition in the form 'I am I', 'Ego = Ego'.

The second absolute principle for Fichte, dependent on the first for matter but unconditional in respect of form, is the principle of negation. Here the axiomatic or necessary hypothetical truth 'not-A is not equal to A' derives from the first principle the existence of the ego, and thus becomes the necessary and therefore certain categorical truth 'not-ego is not equal to ego'. In this principle the mind comes to postulate the non-mind, to treat itself as an object. This opposition of subject and object is necessary for every act of consciousness, else there would be nothing it was conscious of. Finally, uniting the positive and the negative principle, we come to the notion of limitation, or determination, to the third formula which Fichte holds as fundamental to philosophy: 'The ego holds itself to be determined (i.e. limited) by a non-ego and vice-versa.' This principle, for Fichte, is conditional both as to matter and form. The three principles, of course, correspond to Kant's three types of judgment, affirmation, negation and limitation or, as the post Hegelians put it, thesis, antithesis and synthesis.

From the foregoing principles, then, two propositions result:

1. The ego affirms itself to be determined by a non-ego: this is the basis of all theoretical science.

2. Notwithstanding the first principle, the non-ego is itself affirmed and determined by the ego: this is the basis of practical science.

Fichte now feels able to give a psychological and a logico-moral explanation of all the phenomena found in the human mind. When we reflect upon the laws limiting our activity and see them producing the obstacles which the ego affirms as opposed to itself, we have a feeling or sensation. When the mind actually loses itself in such obstacles (objects perceived) and sees in them something produced by a non-mind, we have a perception: continuity and extension, time and space, are (as Schelling also thought) the objectifications of such out-going on the part of the mind. The power by which such sensations are fixed and retained is the understanding; the power of free working in the mind is the imagination; the power which unites understanding and imagination is that of judgment. When we overcome all the limitations involved in these powers and see the mind as pure activity, as free all-producing power, we have the highest faculty in man, pure reason.

The Fichtean philosophy, then, is the triumph of Kant's noumenal will over the rest of the Kantian system. The ego, for Fichte, is *ego agens* and *ego cogitans* in one and the same act, knowing is a form of willing. The ego, which Kant called the noumenal will, for Fichte (as for Kant) constantly strives after self-development: it seeks to realize fully its own nature and to bring into actual existence all that lies potentially in its consciousness, to unite the absolute, the practical and the intelligent self. The postulation of the material world thus becomes for Fichte a (moral or practical) necessity in the mind's (moral) self-development: the ego in striving for its self-formed aim would have nothing *in the face of which* to strive, nothing to give concreteness and the possibility of satisfaction to its practical impulse, if *it* did not create *for itself* obstacles to overcome on the way.

Fichte was not, I think, an outstanding philosophical mind; he is of major importance for our theme here because it is in his earlier system that the pretensions embodied in the Kantian conception of the noumenal will were most aggressively and completely developed, and because it was the Fichte in Hegel that Feuerbach and Marx most clearly saw. The structure and formal argumentation of the first Fichtean system set both the leading themes and the style or conception of philosophical argumentation that were to dominate German philosophical thought from the publication of the second, revised edition of the *Critique of Pure Reason* in 1787 until the dissolution of German Idealism, under the influence of Feuerbach, in the 1840s.[9] In the development of Prometheanism and for an understanding of Feuerbach the attempt to base an entire philosophy on nothing but the internal development and self-alienation of the active consciousness or ego is therefore of crucial importance: in the history of philosophy, the attempt by Fichte, Schelling and Hegel to transform the Kantian Critical Philosophy into a deductive metaphysical system represented a marked falling away of philosophical power, a substitution of merely verbal solutions for the geniune grappling with problems that characterized the Kantian philosophy. It was also, from the point of view of anthropotheism or the deification of the *ego agens*, a self-destructive attempt. In the critique of religion, society, morality and art Prometheanism had a certain force: as the foundation of a philosophical explanation of the universe this kind of subjective idealism was to be found wanting even in Fichte's day. The concept of self-determination, I should argue, is an incoherent concept: it cannot become the basis of a satisfactory philosophical view. The belief in man, or mind, or will, as purely active and never passive requires the removal of the will to a noumenal plane which cannot be connected with the phenomenal plane (the solution of Kant and, in part, of Schopenhauer), or the denial of the ultimate reality of anything outside the active principle (the young Fichte's solution), or as Spinoza saw, the complete denial of genuine independence and multiplicity, the insistence that the self-determined substance must be the only substance of which all things are modes and attributes (roughly speaking, also Hegel's solution). If the mind is to spin a universe out of itself, it must first contain a universe, it must in fact *be* the universe itself. It is thus that Fichte's individual ego becomes in the end a mere aspect of the Absolute Ego, and that the Absolute Ego becomes in his later work (the *Wissenschaftslehre* of 1810, for example) more and more like the God in whom we live and move and have our being, the God who does not 'make' nature but *is* nature, who encompasses everything as part of himself and therefore 'explains' nothing. It is thus, too, that Schelling comes to found his philosophy of identity on the proposition that subject and object are one in an Absolute which contains equally the ego and the non-ego and underlies them both. It is thus, above all, that Hegel once again subordinates the human will and human consciousness to the laws of thought and makes of these the Absolute Idea which is the things in thought and the thought in things. In relation to the Absolute Idea man is nothing more than part of a great transcendent rational system, playing out rôles he did not write and does not fully understand. The *Phenomenology of Mind* begins by unfolding the structure of reason as the structure of domination: the mind externalizes its powers into things and then overcomes them. But in the end domination, too, is overcome and the *Phenomenology* concludes, as Professor Marcuse points out,[10] on a note which is the very opposite of the Promethean dynamic: 'The wounds of the Spirit heal without leaving scars; the deed is not everlasting; the Spirit takes back into itself, and the aspect of particularity (individuality) present in it immediately passes away.'

If German idealism, as Marx thought, accomplished the French

Revolution only in the misty realm of ideas, it nevertheless displayed a sharp enough cutting edge against the pretensions of traditional theology and revealed religion. It did insist on the primacy of reason; rejecting any special and separate field of faith, with its own peculiar validity, it subjected the 'religious consciousness' to tests which left it reeling. Plainly illogical and confused, religion was at best a form of imagination, an attempt to express in fictional or pictorial form truths that were ultimately the proper province of philosophy. Kant had shown the utter inadequacy of the traditional proofs of the existence of God and the inevitable contradictions (paradoxes) that result from treating God as an existing being in relation with 'the world'. He was, at one stage, widely believed to be the author of the young Fichte's devastating *Critique of All Revelation*, published anonymously, which was patently based on Kant's philosophy and openly attacked religion in the name of morality, of the autonomy of man. As they moved with age towards less Promethean positions, Fichte, Schelling and Hegel had all shown – albeit, in their later years, somewhat unwillingly – that the Christian belief in a personal God was but a moment in the development of the Absolute Ego, Absolute Reason or the Absolute Idea, destined to be overcome (even if, in a certain sense also preserved) in the true philosophy. The older Hegel, with all his reluctance to attack Christianity openly or directly, had made the concept of God an episode in history and in the development of philosophy. Heinrich Heine correctly perceived where all this was leading:

> Our hearts are thrilled with compassion, for it is old Jehovah
> himself who is making ready to die. We have known him so
> well, from his cradle in Egypt where he was brought up among
> the divine crocodiles and calves, the onions and ibises and
> sacred cats. . . . We saw him bid farewell to those companions
> of his childhood, the obelisks and sphinxes of the Nile, to become
> a little god-king in Palestine to a poor nation of shepherds.
> Later we saw him in contact with the Assyro–Babylonian
> civilization; at that stage he gave up his far-too-human passions
> and refrained from spitting wrath and vengeance; at any rate,
> he no longer thundered for the least trifle. . . . We saw him move
> to Rome, the capital, where he abjured everything in the way
> of national prejudice and proclaimed the celestial equality of

all peoples; with these fine phrases he set up in opposition to old Jupiter and, thanks to intriguing, he got into power and, from the heights of the Capitol, ruled the city and the world, *urbem et orbem*. . . . We have seen him purify himself, spiritualize himself still more, become paternal, compassionate, the benefactor of the human race, a philanthropist. . . . But nothing could save him!

Don't you hear the bell? Down on your knees! The sacrament is being carried to a dying God![11]

Fichte, as he grew older, passed from his enthusiasm for the French Revolution, his moral attack on religion and his defence of the liberties curtailed by princes to writing the Addresses to the German Nation and becoming the first Rector of the newly founded University of Berlin, meant to provide intellectual backing for Prussia's rôle in Germany. Hegel, whose youthful *Early Theological Writings* (not known or published till long after his death, in 1907) presaged so many of the points made by Feuerbach and Marx, had become the spokesman of Prussian Reaction. The Schelling who had shared Hegel's youthful romantic and radical longings was called to Berlin in 1841 to combat the dangerous appeals to reason which the Left Hegelians had found in Hegel. From what has been said before, it will be obvious that the movement of these three leading figures from the romantic protest of a comparatively subjective idealism to a conservative concern with the structure of totality did not result merely from the sclerosis of age; they were driven to their later positions by logic, by the contradictions of their earlier social and philosophical romanticism. But they were also driven there by Napoleon and the collapse of the initial hopes engendered by the theory, if not the practice, of the French Revolution. They were caught up in the concern for stability that culminated in the Metternich system and Hegel, like the ageing Goethe, watched with growing unease the rumblings that presaged the revolution of 1830. These were no longer the men to consummate the victory of philosophy over theology and of reason over tradition and despotism. One of Hegel's last acts before his death from cholera in 1831 was to denounce the English Reform Bill as introducing formlessness into what should be a political *order*.

Hegel's system, nevertheless, was the intellectual achievement of the age. It was to dominate German thinking until the 1840s and was never to lose its influence on at least some serious German thinkers in each subsequent period. Hegel combined with what appeared to be a subtle, rigorous and thoroughly professional logic an extraordinary fertility and suggestiveness of thought. He made the whole of human culture, both history and the natural sciences, part of philosophy, exemplifying its propositions and giving body to its abstractions. His works became the intellectual baggage of an entire generation – the generation which Feuerbach addressed. The seeds, often even the very formulation, of what they say can be found in Hegel himself, thrown off as a comment in passing, or presented as the 'partial' truth in an ultimately inadequate position or 'moment'. This is true of much in Feuerbach, it is even true of much in Marx, who always recognized that Hegel was expressing important insights in a mystificatory, metaphysical guise. Thus, after Hegel's death in 1831, the battle between conservatives and radicals in German thought was fought as a philosophical battle between Hegelians in Hegelian terms, primarily in the field of religion. The Right Hegelians saw in Hegel the basis for a new and more rational justification of established religion and established authority; the Left Hegelians, on the whole less true to the Master's system, saw in his elevation of reason and in his dialectical method the most potent weapon of criticism. If the Hegelian Absolute Idea, they argued, was manifest only in human thinking then it itself was nothing but a theological distortion of human thinking: there was no Absolute beyond and above Man. In Hegel, religion had been a façade for the Absolute Idea; in truth, then, it must be a façade – for Man. The blunt attack on religion began with David Friedrich Strauss' *Life of Jesus*, published in 1835 and 1836. For Strauss, Christianity is the first recognition that God is Man. The significance of the historical Jesus is that he introduced this idea, an idea which in the gospels became enclothed in myths and spurious miracles. Bruno Bauer went further and rejected the existence of the historical Jesus. For him, the gospels reflected the experience of the early Church in the Roman Empire, where the individual self-consciousness was confronted by powers before which it stood in helpless opposition, so that man became alienated from the world. Christianity, for Bauer, perpetuates this alienation in mythological and miraculous form.

It is in this setting that Feuerbach comes upon the stage.

2. The man and his work

'The significance of the life and thought of Ludwig Feuerbach (1804–72),' Sidney Hook wrote in an important book[1] more than thirty years ago,

> is only now emerging in contemporary philosophy. The rise of Marxism, the development of what is called *Existenzial-philosophie* in Germany (Heidegger, Jaspers), the renaissance of Hegelianism, and the increasing interest in the philosophy and psychology of religion have gradually brought Feuerbach into the field of vision of philosophic consciousness. It would be more accurate to say that he is being restored to his place, for as lonely and modest[2] a figure as he was, during one brief decade the whole of German philosophy and culture stood within his shadow. If Hegel was the anointed king of German thought in the period from 1820 to 1840, then Feuerbach was the philosophical arch-rebel from the time of the publication of his *Das Wesen des Christenthums*[3] to the eve of the revolution of 1848. . . .

The publication of Feuerbach's *Essence of Christianity*, quickly followed by the publication of Feuerbach's *Vorläufige Thesen zur Reform der Philosophie* [*Preliminary Theses for the Reform of Philosophy*, 1842], indeed caused a tremendous stir. It was of Feuerbach in this period that David Friedrich Strauss, himself having caused a furore with his radical left-Hegelian life of Jesus,[4] wrote: 'To-day, and perhaps for some time to come, the field belongs to him. His theory is the truth for this age.'[5] In France in the 1850s, Ernest Renan – unconscious that his own future work was to cause as great a scandal – wrote of Feuerbach, 'if the end of the world were to come in the 19th century, then, of course, he would have to be called the Anti-Christ'.[6] In England, in the same decade, the novelist George Eliot (Marian Evans) was translating Feuerbach's *Essence of Christianity* while her husband, George Lewes, studied him for his history of modern philosophy (in which Feuerbach was not taken very seriously). In Russia, as early as 1847, members of the radical Petrashevskii circle of intellectuals were reading the *Essence of Christianity* and acclaiming the 'anthropological principle' as the culmination of philosophy and the foundation of all social progress.[7] The 'Westernizers', from Alexander Herzen to Granovskii, discussed Feuerbach and Hegel night and day.[8]

To his contemporaries, and to nineteenth-century Europe generally, Feuerbach was the Feuerbach of the 1840s – the Feuerbach, above all, of the *Essence of Christianity* (which went through three editions in seven years) and, to a lesser extent, the Feuerbach of the *Preliminary Theses* and of the earlier *Zur Kritik der Hegelschen Philosophie* [*Toward the Critique of Hegelian Philosophy*, 1839].[9] He was the man who had put materialist anthropology in place of religious idealism, who had shown that God was made in the image of man, that thought was a function of being, that man had feelings and strivings as well as consciousness and that nature confronted man as an independent force, as an objective challenge. To Feuerbach's radical contemporaries – rather more exclusively than to Feuerbach himself, for Feuerbach's interest in religion was more active than his revolutionary zeal – the whole point of Feuerbach's work was to usher in the new religion of man. Feuerbach had proved that God was made in man's image (a simplification of Feuerbach's view to which he himself was polemically prone). He had shown that the human qualities and powers ascribed to God were the divine qualities and powers of man. Anthropotheism, Speshnev wrote to Chojecki,[10] 'at least in its consummate form, as it is found in Feuerbach . . . pulls the whole man, without residue, into God. This is the second assumption of the God-Man, or the Man-God, who, according to legend, takes his body with him to heaven.' The young Karl Marx, within two years of the publication of the *Essence of Christianity*, drew the concrete conclusion on which so much of Feuerbach's popularity rested: 'The criticism of religion ends in the teaching that *man is the highest being for man*, it ends, that is, with the categorical imperative to overthrow all conditions in which man is a debased, forsaken, contemptible being forced into servitude.'[11] Feuerbach himself, in the preface to the first volume of his collected works, issued in 1846, sought to argue that his work should be understood in precisely this way:

It is a question to-day, you say, no longer of the existence or
the non-existence of God but of the existence or non-existence
of man; not whether God is a creature whose nature is the
same as ours but whether we human beings are to be equal
among ourselves; not whether and how we can partake of the
body of the Lord by eating bread but whether we have enough
bread for our own bodies; not whether we render unto God
what is God's and unto Caesar what is Caesar's, but whether
we finally render unto man what is man's; not whether we
are Christians or heathens, theists or atheists, but whether
we are or can become men, healthy in soul and body, free,
active and full of vitality. *Concedo*, gentlemen! That is what I
want, too. He who says no more of me than that I am an
atheist, says and knows *nothing* of me. The question as to the
existence or non-existence of God, the opposition between
theism and atheism, belongs to the sixteenth and to the seven-
teenth centuries but not to the nineteenth. I deny God. But
that means for me that I deny the negation of man. In place
of the illusory, fantastic, heavenly position of man which in
actual life necessarily leads to the degradation of man, I substitute the tangible, actual and consequently also the political
and social position of mankind. The question concerning the
existence or non-existence of God is for me nothing but the
question concerning the existence or non-existence of man.[12]

Feuerbach's swift rise to popularity in the decade preceding the
1848 Revolution was followed by an almost catastrophic slump in
his reputation in Germany immediately upon the defeat of that
revolution. He seethed in chagrin while the public turned to the
suddenly fashionable Schopenhauerian pessimism, later to be
followed by a neo-Kantian revival among more professional
philosophers; he could not understand why his works were not
read and discussed, his positions not developed, his place in the
history of philosophy no longer taken very seriously. He had
become, in Germany at least, primarily a nostalgic memory in the
minds of some socialist radicals, still hoping for a second '48'.[13]

The swift acquisition of a reputation may be as much ground for
suspicion as the sudden loss of it. Was Feuerbach indeed nothing
more than a very minor philosopher, given a spurious philosophical significance by the fact that something in his work appealed to a

CP

transitory mood of the times and made him an ideologue, rather than a philosopher, in a specifically-conditioned struggle against Emperor and Church? Or was he, as Marxists suggest, a man who had the misfortune of being overtaken by history in another sense? Did he simply produce an infinitely abler disciple in the shape of Karl Marx, who soon absorbed him, outgrew him, infinitely extended him and – within Feuerbach's own lifetime – converted the whole Feuerbachian philosophy into nothing but an incomplete prelude to the truth which is Marxism?[14] Or, to put this point in a form more palatable to non-Marxists, is Feuerbach of interest only historically, as a transitional figure between Hegel and Marx, a midwife at the birth of Marxism? Or does Feuerbach's failure stem from an intrinsic weakness in his whole work and outlook: from the fact that he talked endlessly about replacing philosophy first by 'anthropology', then by science, without really doing or developing either discipline himself? Or has Feuerbach simply been unjustly neglected, as Deborin claimed? To answer this, we must look at his life, his fortunes and his intellectual performance. We shall begin with his life and fortunes.

Ludwig Andreas Feuerbach was born on 28 July 1804, in Landshut, Bavaria, where his father, the distinguished German jurist and criminologist (Paul Johann) Anselm Feuerbach[15] had just accepted a chair of law. Anselm von Feuerbach (he was ennobled in 1813) ranks at least as high in the history of legal thinking and criminological studies as his son Ludwig does in the history of philosophy and of ideas, even though he worked in a field where early pioneers lose their relevance much more quickly and become figures of purely historical interest. Before Anselm had reached the age of 25, he had already attracted widespread attention in the learned world with his *Philosophico-Juridical Investigation of the Crime of High Treason* and with his *Revision of the Basic Propositions and Basic Concepts of Positive Penal Law*.[16] He became a *docent* at Jena in 1799, an extraordinary Professor the following year and a Professor *ordinarius* the year after that, when he moved to the chair at Kiel and thence, in 1803, to the chair of law at Landshut. There the Crown Prince Max Joseph and his Minister Montgelas were attempting to bring the Enlightenment (a little belatedly) to Catholic Bavaria. Anselm Feuerbach, a liberal Protestant, Kantian, markedly progressive in his social views, was the first Protestant and the first outsider to be called to a chair at a Bavarian University. The students at Landshut thronged to his lectures, the University employed him in its counsels and accepted his recommendations for further calls to North German Protestant scholars; the Court invited him to redraft the Bavarian penal law in the light of his then revolutionary view that a penal code should treat punishment purely as a deterrent measure, and not as a punitive one. Within a year, however, tensions with colleagues began to build up – apparently based on envy and religious intolerance, but exacerbated by Anselm's undiplomatic character. In September 1805, Feuerbach lost his temper under provocation at the public defence of a doctoral dissertation and stormed from the room, vowing he would give no more lectures at Landshut. He moved to the Court in Munich to become a *Geheimrat* in the Ministry of Justice and to continue work on the Code. In 1807, Napoleon suggested to Max Joseph (by then King Maximilian I of Bavaria) that it would be a fine gesture if the Code Napoleon were introduced into Bavaria. The hint was rightly taken as command; Anselm Feuerbach was charged with the work of preparing a revision of Bavarian civil law in this spirit. He remained in Munich until 1813 when his greatest monument in German legal history, the path-breaking Bavarian Penal Code of 1813, was published and promulgated as law. He had already, in 1806, been appointed a corresponding member of the Russian Law Commission; he had completed his work on the Civil Code; his *Textbook of the Criminal Law Common to the German Jurisdictions*[17] ran through eleven editions between 1801 and 1831; he had written on the criminal law of the Koran, on *dolus* and *culpa*, on St Augustine concerning torture and he had attacked Hobbes' views on the subject's (lack of) right to rebel. He had published, in 1808 and 1811, the two volumes of a collection of remarkable criminal cases, to be followed in 1828 and 1829 by an account of remarkable crimes. In 1831 and 1832 he wrote on the famous case of Kaspar Hauser, whom he befriended and protected in Ansbach until Anselm's death in 1833, and concerning whose origins Anselm Feuerbach's theories still provide some of the most important speculations. These latter writings remain classics of early criminology. In 1814, probably in consequence of Court intrigues and of the jealousy of his former colleague, the Bavarian law professor Gönner, he was moved to Bamberg as Vice-President of the Court of Appeal. In 1817 he moved again, to Ansbach, to become President of the Court of Appeal. In 1822 he visited Paris to study the French legal system and legal practice and he wept at the grave of Rousseau. When he died, he had been loaded with formal honours (if not with real power) and his name was known throughout Europe.

Even apart from Anselm and Ludwig, the Feuerbachs were a gifted family. Anselm's father and grandfather were lawyers; his great-grandfather was an imperial notary and registrar in the land office; the family was directly descended from Johann Henrich Feuerbach, a well-known pastor and *metropolit* in Schotten, sprung of a line of church elders and related to well-known seventeenth-century theologians of the name Feuerbach.[18] Anselm's mother, Sophie Sybille Christine, *née* Krause, also the daughter of a lawyer, was a descendant of the famous jurist Johann Salomo Brunquell. Ludwig's eldest brother, (Joseph) Anselm, born in 1798, became a well-known archaeologist, Professor of Classical Philology at Freiburg and author of a once well-known study of the Belvedere Apollo, *The Vatican Apollo* (1833). The next eldest, Karl (Wilhelm), born in 1800, became a high school professor of mathematics at Erlangen; his ingenious alternative proof of a proposition in geometry is still well known to mathematicians as Feuerbach's theorem. The third eldest, Eduard (August), born in 1803, had, on his father's insistence, dropped an interest in the natural sciences and became Professor of Jurisprudence at Erlangen. Ludwig's younger brother Friedrich, abandoning his theological studies, turned to philology and Oriental literature. He was to become a devoted, if not especially able, propagandist of Ludwig's ideas. Joseph Anselm's son, as we have noted, became the well-known German painter Anselm Feuerbach.

Ludwig Feuerbach, then, was the fourth son of the marriage of Anselm von Feuerbach and his wife Wilhelmine, *née* Tröster. Four more children – the son Friedrich and three daughters – were born after him.[19] For all his liberalism, academic seriousness and concern with dignity, Anselm von Feuerbach was a man of fiery and impulsive temperament, known in the family as 'Vesuvius'. His career in Bavaria, in the University, in Munich and in the Court of Appeal, was punctuated by personal tensions with his colleagues. In 1813 he formed a liaison with Nannette Brunner, the wife of his close friend Hans Kasper Brunner. (Brunner, whose friendship with Anselm was not affected, at periods took part in what was simply a *ménage à trois*.) Nannette bore a son, Anselm, in 1815; she and Anselm von Feuerbach lived together in Bamberg and Ansbach. In 1816, Anselm formally separated from his wife to live with Nannette; he returned to her in 1822, a few months after Nannette's death. All this did not prevent Anselm from being a domestic tyrant; he closely supervised his children's education during the period of the separation from his wife; he later moralized at the young Ludwig much as the far more timid and conventional and infinitely less able Heinrich Marx moralized at the young Karl. Anselm invited Ludwig, then in his student days, not to neglect meeting people from whom he could learn and not to forget that his father was his best friend (cf. W XII, 217–18). These, of course, were the manners of the times.

Ludwig, after primary school in Munich, in 1817 left his mother's house and entered the *Gymnasium* in Ansbach, to be under the eye of his father. By his sixteenth birthday he showed a clear religious tendency. He took lessons in Hebrew from the son of a local rabbi,[20] completed his high school examinations in 1822 and remained in his (now reunited) parents' house for a year before proceeding to study theology at Heidelberg. (In Bavaria, after 1814, an ultramontane Catholic Reaction had become significantly stronger. It had, in turn, produced an illiberal, fundamentalist reaction in the small Protestant community to which Anselm belonged. This climate accounts for some of Anselm von Feuerbach's difficulties in the public service and for the decision to send Ludwig to Heidelberg.) Ludwig threw himself into his studies with such enthusiasm that the father felt obliged to warn him against excess in virtue (W XII, 217). He attended lectures in speculative theology by Karl Daub (an eclectic influenced by the chief contemporary trends, who at that time was passing through a Hegelian phase) and on church history by H. E. G. Paulus, regarded as a distinguished representative of the Kantian rationalism of the Enlightenment. Within a year, Feuerbach was resolved to hear no more at second-hand and succeeded in gaining his father's consent to his transfer to Berlin, to the centre of real thought where Hegel himself lectured. He arrived there in 1824.[21]

There followed an incident of police persecution which, though not terribly significant in itself, was taken by Feuerbach – and by those German liberal intellectuals who knew of it, including

Feuerbach's father – as symptomatic of the Philistinism and illiberalism of the times, stretching from the Congress of Vienna to the revolutions of 1848. The secret investigation commission set up by the Prussian Government under von Kamptz had received a report that several of the brothers Feuerbach were members of a secret organization. Karl, already a mathematics teacher at Erlangen, was arrested in May 1824 and transferred from one prison to another until he attempted to commit suicide in December 1824. (He was finally released without any evidence of 'subversive activities' being brought against him.) Ludwig, who had arrived in Berlin on 18 April 1824, was placed under police observation (though not prevented from attending lectures); reports on his movements were sent to the secret police; his acceptance as a matriculated student was delayed first on technical grounds, then on the ground that he was under police investigation. Status as a matriculated student was finally granted him on 19 May after he had deposed in an examination at Police Headquarters that he was not a member of any secret organization. Then, in June, he was summoned before a University disciplinary commission: the Kamptz commission claimed to have new evidence of his membership of a secret organization, a passage in one of his letters (seized from the recipient in Darmstandt) in which he referred to political events being discussed in 'the circle of the able'. The University commission was persuaded that the 'circle of the able' (*Kreis der Tüchtigen*) was not a secret organization, but a normal enough way of saying that the discussion took place among the more intelligent students, though matters hung in the balance for a month. On 28 July 1824, his twentieth birthday, Feuerbach was finally admitted to the Faculty of Theology in Berlin. His father, not apprised of these events by Ludwig until they were safely behind, heard of them with the deepest indignation. 'What times are these,' he wrote in reply to Ludwig's letter (W XII, 234), 'in which a young man, no matter how decent, living no matter how innocently, concerned only with himself and his studies, able to show formal, public testimonials to his lawful, irreproachable, even exemplary behaviour, in spite of all this is not secure from the attacks and persecutions of spies?'

While still a theological student, Ludwig Feuerbach attended Hegel's lectures regularly and with enthusiasm; he became an Hegelian and felt that he could no longer reconcile studies in theology with his interest in philosophy. Later, in 1846, he wrote of this period:[22] 'I entered the University of Berlin in a highly divided, unhappy, undecided state; I already felt in myself the conflict between philosophy and theology, the necessity of sacrificing either philosophy to theology or theology to philosophy.' In seeking his father's permission to come to Berlin he had (cunningly?) referred to the opportunity of hearing the great Schleiermacher in Berlin's Theology Faculty; after hearing Hegel as well, he found that 'the theological mishmash of freedom and dependence, reason and faith, was completely repellent to my soul with its demand for truth, i.e., unity, decisiveness, absoluteness'. Breaking the news to his father was a matter of some delicacy. There is no sign that Anselm von Feuerbach was willing to recall that thirty years earlier he himself had quarrelled with his parents and had been cut off from support because he insisted on doing philosophy instead of jurisprudence at Jena. Ludwig wrote to his old teacher Daub, who conceded that he had felt, at Heidelberg, that Ludwig would not stay long at theology. The matter was referred to the Berlin lawyer Eduard Hitzig, a friend of Anselm, who testified to Ludwig's seriousness. Anselm gave his consent, though with bad grace, and Ludwig transferred to the Philosophy Faculty in 1825. In the same year, however, King Maximilian I died. His successor to the Bavarian throne refused to renew the government stipend granted to the Feuerbach children for their studies, and the family faced financial difficulties. In the middle of 1826, Ludwig Feuerbach left Berlin for Erlangen, where his studies could be pursued more cheaply.[23] He gained the degree there in 1828 with his thesis *De ratione una, universali, infinita*, published in the same year. At Easter, 1829, Ludwig Feuerbach became a *docent* in philosophy at Erlangen, opening his academic activity with lectures on Descartes and Spinoza. He went on to lecture on logic and metaphysics in the following semester, which he did regularly until 1832.

At this stage, Feuerbach would have been regarded as a member of the Hegelian school. Two of the main themes of his subsequent philosophical development, his rejection of Christianity and his belief in the objectivity of nature and the importance of knowledge through the senses, however, were slowly being adumbrated in his work. His inaugural dissertation *Of Reason, One, Universal, Infinite*, took up an Hegelian theme in an Hegelian way – reason as the

activity of the universal, as that which comprehends nature and
gives it significance and unites thinking and being. What the
senses bring us was still seen as inadequate and incomplete, but
Feuerbach did deviate significantly from Hegel in using the
Hegelian conception of reason to attack Christianity, to put the
claims of philosophy against those of religion. Reason, he argued,
is that which enables man to break through the borders of individuality, which unites him with other men, while Christianity is
the religion of egoism and individuality.[24] Then in 1830, Feuerbach
published anonymously his *Thoughts on Death and Immortality*[25]
with an appendix of satirical-theological epigrams, in which he
announced that religion was merely a kind of insurance company
and that theology could free itself from an unbearable dualism by
negating itself forthwith. The appendix immediately aroused the
wrath of the censor. The work itself, though strongly Hegelian in
form, was well understood to deny the immortality of the soul, to
affirm that man's only dwelling-place was on this earth and that
the only immortality lay in human culture, which was handed
down from generation to generation and in which a man's 'spirit'
survived his person. Even Feuerbach's father was shocked, both
by the book's denial of immortality and by the effects it was likely
to have on his son's career. On the latter point he was right; denied
promotion at Erlangen, Feuerbach absented himself from the
University in 1832 and became increasingly aware of the fact that
the combination of theological outrage and Prussian conservatism
was closing all prospects of a serious University career to him. He
toyed with the idea of emigrating to Paris, under the naïvely
mistaken impression that Holbach and Helvétius, whom he
already admired, had been able to work and publish in peace there,
that Paris, indeed, had long been the city of intellectual freedom.
He formed a close friendship with Christian Kapp, extraordinary
Professor of Philosophy at Erlangen, and later Professor of Philosophy at Heidelberg. Kapp did everything possible to recommend
Feuerbach for University posts – but in vain. Feuerbach returned
to Erlangen, without making use of his right to lecture, but he did
attempt to further his academic prospects by publishing a series of
academic works in the history of philosophy – the *History of
Modern Philosophy From Bacon To Spinoza* (1833), which was
based on his lectures at Erlangen and well-received in the professional journals, a second volume of the history, dealing with the

philosophy of Leibniz (1837) and his study of Pierre Bayle (1838). Except for a semester in 1835–6, when his friends persuaded Feuerbach to give a series of lectures at Erlangen for those students who wanted to hear him, Feuerbach remained firm in the resolve that he would not lecture at Erlangen as long as he was left in the lowly position of *Privatdocent*. All attempts at gaining him promotion or having him appointed to more senior philosophical vacancies in such centres as Marburg, Heidelberg and Freiburg foundered on objections to his irreligiousness. In Erlangen, in 1836, a third attempt to have Feuerbach promoted to an extraordinary professorship came to nothing. The Pro-Rector, J. G. V. Engelhardt, a Professor of Church History, wrote to Feuerbach saying that the only objection to Feuerbach's appointment was the claim that he had been involved in the publication of the *Thoughts on Death and Immortality*; could Feuerbach put him in a position to reject these charges as false? Feuerbach took this to be a polite refusal to appoint him.

Meanwhile, in 1834, Feuerbach had met Bertha Löw, a year older than himself, who after the death of her father in 1822 had inherited a share in a porcelain factory in Bruckberg. A friendship and a correspondence sprang up. Soon the couple regarded themselves as engaged. Feuerbach continued to wait for the offer of a post and to publish his philosophical writings. In 1837 he threw himself, for a while, into the study of anatomy and physiology as conscious compensation for the philosopher's one-sided concentration on mind and spirit.[26] On 12 November 1837 he and Bertha were married at Bruckberg, Feuerbach's joblessness notwithstanding. For the next twenty-three years, they were to live modestly but comfortably in rural seclusion in the castle at Bruckberg, relying on the profits of the porcelain factory and the proceeds of Feuerbach's writings. Feuerbach, convinced that he was quite unlikely to be offered a University post worthy of his talents (another attempt by his friends in 1840 to secure him a chair failed), increasingly began to hold himself up as an independent thinker, free of the narrow professionalism and stultifying division of the sciences imposed by University organization and hallowed by University life. He claimed to be discovering greater insight and native intelligence in common men, peasants and artisans, than in the philosophers of the schools; he sang paeans of praise to nature and the natural life. 'Once in Berlin and now in a village! What idiocy! But no, dear friend!' he wrote in the *Philosophical Fragments* concerning Bruckberg (W II, 379–80).

> See, the sand which Berlin's State philosophy . . . threw into my eyes I wash out completely with the spring of Nature. I learnt logic at a German University, but optics, the art of *seeing*, I learnt for the first time in a German village. The philosopher, at least as I understand him, must have Nature as his friend, he must know her not only from books but face to face. I had long pined for such a personal acquaintance; how happy I am that this need can finally be satisfied.

The move to Bruckberg began Feuerbach's evolution as an independent philosopher; the first ten years there marked the high-point of his philosophic career and were probably the happiest period of his life. His *Thoughts on Death and Immortality* had established Feuerbach as a coming young man; his *History of Modern Philosophy*, warmly received in Hegelian circles as in many respects better than J. E. Erdmann's,[27] established his reputation as an important Hegelian. Until 1838, however, his writings suggest no strongly independent Feuerbachian position: his historical work, though less inclined to force philosophical thinkers into a Hegelian pattern than Erdmann's, stands on unmistakably Hegelian ground, still pouring a fair measure of contempt on 'thoughtless empiricism'. Feuerbach had defended Hegel against Bachmann in a review published in 1835; his lectures at Erlangen in 1835–6 had still been quite Hegelian in spirit. But at the end of the Leibniz book, Feuerbach began to sharpen his contrast between philosophy and theology; in the Bayle book this came to the foreground. 'Bayle' became a pseudonym for Feuerbach himself, who was now clearly moving towards a rejection of idealism as itself a theological form of philosophy. The 'Contribution to the Critique of Hegelian Philosophy' (1839) marked an unmistakable break with Feuerbach's Hegelian period; it set him up as an independent and fundamental critic of idealism in general and of the Hegelian philosophy in particular. The *Essence of Christianity* two years later sealed this reputation and made Feuerbach the most talked-of philosopher in Germany, among both radicals and their theological opponents. His *Preliminary Theses for the Reform of Philosophy* and his *Basic Propositions for the Philosophy of the*

Future followed in quick succession, both published in Switzerland because of censorship. This was the period in which Karl Marx wrote: 'You have no other way to truth and freedom than through the fire-brook [*Feuer-bach*]. Feuerbach is the purgatory of to-day.'[28] But although Feuerbach had given some articles to the Young Hegelian Arnold Ruge for his radical *Annals*, he held himself somewhat aloof from the activity of Ruge, of the young Karl Marx and of those others who were anxious to flourish the weapon of criticism in the periodical press. A letter from Marx in 1843, asking Feuerbach for a critique of Schelling for the *Deutsch-französische Jahrbücher*, received a courteous answer, but the request was clearly declined.[29] Feuerbach held, in the main, to his studies in the field of religion, revising the *Essence of Christianity*, defending or explaining it in the light of criticism, publishing several articles on religion and theological matters, issuing the *Essence of Religion* in 1846 and, in the same year, bringing out the first two volumes of his *Collected Works*. He knew that the *succès de scandale* of the *Essence of Christianity* had killed whatever lingering hopes there may have been of his appointment to a University chair through Kapp's continuing efforts; he (rightly) did not take seriously Ruge's talk of founding a 'free academy' at Dresden in order to lure Feuerbach out of his nest at Bruckberg.[30] The *Essence of Christianity*, however, was going splendidly – three editions in seven years. Feuerbach had no doubt that it was an epoch-making work. His revisions of the second and third editions were along three lines: he toned down the Hegelianisms still strong in the first edition; he tried to make the style more popular and accessible, and he tried to clinch his arguments by a growing mass of quotations from religious and theological thinkers themselves. 'My work will be much improved in the second edition,' he had written to his publisher in January 1842 (cited in Bolin's memoir, W XII, 83).

I have already given a stronger basis and further development to much of the material, and I have done this so clearly that the work must be accorded the status of an unavoidable, evident truth, of a scientific, even more than scientific, of a *world-historical, fact* . . . I am only still undecided about the arrangement of the whole. Strictly, I should have put the negative part [the criticism of theology, which comes last in the book]

first and the positive part last, then the stupid would see that
this book contains the elements of a *positive*, obvious philosophy, fresh from life and true theoretically as well as practically. But what worries me is thinking about the damned
censorship, which will believe that it is confronted by the very
devil himself if I put the negative part first.

In the end, he did not – but he was to spend much of his time
between 1841 and 1848 emphasizing that the *Essence of Christianity* was not primarily an atheistic assault against religion, but a real
attempt to preserve the moral and cultural content of religion, to
help religion break out of what had become a confining chrysalis.

It was Feuerbach's view that the real content of religion could
only be expressed through the establishing of democratic politics –
through making politics the religion of mankind – and Feuerbach
had himself suffered from censorship and police investigation.[31]
Nevertheless, throughout the period 1843–8 Feuerbach was
extremely sceptical of the prospects for political revolution in
Germany. He had liked Ruge's criticisms of the 'German-
Christian juste-milieu', he wrote to Ruge in March 1843 (W XIII,
120), but warned: 'I remain firm in my opinion: in Germany
theology is the only practical vehicle for politics, the only vehicle
likely to lead to success, at least in the near future.' He had, of
course, extensive personal acquaintanceship with many of the
representatives of liberal and of radical Germany, and his thought
was widely recognized to have had great influence upon them. On
a visit to Heidelberg, he had met the great poet Georg Herwegh,
living as a political exile in Switzerland, whose poetry shows
strong signs of Feuerbach's influence. Several of the men involved
in the 1848 Revolution in Germany were friends of Feuerbach.
When the Revolution came, he welcomed it, but with caution
about its prospects. On 3 March 1848 he wrote to his publisher,
Otto Wigand (W XIII, 156): 'Vive la République. The French
revolution has also brought out a revolution in me. As soon as I
can, as soon as I have settled all my affairs here, I go to Paris,
without wife, without child, without books, without—.' He confesses that there are other grounds that are driving him out of
Bruckberg (the beginnings of financial difficulties, it seems) and
adds, 'But where shall I make my domicile? In a town of German
Philistines? Never again. In a German village or in Paris. Those

were always my chosen alternatives. My honour demands this.' A
few weeks later he was writing to Herder: 'Now is no time for
philosophy, though this is the time above all not to lose one's
head' (W XIII, 157). Paris forgotten, Feuerbach travelled to
Leipzig to see Wigand. In the newspapers he read that Breslau
University was considering calling him and Arnold Ruge to chairs;
everybody was predicting that Feuerbach would now become an
academic luminary in the free Germany. In Ansbach, the popular
assembly proposed Feuerbach as a delegate for the Frankfurt
Diet; the Frankfurt newspaper *Didaskalia* contained a flowery
appeal, signed by 'several Heidelberg students', calling on the
'noble thinker, you who in the years of servile learning never
departed from reason and science by seeking to justify the *status
quo*', to recognize that 'the hour of your effectiveness has struck', to
leave his rural retreat and come forth as a delegate to the National
Assembly. 'It was you, with a few others, who offered us comfort
and a refuge when we left the dishonoured lecture halls of German
universities, revolted by the lies of the learned, and sought truth'
(W XII, 114).

Feuerbach did not become a candidate, but he did travel to
Frankfurt. There, he held discussions with Ruge and Carl Vogt
(who were members of the National Assembly) and he attended
the Democratic Congress in Frankfurt organized by the radical,
free-thinking wing of German democracy to protest against their
insufficient representation in the National Parliament. To the
proceedings of this Congress, however, Feuerbach lent the distinction of his name rather than the active participation of his
voice; he sat there almost completely silent. Political activism did
not impress him: he was anxious to be writing again. Plans by the
Baden Ministry of Education to have him called to a chair of
philosophy were still moving slowly; he expected nothing from
them. The progress of the 'revolution' in general appalled him.
'Politics has driven me out of Frankfurt,' he wrote to Otto Wigand
from Darmstadt in September 1848. 'I couldn't stand it any longer
after these latest, sad events. *German* freedom and unity is a
devilish mockery of freedom and unity. We are on the path that we
already took in 1832: we have raised ourselves only to sink all the
deeper.' Feuerbach, of course, was proved right. The revolution
failed; Feuerbach was not called to a university post; officialdom
remained officialdom. Feuerbach's recognition came from the

students at Heidelberg who invited him to give a series of public lectures on the essence of religion as a symbol of the new, free academic life. The lectures, given twice a week in the City Hall, took place from 1 December 1848 to 2 March 1849; they were attended by a wide-ranging audience of academics, students, townspeople, workers; they were the last high-point of Feuerbach's public activity. (Among those attending the lectures, and enormously impressed with their content, if not with their 'bad, laboured delivery', was the physiologist Jacob Moleschott, with whom Feuerbach quickly struck up a close friendship and whose medical materialism Feuerbach soon accepted with enthusiasm.)[32]

Back in Bruckberg, Feuerbach watched the expected collapse of the Frankfurt Parliament and the re-establishment of German Reaction with some detachment, seeking consolation in his scientific studies and in his work on religion. Moleschott sent Feuerbach his popular textbook on foodstuffs, published in 1850. Feuerbach reviewed (or rather summarized) it under the title 'Natural Science and the Revolution' and wrote: 'Foodstuffs become blood; blood becomes heart and brain, the stuff of thought and attitudes. Human fare is the basis of human education and attitudes. If you want to improve the people give it, instead of homilies against sin, better food. *Man is what he eats.*' (W X, 22.)

In October 1851 Feuerbach published the Heidelberg *Lectures on the Essence of Religion* as the eighth volume of his collected works; in the preface he announced that he had taken part in the political and non-political events surrounding the revolution 'only as a critical by-stander and listener, and this for the simple reason that I cannot take part actively in thoughtless and unsuccessful enterprises, and that at the beginning of these activities I already foresaw, or sensed beforehand, their upshot' (W XII, 132–3). Feuerbach went on to explain, ostensibly in reply to a demand from a well-known Frenchman to explain why he had not played a more active part, that if a revolution broke out again, it would be a great and successful one, spelling the end of monarchy and of the hierarchical organization of society. This revolution would not come in Feuerbach's lifetime, however. Meanwhile he was taking part in a great and successful revolution the results of which would be felt only in the course of centuries. For just as he did not believe in miracles and gods in religion, Feuerbach wrote, so he did not believe in miracles and gods in the field of politics. The

March revolution had still been a child, even if an illegitimate child, of Christian faith: how could the Frenchman expect Feuerbach's unbelieving spirit to be linked with the spirit of the Parliament at Frankfurt?

Meanwhile, Feuerbach's brother Eduard had died and the work of bringing out their father Anselm's biographical remains had fallen to Ludwig. He completed it in 1851; the two volumes were published and (combining the appeal of Anselm and Ludwig as co-authors) were expected to sell well. Like the Heidelberg lectures, however, they had in fact very limited success, confirming the marked decline of Feuerbach's reputation and appeal since the defeat of the 1848 revolution. Feuerbach for a period toyed with the idea of emigrating to America. There – with the post–1848 emigrations – he possibly had as many admirers as in Germany, and a number of correspondents. Christian Kapp's nephew, Friedrich Kapp, himself an admirer and close friend of Feuerbach, had gone to America and Feuerbach's publisher, Otto Wigand, feeling the pressure of the new reactionary climate on his publishing house, was thinking of emigration. Nothing came of it, however; Wigand remained in Germany; Feuerbach was by now in sufficiently straitened financial circumstances to lack the fare for a visit of exploration to America. He remained in Bruckberg, spending almost five years on his study of the material foundations of Greek religion, the *Theogony*, published in 1857 as the ninth volume of his *Collected Works*. It was regarded by the critical public as adding nothing new to his critique of religion and had no success whatever.

Meanwhile, the porcelain factory had been doing increasingly badly. Feuerbach's own money had been put into the sinking ship without proper security; it was lost in turn and liquidation could finally not be avoided. The years 1858–9 saw the final failure of the business; in 1860, Feuerbach and his family had to seek a new, and more modest, place to live. They chose a small place at Rechenberg, near Munich, but were in desperate financial straits and could not move without help. Friedrich Kapp's family came to their aid through a wealthy acquaintance and admirer of Feuerbach, Otto Lüning, who discreetly raised a collection among Feuerbach's followers in the newly-founded *Deutscher National-verein*, though he had some difficulty in persuading Feuerbach to accept the money. The Feuerbachs moved to Rechenberg, where they were still visited by occasional admirers, including Bolin, Friedrich Kapp (on a visit from America), the somewhat confused exiled Russian nobleman Jacob von Khanikoff, and others. At this stage, too, Feuerbach formed a friendship with his enthusiastic follower, the peasant philosopher Konrad Deubler, who had suffered a great deal from police persecution in the 1850s (it was one thing to be a middle-class radical, quite a different thing to be a peasant or working-man wanting to read and discuss). In his philosophical preoccupations, however, Deubler is completely uninteresting. From Switzerland, Ferdinand Lassalle sent Feuerbach his writings, as a mark of respect. In 1866 Feuerbach issued the tenth volume of his *Collected Works* with writings from the Rechenberg period, collected under the title 'God, Freedom and Immortality from the Standpoint of Anthropology'; it fell very flat indeed, failing to arouse interest even among Feuerbach's admirers. By now the years were passing on the whole quietly and uneventfully; Feuerbach worked on ethical fragments, but his financial future was again very worrying; friends tried to gain him a national pension in recognition of his services to German culture, but without success. They considered a popular edition of his works, but no one was too hopeful of its intellectual impact or commercial success. In summer, 1870, Feuerbach suffered his first stroke, leaving him confused and apathetic; a social democratic paper in Würzburg published the news under a headline indicating that the great democratic thinker was sick and in condition of desperate material need: contributions from Germany, Belgium, England, Austria and the United States came in, making it possible to seek proper medical care for Feuerbach. His condition, however, became progressively weaker: he died, in Nuremberg, on 13 September 1872. His wife survived him by eleven years. She was buried next to him in Nuremberg.

PART TWO

The Critical Philosophy

3. Ludwig Feuerbach's critique of religion

'God was my first thought; Reason my second; Man my third and last thought,' Feuerbach wrote in a famous passage of the *Philosophical Fragments* which he collected to illustrate his intellectual development (W II, 388). He had, of course, abandoned the study of Protestant theology almost at the outset of his University career. 'Palestine is too narrow for me – I must, I must go out into the wide, wide world and only the philosopher carries this world on his shoulders,' he wrote to his father in 1825 (W XII, 243; cf. W II, 362). Nevertheless, more than twenty years later, Feuerbach himself emphasized that all his writings, including his studies in the history of philosophy and his criticism of idealism, 'have only one aim, one will, one thought, one theme. This theme is religion and theology and whatever is connected with them' (W VIII, 6; GW VI, 12). Feuerbach was right. The criticism of religion does lie at the heart of his thinking and his writing. It is the central position towards which his whole philosophical *Weltanschauung* first tended and around which it then further developed. It is the focus that gives definition and shape to the rest of his views. Though not historically his earliest position, it can most usefully come first in any exposition or assessment of his philosophy in general. Religion became for Feuerbach the fundamental phenomenon in the history of human culture; to understand it was to understand man. It was for this reason that Feuerbach was anxious to deny that he was an atheist: he had not come to destroy religion, but to explain it. Thereby he would show how its fantasy-promise could be fulfilled in reality. 'Religion,' he writes in the preface to the second edition of the *Essence of Christianity*,

is the dream of the human mind. But even in dreams we do not find ourselves in emptiness or in heaven, but on earth in the realm of reality; we only see real things in the entrancing splendour of imagination and caprice instead of seeing them in the simple daylight of reality and necessity. Hence I do nothing more to religion – and to speculative philosophy and theology as well – than to open its eyes . . . i.e., I change the object as it is in the imagination into the object as it is in reality (W VII, 287; EC xxxix).

Feuerbach's technique, then, is that of the man who is seeking the empirical sources of human beliefs, that in terms of which they are to be appraised and understood. By 1841, he is, in his presuppositions and his general approach, unquestionably in the broad sense an empiricist. He does not believe that there is anything outside or above the ordinary world of our senses, anything that does not exist in space and time. This is one aspect of what he means when he says he is a materialist.[1] We shall see later that Feuerbach was not in the 1840s, if ever, a crude materialist, wishing to reduce everything to matter. Certainly in his critique of religion there is no suggestion that only matter is real, that reason, conscience, consciousness, hope and faith are in some way unreal. Feuerbach has rather the empiricist's suspicion of high-sounding abstractions; he rejects all that which claims, in principle, to be above or beyond sensory knowledge, to exist outside empirical reality and in abstraction from it. Non-empirical views seem to him – in my view rightly – a form of self-mystification, a projection of real components into an illusory world. They are based on an abstraction of functions and relations from the empirical processes which have these functions and relations. In two early essays, Feuerbach argues that speculative (i.e., idealist) philosophy and speculative theology are merely drunken philosophy which needs to become sober. They are forms of self-mystification, of faith which abstracts and reveres itself. Fichtean idealism correctly recognizes that self-consciousness is absolute for man, that for man it is the only measure of all things. Fichte, however, then reverses the true relation of subject and predicate and says, 'the absolute is self-consciousness'. The Hegelian philosophy is not open to the objection that it projects the human species into the godhead but it, too, reverses the relation of subject and predicate. Instead of saying that man knows himself in God, it says that God knows himself in man; instead of saying reason is absolute, it says 'the Absolute is Reason'; instead of saying that man produces reason, it says that reason produces man.[2] Speculative philosophy fails to see that the relationship between philosophy and theology is the relationship between thought (reason) and fantasy, or, as Feuerbach puts it, between healthy and unhealthy states of mind.

Feuerbach's initial aim is analytic and in a non-vicious sense reductive. He does not confront religion as an external critic, as one who is simply concerned to show that there is no God. This, Feuerbach believed, was work successfully completed by the eighteenth-century Enlightenment. The point now was to understand religion, to show its genesis in something non-supernatural in terms of which it could be explained and understood, thus undermining the supernatural pretensions of religion at the same time as accounting for them. Feuerbach's method, applied and extended by such thinkers as Marx and Freud, has become one of the standard ways of dealing with 'ideologies' as opposed to theories – we show how they arose and what needs they satisfy or what longings they appeal to.[3]

Feuerbach's form of exposition, especially in his writings on religion and on the reform of philosophy, was literary rather than philosophical. He preferred the telling image to a careful distinction, the illuminating insight to the deductive argument. His favourite mode of philosophical expression was the aphoristic sentence or paragraph. As Lange put it,[4]

> To a clear logic Feuerbach never attained. The nerve of his philosophizing remained, as everywhere in the idealistic epoch, divination. A 'consequently' in Feuerbach does not, as with Kant and Herbart, carry the force of a real, or at least an intended, inference of the understanding, but it means, as with Schelling and Hegel, a leap to be taken in thought.

The aphoristic and comparatively unsystematic character of Feuerbach's writing was no doubt aggravated by the Hegelian tradition in which he began his work and especially by that philosophically extremely troublesome German word *Wesen*, which can mean a being or thing, a way of existing or a metaphysical essence,[5] or all three of these with confusing impartiality. All too often, this leads Feuerbach into the stylistic trick of over-emphasizing his points to the exclusion of everything else, including the points he will be emphasizing in the next paragraph or chapter. He is a man saying 'the real truth of religion is A' and a little later, 'the real truth of religion is B' – when all he means is that both A and B are of vital importance to the understanding (or the historical development) of religion. The result of this was noted by as sympathetic a reader of Feuerbach as the Russian positivist P. L. Lavrov, who wrote[6] that Feuerbach's effect on the reader was more like that of a speech in the pulpit than like that of a University lecture – Feuerbach's style abounded in conceptions and mannerisms typical of sermons. Engels, recalling the impact which the *Essence of Christianity* made in Germany in the 1840s, emphasized the same point:

> Even the shortcomings of the book contributed to its immediate effect. Its literary, sometimes even highflown, style secured for it a large public and was at any rate refreshing after long years of abstract and abstruse Hegelianizing. The same is true of its extravagant deification of love, which, coming after the intolerable sovereign rule of 'pure reason', had its excuse, if not justification.[7]

Irritating as Feuerbach's literary imprecision and hyperbole can be, and fatal as they were to any ambition that he may have had of becoming a philosopher of the first rank, we should not allow them to blind us to the importance and fruitfulness of a great deal that Feuerbach is saying. His method, indeed, was in part forced upon him by his material and his aim. He was dealing with religion as a fantasy or symbolic dream; he was therefore interested not only in arguments, but in passions and in fantasies, and his problem was to understand and communicate their content rather than to criticize their coherence. The result is a certain preoccupation with the material being analysed or communicated at the moment and a lack of systematic exposition and philosophical nicety. Feuerbach in consequence has to be read sympathetically; his work is a mixture of illuminating insights and important if undeveloped logical criticisms, often buried in extravagances of style and overemphasized illustrations. Many of his insights, also, stand independently of the rather loose 'system' or 'method' in which they are embedded: to 'summarize' Feuerbach into a set of very general propositions would be to miss much that is most interesting and suggestive in his work. In what follows, I have endeavoured, therefore, to keep much of Feuerbach's detail, to leave, as far as possible, the living flesh on what would otherwise be a striking but somewhat brittle skeleton.

*

The *Essence of Christianity* is Feuerbach's best-known work on religion. To a considerable extent, it is self-contained. It was read at the time with an enthusiasm only matched by the lack of care with which its readers assimilated Feuerbach's position. Its overemphasis was always taken seriously, most of all by its admirers; its qualifications were usually neglected. A great deal of the criticism levelled at Feuerbach was consequently misplaced, and he spent an inordinate amount of his time in the next four years explaining what he had really said (or meant). For Feuerbach's view of religion generally, we should take the *Essence of Christianity* together with those of his later works that also take account of polytheism – the *Essence of Religion* (1845), the *Lectures on the Essence of Religion*, delivered at Heidelberg in 1848–9 and published in 1851, and his study of the material foundations of Greek religion, *The Theogony* (1857).[8] We should also consider some of his more minor writings on Christianity and on the reactions to his *magnum opus* – e.g., 'On Philosophy and Christianity' (1839), 'Toward the Appraisal of the Work *Essence of Christianity*' (1843) and 'The Essence of Faith in Luther's Sense' (1844). Taking this general corpus of work and attempting to keep some of Feuerbach's language and style without allowing it to obscure his points too much for the modern reader, we may say that Feuerbach's position on religion was this:

Religion is a dream, a fantasy-picture which expresses man's situation and at the same time provides a fantasy-gratification of man's wish to overcome that situation. Religion is therefore primarily practical rather than theoretical: it is an 'art of life'. In religion man recognizes his helplessness, his dependence, and he seeks to overcome it by calling in the aid of the imagination. Sacrifice and prayer thus stand at the very centre of religion and reveal to us its essential character and aim. The ground of sacrifice is dependence, the result of the (successful) sacrifice is confidence, self-feeling, independence (W VII; 462). The same is true of prayer – 'not, certainly, the prayer before and after meals, the ritual of animal egotism, but the prayer pregnant with sorrow, the prayer of disconsolate love, the prayer which expresses the power of the heart that crushes man to the ground, the prayer which begins in despair and ends in rapture' (EC 122; W VI, 147).[9] Men rush to religion in their need, because it is in their need that they feel their wants most strongly and yet discover that they are helpless save in fantasy (W VII, 466). The Soviet Marxist writer Deborin[10] in this respect accurately expressed Feuerbach's position: religion 'has for its presupposition the contradiction between "can" and "want", between the means that can be used to achieve an end and wishing for that end, between reality and imagination, between being and consciousness'. Because religion expresses a wish, it is not merely a mechanical projection of that which man finds on this earth; it incorporates a moral judgment as well. What man praises and approves and therefore wishes for is God to him; what he blames, condemns, is – for him – not divine. The religious fantasy, in expressing a moral judgment, also becomes a form of compensation. In a number of striking passages, Feuerbach emphasizes that men seek in heaven what they cannot find on earth. They compensate for their frustrations. 'The more empty life is, the fuller, the more concrete is God. The impoverishing of the real world and the enriching of God is one act. Only the poor man has a rich God' (W VI, 19; EC 73) – just as it is the chaste monk who worships the most sensual Heavenly Virgin.

Religion, then, is in the fullest sense fantasy. By being fantasy, by being in essentials completely and ruthlessly man-centred, it comes into conflict with science and philosophy. 'Every object, of course, can be apprehended and known by man only in virtue of its relation to man – even in science,' Feuerbach writes (W II, 282). But in philosophy and in science this man-centredness is controlled by reason and objectivity, by a concern with what actually is the case. To philosophy and to science, the distinction between the true and the false is fundamental. In religion, there is no such control and no such concern. In religion, 'feeling elevates itself into a god . . . it cannot abide anything which contradicts it, *its* wishes alone are the only valid laws. The law of the heart as distinguished from the real laws of the world finds its outward expression in the miracle. The miracle is therefore the *natural*, and for that very reason the essential, conception which religion has of the world.'[11] 'Man wants to be God, that is the secret source of

God; man shall be God, that is its [religion's] frank and clearly-expressed ultimate purpose' (W IX, 361-2).

Religion, then, is a form of wishing – the expression of a lack or need and an attempt (in the imagination) to overcome that lack or need. 'Wishing,' Feuerbach writes, 'is the slave of need – but a slave with the desire for freedom.' Religion is hence practical and not theoretical, revolutionary activity and not mere contemplative knowledge. It is an attempt to work over reality into something satisfactory to man. But it does so in fantasy, because man is not yet ready, not yet powerful enough or knowledgeable enough, to do it in reality. When man does become knowledgeable and powerful enough, religion withers away and dies; its place is taken by politics and technology as the expression of firmly reality-centred human wishes and as the ground for a real as opposed to an imaginary transformation.

Religion, for Feuerbach then, is in the first place grounded in dependence; it arises in consequence of man's recognition of his helplessness and could not arise if he were not helpless. It is man's dependence, as Schleiermacher[12] saw, which is the whole foundation of religion. The concept of dependence in Feuerbach, however, as he himself emphasizes, is 'no theological, Schleiermachian, mystical, indeterminate, abstract feeling' (W VIII, 55; GW VI, 53-4). It is not Schleiermacher's vague metaphysical 'dependence', as felt by the finite when confronted by the shoreless infinite. It is the concrete empirical dependence of man on nature and other men. What distinguishes man from animals, according to Feuerbach, what explains why men have religion and animals have not, is that man is *conscious* of his dependence. Further, man has memory, he can fix past events in his mind. His experiences of the past can therefore provide the material from which he constructs his hopes for the future. Thus the belief in an after-life expresses the wish that the dead were still alive, that the past would continue into the present and the future. Fear of death is a primary fear at the base of religion: 'The grave of man,' Feuerbach writes, 'is the birthplace of the gods.'[13]

Feuerbach, it is true, tends to play fast and loose with the notion of dependence, just as he plays fast and loose with the notion of man-centredness. The theory of religion that he is outlining is one that seeks to present, but fails carefully to distinguish, both the *cognitive* and the *emotional* or affective roots of religion.[14] Feuerbach finds dependence and man-centredness in both, but the senses in which he uses these concepts vary.[15] Thus, on the cognitive side, he means by dependence merely that man selects for attention, or notices, those things which are important to him, which impede or further his interests. (This, in itself, as we shall see, was one of Feuerbach's more interesting contributions to a theory of knowledge.) Feuerbach does emphasize that man is in principle capable of deifying anything that strikes him, even if this leads to particular religious beliefs in which we find the deification of things quite indifferent to the progress of human culture. 'Yes, things and beings can be adored when there is no other reason for adoration than a certain mood or idiosyncrasy. If religion is nothing but psychology or anthropology, then it is obvious that idiosyncrasy and mood must also play a certain rôle in it' (W VII, 57), though not, of course, a fundamental or systematic rôle. Man, then, is here treated as dependent on things that do not necessarily make him feel helpless, and Feuerbach admits that such things can play a rôle in religion. On the affective or emotional side, however, it is nearly always dependence as helplessness that is emphasized. If he were not helpless, man would not *wish*, but *act*. Similarly, Feuerbach is working with two conceptions of man-centredness. On the cognitive side, man-centredness means no more than dependence meant there: the fact that man knows those things that concern him or come into relation with him and that man can only know them as they concern him or impinge upon him. On the affective side, man-centredness has a stronger meaning: it means that man makes his own wishes law. By combining the cognitive and the affective, and by combining the two different senses of man-centredness, Feuerbach came to his main slogan in the field of religion: 'the secret of theology is anthropology'.

Feuerbach was well aware, however, that the slogan could lead to misunderstanding. Reviewing the development of his thought and writing on religion in the first three of his lectures on the *Essence of Religion*, he said:

My teaching or my view of life can be summed up in two words: nature and man. The being (*Wesen*) which I regard as preceding man, the being which is the *cause* or *ground* of man, to which man is indebted for his origin and his existence, that being is in my view *not God* – a mystical, vague, ambiguous word – but nature – a clear, empirical, unambiguous word and being (*Wesen*). The being, however, in which nature becomes a personal, conscious, rational being – that is man (W VIII, 26; GW VI, 28–9).

Religion for Feuerbach, is a man-centred view of the world, it is not ultimately the worship of God but the worship of man. However, it necessarily involves nature. As a Continental writer, discussing Feuerbach, puts it: 'In the notion of God man relates the world to himself, so that the aspect of the world "for us", "from our standpoint" takes the ascendant instead of the world "in itself".'[16] This process of relating the universe to himself is a gradual one, in which man slowly becomes conscious of his position, of the fact that he is not only a natural part of the universe but also its latest and highest being, comprehending all of it within himself.[17] Man, Feuerbach stresses again and again, is part of nature and also dependent upon it, but man is also a conscious being constantly striving to liberate himself from thraldom to physical necessity and to dominate nature in his own interest. The history of religion, as we would then expect, reflects the history of man.

For Feuerbach – here quite conventional for his time – there are two great stages of human history: the stage in which man is primarily dependent upon nature, in which he is a simple primitive, and the stage in which man becomes truly socialized and becomes primarily dependent on other men (or as Feuerbach would put it, conscious of his humanity). The first stage finds its religious expression in polytheism as the worship of nature and of natural forces. The second stage finds its expression in monotheism as the worship of (spiritualized) man.[18] In the first stage, physical properties are emphasized, man deifies physical necessities; in the second stage moral or spiritual qualities become predominant, and man deifies what seem to him moral necessities.[19] He always does so, according to Feuerbach, in the light of feelings or emotions, for he is always wishing. 'In every wish we find concealed a god; but in or behind every god there lies concealed nothing but a wish' (W IX, 21). 'Whatever the object of religion may be, be it even a snail shell or a pebble, it is an object of religion only as an object of the emotions, of the imagination' (W VII, 470). When the ancient Mexicans created a Goddess of Salt, they were doing nothing more than worshipping salt itself – but worshipping salt *as the object of human wishes.* In other words, they were worshipping the economic, medical and technological functions of salt, as well as the aesthetic beauty of its crystals, all of which impress man as 'divine, i.e., benevolent, splendid, valuable and worthy of admiration' (W VII, 439). Similarly, when the Christian celebrates the miracles performed by Jesus, he is expressing human, earthly wishes. He is wishing that water were wine and that the dead were alive; at the same time he is celebrating the power of the human imagination,[20] which, just like Jesus, can make these things come to pass in a flash (W VI, 151–62; EC 126–34; W VII,12, 33). Primitive peoples concentrate on physical properties, on the physical powers of nature before which they still feel enormous helplessness. But because primitive peoples do not find their life dependent on earth in general, but on particular mountains, fields, streams, etc., they deify *particular* mountains, fields and streams. They invest them with *manitous* or spirits – they worship them not as inanimate objects but as they appear in human fantasy and imagination (W VII, 434–6). Because man depends on the seasons for his agricultural existence he dramatizes seasonal festivals. Because primitive man appreciates full well the rôle that the domestication of animals played in making him human, in distinguishing him from other animals, primitive man deifies these domestic animals and prays to them as though they were human. It is out of specific needs that man fashions the objects of his worship. Because of this concreteness, religions differ and each religion finds the other laughable. The Greeks laughed at the gods of the Egyptians not because Egyptian gods were different but because Egyptian needs were different – to the Greeks the Egyptian God is laughable because he does not correspond to Greek needs. In the ultimate sense, then, it is always man and his needs that are the ground of religion, the terms in which it is to be understood. As man changes, religion changes. Man ceases to be wild, primitive, determined (as Feuerbach believes) by momentary impressions and feelings and comes to be governed by laws. Religion, following suit, ceases to portray nature-gods as arbitrary, capricious, inexplicable – it makes them exercise understanding and reason and subject their own will to principles (W VII, 476). Again in the polytheistic stage, as man turns from what Feuerbach calls a pure physical existence to a political one, distinguishing himself consciously from nature, so his gods become political beings increasingly distinguished from nature. The forces of nature, which were earlier personified directly, now become mere attributes of political and moral forces: Zeus is no longer Thunder itself, but king of the gods and father of kings, using thunder to support the claims of royalty.[21] Man in this stage is still impressed by the splendours of nature and the power of natural forces, he still treats them as divine. But they are now divine in a subsidiary way, they are regarded as having secondary importance beside the political and the technological powers of man. They are no longer the things on which man feels most dependent. But even in the later stages of polytheism, man's mastery of nature is not complete. Just as man does not yet place himself completely above and outside nature, so his gods are not yet placed entirely above and outside nature. 'The pagans were not yet absolute, necessary, radical supernaturalists' (W VII, 477).

It is in monotheism that we find the completion of man's comparative liberation from nature, the turning of man's attention inward, to his own character. True monotheism, according to Feuerbach, arises only where man has already made himself the aim, the centre and the unifying force of nature. Polytheism, the religion of nature, converts real objects and forces into beings of the imagination – its function is to assuage man's fears by humanizing nature. Monotheism makes imaginings and thoughts into real beings, or rather, it makes the human powers of thought and imagination the most real, the absolute, the highest being (W VII, 478). Polytheism worships man only indirectly, by humanizing nature; monotheism worships him directly, by subjugating nature to a Divine Person. Polytheism takes as the model for humanization the physical individual, monotheism the universal human spirit. Polytheism recognizes the individual as part of the species; monotheism dramatizes the unity of the species and the individual, it personifies mankind into a man, whom it calls God.

In Judaism, which is the first stage of monotheism, human nature (according to Feuerbach) is deified only in a narrow, national, egoistic form. Jehovah is the representation of the Israelite national consciousness, of man as a national and not as a universal being.[22] Jehovah is the God of the Jews, the personification of their unity, of their national conscience, of their tribal laws – the focal point of their politics. Thus, in the Old Testament nature, providence and miracles are all represented as servants of Israel, as means to the satisfaction of man's practical, egoistic needs (W VI, 143-4; EC, 120).[23] Christianity, in cleansing Judaism of national egoism, or of national limitations, produced a new religion, a religion of man as a universal being in place of the religion of the Israelite (W VI, 144; 120-1).[24] Christianity, from its very inception, proclaimed that man had become God – and this is the real meaning of the Christian slogan that God has become man. In Catholicism, this message is still obscured by theology,[25] by the concern with that which distinguishes God from man. In Protestantism, the message becomes clear:

> The God who is man, the human God – i.e., Christ – he alone is the God of Protestantism. Protestantism is no longer interested in the question that concerns Catholicism, the question what is God *in himself*. Protestantism therefore no longer has a speculative or contemplative tendency like that of Catholicism; it is no longer theology but essentially only *Christology*, i.e., religious anthropology (W II, 246). *Homo homini deus est*.[26]

It is with the God of the Christians, and especially with God as Luther saw him, that Feuerbach is concerned in the *Essence of Christianity*. The God of Christianity, Feuerbach argues, is essentially but universally man – man stripped of his individual limitations, man as a species-being, man as an expression of the essentially human.[27] (It is part of Feuerbach's view, going back to his dissertation, that the essential human capacities are always universal and not individual, that they are properties of the species and connect men with each other instead of dividing them.) The final stage of religion, then, is the one that most obviously, almost openly, takes man's powers, qualities and essential characteristics and treats them as divine, i.e., as worthy of admiration and respect. This is the real content of religion and what is morally positive about it. What is distinctive in religion, what distinguishes it from true anthropology (either in its theoretical sense, as the science of man, or in its practical application, as politics), what brings religion into conflict with anthropology, is that these human powers, qualities and characters are projected, alienated, taken away from man, and set up as having independent existence outside of man.

Religion is thus not yet a direct appreciation by man of his own worth; it is only 'the first and moreover indirect self-consciousness of man' (W VI, 16; EC 13). This indirectness, the fact that man does not consciously realize that he is the object of his own worship but thinks that he is worshipping something above himself, provides the specific distinguishing characteristic of religion. This alienation, however, is only a perverted representation of the relationship between the individual and his species. 'The contradiction between the divine and the human is an illusory one . . . this contradiction is nothing more than the contradiction between the essentially human, between humanity, and the individual' (W VI, 17; EC 13-14).

Religion not only *is* anthropology, in order to perform its social function it *needs* to be. If God had no human properties, he would have no message, no meaning, for man. If God were wholly other than man, the perfection of God would neither depress nor inspire man. God would be irrelevant, he would have no moral significance. The moral force of religion depends upon its creating the consciousness of a rift or split between God and man; but such a rift can take place only between beings that have common properties, 'that could be one, that should be one, that therefore in essence and in truth are one' (W VI, 42; EC 33). The properties of divinity, then, are those human properties which man sees as divine because he sees them as having moral value or aesthetic beauty, as transcending his own individuality, as ends in themselves, or as essential aspects of his own being as a man. 'A quality is not divine because God possesses it, but God possesses it because it is in itself divine, because without it God would be a deficient being' (W VI, 26; EC 21).[28]

If religion is a projection of man as a 'species-being' (*Gattungswesen*), as a representative of humanity, then – according to Feuerbach – we must seek the key to the analysis of religion in the analysis of man as a species-being. Nevertheless, this Feuerbachian conception of the species-being, important as it seemed to many subsequent thinkers, especially to religious philosophers, has no particularly subtle or interesting connotation in Feuerbach. He uses a striking phrase, the phrase that 'man is both I and Thou', to bring together a number of different notions about man: the fact that man can see himself both subjectively and objectively, the fact that the human individual is somehow incomplete without both sexual and intellectual love, which requires recognition of and striving towards another, and the fact that thought, reason and speech use a language common to the species and are thus dependent on the existence of others. But when it comes to Feuerbach's analysis of man as a species-being, of man as an expression of the essentially human, he is quite traditional and conventional. The distinctively and essentially human for Feuerbach consists in the three traditional faculties of man, cognition, conation and affection – or, as Feuerbach puts it, Reason or Understanding, Will, and Love (or as he more commonly calls it, the Heart). These are the characters that are essential to man and yet transcend man as an individual. They are characteristics of the species and as such turn each man's attention beyond himself. They are characteristics that are perfections because they are ends in themselves. They are characteristics that are infinite, both because they are in principle boundless and because they possess man instead of being merely possessed by him. Man is seized by understanding, by love, by strength of will. Out of these characters he fashions his God. God is infinite knowledge, infinite will, and infinite love.

God, in the first place, is put over and above man as an alien being. What is the human characteristic that can be set over and above man, that leads to a split in man's conception of himself, that enables man to recognize his dependence and unworthiness? It is Intelligence, i.e., Reason or Understanding. God, then, is in the first place the human understanding conscious of its own perfection. It is free of the lusts and sufferings of the heart, it enables man to rise above them and even to come into conflict with them. The infinite spirit, then, is nothing but the human understanding freed from individuality and suffering.[29] This is the God of the theologians, God in his metaphysical guise, God as the *ens realissimum*.[30] We can no more make a picture of God in this guise, we can no more anthropomorphize the *ens realissimum*, than we can make a picture of the understanding. The independence of God, then, is the independence of the understanding; the unity of God is the unity of the understanding. God's infinity is its infinity and his necessity is its necessity – for without the understanding there is nothing, just as without God there is supposed to be nothing (W VI, 47–9; EC 38–41). The metaphysical God who is the understanding is primary in the eyes of the theologian, but he is not the God of religion. 'God as God – as the infinite, universal understanding devoid of all anthropomorphisms – has no more significance for religion than the general proposition from which it begins has for a particular science' (W VI, 54; EC 44). The understanding lays the ground for God's otherness, which relates only to God's *existence*. Religion is concerned with God's *essence* and this is grounded in feeling. God as understanding therefore appears in Christianity primarily in his aspect of moral perfection; he is the personification of the moral law, of the moral consciousness of man. This provides a bridge to will and love. For when the concept of God is treated as that of a moral being, when it is grounded in the idea of moral perfection, it passes over into a personification of the will. God becomes the perfection of the will, calling on man to act practically in accordance with man's moral consciousness, i.e., calling on man to become God. But God, in calling on me to become what I might be, tells me what I am not. As the personification of the understanding and of the moral will, God therefore depresses man instead of raising him up. This depression is the more agonizing because the idea of God sets up against man what are essential characters of man's own being. The threatened tension can be overcome only by infusing God with the third, and for Feuerbach most vital, of human characteristics – love. Love is 'the tie, the principle of mediation, between the perfect and the imperfect, the sinless and the sinful, the universal and the individual, the law and the heart, the divine and the human. Love is God himself and outside it there is no God. Love makes man God and God man . . . love is the true unity of God and man, of spirit and nature' (W VI, 59; EC 48). While law damns, the heart (love) has compassion; the law affirms me as an abstract being, the heart affirms me as a real existing being. Law makes man dependent; love makes him free. For religion to perform its function, then, God is and needs to be love – real love, the love of flesh and blood, the love of man and woman, and not merely an abstract metaphysical category. Only real beings have compassion, only a God of flesh and blood can perform his religious function and pardon sin. It is no accident that the religious imagination portrays the blood of God as cleansing us from sin, for only human blood can make God compassionate. The Incarnation thus stands revealed in Feuerbach's analysis as a central and essential religious symbol – it is the thinly disguised avowal of the fact that God is man. This avowal is not mysterious or irreligious; the

EP

Incarnation is the natural conclusion that ultimately had to be drawn from the human premises on which religion is erected.

Once we recognize that the Incarnation portrays and reveals the human essence of God, that it is a symbol for human love and its power, then we can understand 'the secret' of the Trinity: 'God the Father is *I*, God the Son *Thou*. The *I* is understanding, the *Thou* love; but only love with understanding and understanding with love are the mind [or spirit], are the whole man' (W VI, 82; EC 67). Because love requires two people, because it is the relation of I-Thou, the relation between one human being and another, it was therefore necessary that God should be differentiated into two, the Father and the Son. (The Holy Ghost, the third person of the Trinity, according to Feuerbach, is not a separate third personality at all, but is the symbol of the relationship between the Father and the Son and of the relationship between man and God. This, Feuerbach argues, early theologians themselves saw.)

In the remainder of the *Essence of Christianity*, Feuerbach seeks to bring out the empirical, human content of various specific religious conceptions. The act of creation, he argues, is a celebration of the powers of the human will – not of the rational will but of the imaginative will, which is totally indifferent to physical means and causal laws, which creates apparently *ex nihilo*, just as God is supposed to create *ex nihilo* (W VI, 121; EC 101–2).[31] In so far as the creation is portrayed as being for man's sake, and in so far as it is portrayed as an act of imaginative will indifferent to causality, it provides a fantasy-gratification of man's desire to master nature and to escape from causal necessities. God as *logos* is a celebration of the powers of the (human) word, which is in man and yet above man – the word which is power, which creates revolutions, which is alive after men are dead. The miracle, as we have already seen Feuerbach arguing, is a fantasy wish-fulfilment and at the same time a celebration of the power of human fantasy. In creating or accepting the account of a miracle, man denies the independent reality of nature and of natural laws, he makes nature and its laws entirely subservient to (human) will. The Virgin-Mother is another wish-fulfilment, a fulfilment of the wish that unspotted virginity, honour and the feeling of shame might be combined with natural love and motherhood – as they rarely are in reality. Christianity thus is above all the religion of subjectivity (W VI, 180; EC 150); Christ is the personified essence of this subjectivity, he is the difference between Christianity and heathen-dom. The Christian increasingly centres attention exclusively on himself; the heathen sees man in his relation to the universe and to other men. The conflict between Christ and the law expresses the wish of the Christian to be free of the law, while Christ's power of saving and redeeming – which also has its natural content – is not so much a celebration of the power of morality as of the power of example. Feuerbach, as we have noted, consistently mixes cognitive and emotive reduction: the human content of a religious symbol is sometimes the human experiences which it transposes in imagina-tion and sometimes the human wish which gives shape and form to the transposition. Ideally, Feuerbach would like each religious symbol to be human in both senses, with the emotive wish determining the selection and arrangement of cognitive content. But he is prepared to concede, at any rate implicitly, that what Freudians have called the reality-principle can break through into the religious imagination in a way counter to the wish. Thus he emphasizes that the conception of Providence is a recognition of the inhuman necessity of nature, that the concept of Grace as an arbitrary act of God's is a recognition of the fact that the course of nature may be unpredictable to man and not controllable by him (though only because it is not yet, for him, reducible to laws).

So much, then, for the anthropological reduction of religion in general and of Christianity in particular. What religion celebrates is man; what it makes attributes of the divine are in fact the divine (valuable, splendid) attributes of man. For 'God is love', we must read 'love is divine'; for 'God is compassionate', we must read 'compassion is divine' – i.e., valuable, splendid, good in itself. Religion, according to Feuerbach, takes these properties from man and ascribes them to another being set over and above man. It takes the species-characteristics of man, his essential humanity, and converts these into a divine person distinguished from man. It thus has certain necessary inhuman consequences. *Religion is an expression of man's alienation*; what religion celebrates in man it at the same time takes away from him and gives to another. Since the properties of God and man are identical, it can enrich God only by impoverishing man (W VI, 32; EC 26).[32] Thus 'man affirms in God what he denies in himself' (W VI, 33; EC 27). The Virgin represents the love that the monk denies him-self in this world. The nun becomes the bride of Christ, i.e.,

substitutes an unearthly love for real earthly love. God is given the
personality and dignity that man denies to himself. God behaves
with the egoism that man renounces; God knows everything, man
knows nothing.

> God is not what man is and man is not what God is. God is
> the infinite being, man the finite; God is perfect, man is imper-
> fect; God is eternal, man is temporal; God is almighty, man
> is powerless; God is holy, man is sinful. God and man are
> extremes: God is the absolutely positive, the essence of all
> realities, while man is the negative, the essence of all nothing-
> ness (W VI, 41; EC 33).

By projecting all that which makes up the perfections of the human
species (and which should therefore seize and inspire man) into
the transcendent sphere and objectifying it as God, man reduces
himself to a pitiful, miserable, sinful creature. Because religion
ends by depressing the dignity of man instead of elevating it,
religious faith becomes not the expression of love but the very
contrary of it. All the horrors of Christianity have flowed out of
faith and out of the associated doctrine that only God has dignity
and man is sinful (W VI, 310; EC 257–8). There is in religion no
inner connection between faith and the moral sense; faith is
indifferent to good and can even contradict the moral law. Not
faith but the moral sense says to man, 'your faith is as nothing if you
do no good'. Even where religion enjoins good works, they are not
to be done for their own sake or for the sake of man, but for God's
sake. Love in religion does not flow out of its true root – the consciousness of the species – but out of the relationship to *another*
allegedly non-human being; it is mediate and not immediate. Must
we really love each other only because Christ loved us all?

Religion, Feuerbach has argued, is a wish-fulfilment, a reaction
to frustration and an attempt to overcome it. Feuerbach does not
deny that Christianity as a religion of feeling can offer man
comfort; comfort is precisely what the feelings often seek.

> It feels more comfortable to suffer than to act, more comfort-
> able to be saved and freed by another than to free oneself . . .
> more comfortable to love than to strive; it is more comfortable
> to know that God loves one than to love oneself with that

simple, natural self-love which is innate to all beings, more comfortable to see oneself reflected in the loving eyes of another personal being than to look into the curved mirror of one's own self or into the inner depths of the still waters of nature; it is more comfortable altogether to let oneself be determined by one's emotions – as though they were another being, yet basically the same being – than to regulate oneself by reason (W VI, 168–9; EC 140).

But in so far as religion treats feelings, love, human attributes as mere attributes of God, it subordinates them to mere attributes of a being that is supposed to have reality without them and independently of them. Religion does not only depress man *vis-à-vis* God; it even depresses the divine predicates *vis-à-vis* God.

As long as love is not raised to the level of substance, is not made a being itself, so long there lurks behind love a subject that is something even without love, a loveless monster, a daemonic being distinguishable and actually distinguished from love, which sates itself on the blood of heretics and unbelievers. It is this being which is the phantom conjured up by religious fanaticism (W VI, 64; EC 52–3).

It is as a rebellion against this loveless monster within religion itself, it is as a recognition of the fact that *love seizes God* instead of being merely subordinate to him, that the Christian doctrine of the Incarnation is to be understood. Religion, and especially theology, however, need both to affirm and to deny the Incarnation, to say that God is love and to say that God is something above love, something that can be distinguished from it. The element of alienation, of setting something over and above man that should be man's, increases as religion comes to reflect on itself, as it seeks to acquire a theoretical basis, as it becomes *theology* (W VI, 238; EC 197). Because Feuerbach regards this increase in alienation as having fundamental significance, he divides the *Essence of Christianity* into two parts. The first analyses the content of religion and the second aims to confute theology and to bring out the way in which it stands in contradiction to the function and content of religion. In theology, according to Feuerbach, that original unselfconscious separation of man's qualities from himself which lies at the root of religion becomes a studied, intensified separation, a separation not only of location, but of essence. The theological proofs of God's necessity are meant to make God self-sufficient, to sever God from man according to his very essence. They thus consummate the alienation of man's highest qualities from man and depress even further the sinful (because now incomplete) man that is left. Hence Feuerbach speaks of himself as the enemy of theology, but not of religion. He is opposed only to the *form* of religious expression. The theologians convert this form into the essence of religion. Feuerbach is not opposed to the *real* essence of religion, to its *content*, i.e., to the longings and ethical valuations that man expresses in religion. The logical contradictions of theology rest on the very fact that theology seeks to separate God from man while having to recognize, in the spirit of religion, that God is for man and of man. Thus we have, for example, the contradiction in the theological doctrine of revelation. The *need* for revelation, the claim that man cannot know God except with God's help, is intended by theology to consummate God's separation from man. The *fact* of revelation, on the other hand, shows man at the centre of God's thought. It makes God dependent on man, on man's power of understanding; it forces God to think with man's thoughts (W VI, 250; EC 207).[33] The 'mysteries' of theology all rest on this separation of God from man and nature. What creates the 'mystery' is simply the fact that a familiar, natural or human quality is posited as an unfamiliar, supernatural, divine quality; it becomes mysterious for this and no other reason (W VI, 257–8; EC 214).[34]

The doctrine of the Sacraments, Feuerbach argues, expresses particularly clearly the contradiction that lies at the heart of religion. The Sacraments are earthly transactions and at the same time unearthly transactions; the bread and wine of communion are bread and wine and yet not bread and wine. The allegedly mysterious contradiction here is in reality the unmysterious contradiction between objectivism of religion and its subjectivism, between what things really are and what man wishes they were, what he makes them in fantasy. Theology mystifies and confounds all by treating as objective what is subjective.

The viciousness of the alienation in religion, according to Feuerbach, expresses itself in one other important way. God is the human essence transplanted into heaven. In implicit recognition of this man denies to himself, or at least seeks to suppress as worldly, that which he denies to God. In Christianity man is reduced to the individual, to a single person (God) who has aspects, but contains no distinction of sex. Christianity therefore does not recognize sexual distinction and sexual union *as part of the human essence*, does not see that two sexes make up man. It therefore robs man of sex, it puts celibacy at the centre of the Christian conception of life.

> Just as the true Christian has no need of education, because it is a worldly principle contrary to feeling, so he has no need for (natural) love. God fills his lack, his need for education; God also fills his lack, his need for love, for wife, for family. The Christian identifies the species directly with the individual: he therefore rejects the difference between the sexes as a burdensome, accidental accretion (W VI, 202; EC 167).

In heathendom Zeus and Here were the great model of every marriage, in Christianity marriage is excluded from heaven and treated here on earth as having only a moral, but not a religious, significance (W VI, 203; EC 168).

The reduction of the human essence to a single individual Feuerbach regards as another source of logical difficulty. The infinity, perfection, omniscience and omnipotence which Christianity ascribes to *one* being are not possible characteristics of any *one* empirical being: they represent the consummation of the capacities, talents and potentialities not of man as an individual, but of man as a species, of man as the human race. The human race, not man or any other individual being, is – in relation to the individual – eternal. The human race seems to the individual to combine all moral qualities, to be potentially capable of anything and to have potentially the sum of all knowledge. To make these the characteristics of a single person is to open the way to paradox and absurdity (as the Sunday-school child sees when it asks, 'Can God build a wall so strong that he cannot pull it down?' or 'How can God be all-powerful if he cannot change his mind, and how can he have been perfect or omniscient if he really "changed" it?').

*

Feuerbach can be read sympathetically or unsympathetically. One can fasten on his insights or one can emphasize his exaggerations, his historical simplifications, his overenthusiastic and often *prima facie* inconsistent reduction of phenomena to their real essence or nature.[35] The 'essence' of religion, according to Feuerbach, is sometimes man, sometimes love, sometimes dependence, sometimes nature and so on. Here Feuerbach's grammar and style should not be taken too seriously. His *is* often sounds as though he meant it to be the *is* of identity, but he is perhaps rather to be understood as a man analysing a complex social phenomenon who finds that a great deal can be said about it at different levels. Feuerbach can thus emphasize different aspects; he can find in the phenomenon the interplay and mutual dependence of 'opposites' which are not in fact exclusive. Religion can in principle be the product of man's self-knowledge, the expression of man's dependence, the gratification of a wish, the poetic elevation of the things man admires, and so on. These elements may all mingle in it, and mingle not merely in a mechanical way but influence each other, uphold each other in mutual relationships, etc. Feuerbach presents each of these reductions so forcefully, with so much rhetoric, that he appears to regard each of them as the true *essence* in terms of which the whole of religion should be explained. Sometimes Feuerbach attempts to pull all these 'essences' together by treating them as expressions of man (man's relationship to nature, in this connection, is for Feuerbach also part of the 'being' or 'essence' of man). But leaving aside his activist proclamation of anthropology as the new religion of mankind (for which this conception of a human essence may indeed be necessary), the juggling with what appear to be essences is in part only a rhetorical trick and a habit of style. It does not seriously affect his critical evaluation of religion in its most general implications. Feuerbach himself is conscious, at times, of the complexity of the material he is analysing. In his *Lectures on the Essence of Religion* he writes:

> In the field of religion, we find ourselves at first in a chaos of the greatest and most confusing contradictions. Despite this, deeper examination shows such contradictions to be reducible to the motives of fear and love and these, though in accordance with the differences in mankind they attach themselves to different objects, can be reduced to the feeling of dependence (W VII, 54).

Such 'reduction' is much more complex than Feuerbach admits, and cannot be accomplished without residues. This is no more fatal to Feuerbach's general view, however, than the fact that Feuerbach's historical stages are not always consistent or faithful to the whole of the material. The strength of Feuerbach's position lies in its general approach and in the intimate connection that he can establish between the nature of religious claims and the approach that he considers appropriate in studying them and explaining them. There is no question of Feuerbach confronting religion from outside, with an approach developed in different contexts or based on principles drawn from other fields.[36] The principles of analysis that Feuerbach uses and the general conclusions to which they lead him I would regard as Feuerbach's greatest contribution to thought and as a lasting and correct *statement of approach* to religious phenomenon.

The specific character of religion, for Feuerbach, lies in its claim to deal with the *supernatural*. The chief contradiction in the heart of religion – the contradiction to which Feuerbach returns again and again – is that religion cannot give the supernatural any *content* except a *natural* one. It is thus forced to vacillate between two inconsistent positions. By making God supernatural it makes him indescribable and uninteresting (i.e., irrelevant to any human concern or human experience); by making God describable and uninteresting it turns him into a *natural* being, but into one that is logically impossible. Religion as religion cannot abandon either of these two inconsistent positions: it needs a God who is within the world and yet not within the world, a God who is human and yet not human, a God who is infinite and yet specific, perfect and yet capable of understanding weakness, suffering and sin. To protect the supernatural claims of religion, theologians take refuge in the position that 'God is wholly other' (than man). They sever God's supernatural existence from God's natural predicates, or they deny that the predicates *we* attribute to God are anything but products of our imperfect understanding, or they deny that God has predicates at all. But a being that has no predicates is no being: 'to be' *is* to have predicates; to say that God has no properties is to say that there is no God. Neither can we separate God's existence from his predicates, say that the former is supernatural and that the latter are natural. A being is no more than all those things that might be predicated of it. We cannot say, 'everything about God is natural, but he himself is supernatural', because there is no 'he himself' over and above the properties that make him up. There is, in other words, no colourless, propertyless, unspeakable and unknowable 'essence' or 'being' or 'substance' behind all properties in which these properties inhere: an 'essence' or 'being' is nothing more than a collection of properties bound together in space and time. Properties are related to each other, not to some propertyless 'substance' behind them which would have to be both something and nothing. Neither can we say that God has properties but we know them not. If this were so, then in not knowing the properties, we would not know the 'God' who is supposed to have them: knowing neither, we could certainly not claim to know a relation between them. We would not even have grounds for speaking of 'God'.[37] The same kind of thing, Feuerbach argues, can be said about the attempt to treat God's infinity as a supernatural trait. First, God's infinity contradicts his personality, his individuality. If God is infinite, there is not anything which he is not, i.e., he includes all things. If God is an individual, a person, a specific thing, he must have limits, he must be distinguished from other things by not being what they are. Secondly, an infinity can only be an endless series of finite – i.e., of real, natural – properties or events. The infinite makes sense only *in* space and time, not outside them. As Feuerbach puts it, 'Only in empirical reality, in time and space, can an infinite, a really infinite, being find room' (W VI, 28; EC 23). In so far as an infinite being is supposed to have all properties, to unite in itself opposites and contradictions, it can do so only be going on and changing in time, i.e., by being temporal and historical. The same man can be black-haired in his youth and white-haired in old age. 'Not Hegelian dialectic,' says Feuerbach, 'but time is the means for uniting opposites and contradictions in one and the same existence' (W VI, 28–9; EC 23).

The general position against the religious postulation of an infinite being held to be supernatural, then, is this: Infinity is not a property to be distinguished from the finite, it is merely an extension of the finite in numerical terms, it is an endless addition of more finite properties or events, it does not rise above finitude but merely keeps extending it in space and time. God as presented by the theologian has in reality not a supernatural quality, but *more* natural ones. The same, Feuerbach argues, applies to God's alleged perfection. Perfection, too, is not *a* quality or a supernatural trait: it is simply a collection, in the imagination, of all those qualities which man admires, posited in the imagination as though they were accompanied by no defects and faced by no impediments. God, as Feuerbach holds Spinoza saw, never rises above Nature (here including man), but merely encompasses more and more of it.

There is, then, no supernatural. Religion has to be explained and analysed as a natural, human phenomenon – as a false belief, or, on the positive side, as a fiction. Religion is transcendent only in the sense in which false beliefs are transcendent: it cannot be interpreted as a direct representation of reality. Religion is to be treated on the analogy of dreams, fantasies, works of fiction or imaginative art. They, too, are natural – they do not portray a totally other world, they merely select and rearrange materials drawn from this world. We look at them and we ask, 'Where did their creator get the idea?' and 'What is it that he wants to express?' The same, Feuerbach says, should be done with religions. *The answer our examination will give us, in religion as in dreams, will contain no supernatural residue.* Man gets the ideas contained, rearranged and elaborated in religion precisely where he gets all other ideas – from human experience.[38] Feuerbach often puts his position, especially in the earlier 1840s, as stating that the content of religion is man or that religion must be reduced to man. This pithy formulation suited him for policy reasons, because he wanted to proclaim a new religion of man: the religion of democratic politics that would free man from subordination to fetishes he had himself created. But what he meant – as is clear from some passages of the *Essence of Christianity* and even clearer from the preliminary work and the Heidelberg lectures on the essence of religion – was that religion must be reduced to human wishes and thus ultimately to *human experience* (which, for Feuerbach as for Marx, is all that shapes man – e.g., 'Nature' – and can therefore be included in the term 'man').[39] Human experience is both of man's 'inner' states and of the 'external' world: the analysis of religion can therefore draw on everything that is empirical, on anything that is the object of human knowledge as it is known to man. Feuerbach is simply arguing, in the first instance, that religion is to be treated empirically like all other human phenomena, and as all religions have in fact treated those previous or other religions which claim a different supernatural content or inspiration. In reducing religion to its 'latent' as opposed to its 'manifest' content, we must realize that religion reflects reality only *as seen by man*: it thus embodies those aspects of nature, for instance, that strike man, those that he notices because they satisfy or impede his interests. [40]

The analogy of dream-analysis also enables us to explain and justify Feuerbach's hostility to theology. Dreams stand to reality at one remove; theology stands to it at second remove. Where dreams can illuminate reality, once they are properly interpreted, theology obscures reality by resisting such interpretation, by treating the fantasies that constitute religion as direct representations of (another) reality. Theology as theology (and not as containing, in a subsidiary way, philosophical argument, ethical enquiry, etc.) is necessarily obscurantist: it seeks to take as the very foundation of its subject that which makes no sense, and to strip away everything that does make sense. It treats error as truth, fantasy as reality: it seeks to separate the form of the dream from its substance, or rather to treat the form as though it were the substance. It thus loses the clue to the real meaning of the dream; it impedes study instead of promoting it. Theology is mystification. Where 'religion' gives words their natural meaning, theology gives them a non-natural one. Hence Feuerbach completely rejects the view that philosophy and theology can be reconciled. For him they are diametrically opposed. Philosophy is concerned with reason, with objectivity, with what is the case, theology seeks to rationalize – in the Freudian sense – the demands of the emotions, to put feeling above understanding.

> Every mediation between dogmatics and philosophy is a *concordia discors*, against which one must protest in the name of religion as much as in the name of philosophy. All religious speculation is vanity and lying – a lie against reason and a lie against faith – a game of chance, in which faith swindles reason and reason swindles faith out of that which belongs to each.

The *Essence of Christianity* and a great deal of Feuerbach's subsequent work, as we have seen, were devoted to demonstrating that the Feuerbachian (i.e., the empirical) analysis of religion could work, that religious conceptions could always be explained in terms of human experience. In principle, Feuerbach seems to me entirely successful. The concept of saving grace does embody the arbitrariness that man experiences in his relations with nature and 'fortune' and the dependence he feels in them; the moral qualities of God are the moral qualities man meets in man, abstracted from surrounding defects; the purity of the Virgin is the purity of virgins, again abstracted from surrounding defects. Even those religious conceptions that claim to embody the transcendence of God embody nothing more than an empirical transcendence. Creation *ex nihilo* is, indeed, a fantasy woven around the powers of the human imaginative will, which conjures up realities without having to build them;[41] God's infinity is the infinity of nature and the comparative infinity of the human race and of a particular society from the point of view of the individual; God's omniscience is the theoretical omniscience of the knowing mind, which knows no limits in principle; God's omnipotence is the omnipotence of the imagination and the comparative omnipotence simple men ascribe to the mighty. The 'mystery' alleged to lie at the heart of religion is nothing but the projection of an emotive response – as when we call a surprising event 'unbelievable' because we found it hard to believe it would happen (cf. W VI, 257–8; EC 214).

All too often, however, Feuerbach writes as though a complex historical phenomenon like religion, stretching over many periods and many different societies, can be reduced to a few simple 'keys'. It is not surprising that the reader should become conscious of the fact that these keys are not the same keys in different portions of Feuerbach's work. The transcendence of God, for example, is sometimes derived from the transcendence of nature, sometimes from the transcendence of the understanding and sometimes from the transcendence of the human species as viewed from the standpoint of the individual. It seems to me that Feuerbach's detailed reductions can only be treated as examples, as illustrations, that bring out possible contents of religious symbolism or, if one prefers, aspects of religion. One of the peculiar strengths of religious symbolism is that it can combine contents from different areas of human experience or at different levels of human thinking. Religious conceptions are like the plots of Kafka's novels – their very impact comes from the fact that they express or are capable of suggesting a variety of human experiences; they are allegories with more than one possible interpretation, reflecting the universality of certain feelings and of certain aspects of certain situations. Feuerbach, I should argue, has shown that in any particular case we have no difficulty in accounting for a particular religious conception by seeking a natural experiential phenomenon or set of phenomena which it takes over and transports into what is allegedly another world. Feuerbach, indeed shows more than this. He shows that religion *must* give such experiential content to its conceptions if it is to be understood. He shows that the history of religion in modern times necessarily vacillates between a super-naturalism that is empty and a naturalism that is irreligious or, as Feuerbach would have put it, anti-theological. Here Feuerbach does isolate what an Hegelian would call a 'moment' (an inescapable logical tendency) in the development of religious traditions. There is, Feuerbach writes (W VI 38; EC 31), a religious systole and diastole similar to that of the blood – God acts according to his own nature and laws, that is the religious repulsion; God acts in me, with me, for me, through me, on me and on my behalf, that is the religious attraction. The content that can be poured into religious conceptions and the social effects that these conceptions can produce are richer and more varied than Feuerbach empha-sized in the main trend of his work – but I do not believe that this in any way affects the fundamental line of his criticism. The supernatural *is* made up of the natural; that which is supposed to distinguish it, to make it specifically supernatural or divine, can never be expressed coherently. There is still, more than a hundred years after Feuerbach's best-known work on religion, no better clue to the vacillations of Christian theory, especially to the strug-gles that we find going on in respect of the New Theology today, than this contradiction – rooted in the inescapable conflict between the natural content and the supernatural pretensions of religion. This content Feuerbach understood very well indeed, and he was able to bring it out from the history and character of religion itself. The best confirmation of Feuerbach's claim, indeed, lies in the struggles within Christianity, in the conflicts that Christians them-selves go through.

When it comes to Feuerbach's detailed analyses, they suffer both from his tendency towards unsystematic over-emphasis and from the cultural limitations of an early nineteenth-century thinker. The human experiences to which Feuerbach reduced religion, though not excluding man's relationship with nature and man's social organization, are certainly predominantly individual experiences. Outside of Israel, Feuerbach does not really ascribe much signifi-cance to any form of human organization that stands between the individual and the species. He completely ignores the familial connotations evoked by the conception of God the Father and God the Son – he seems to have been quite unaware of authority-relations in the family and of the rôle of love, fear and hate in the family situation (perhaps because he knew too much of them and was anxious to overcome them). In Feuerbach man has, besides thought and will, feeling and sex and a consciousness of being a member of a species – but for the purposes of systematic discussion he usually has no concrete social organizations, no economic, cultural, or bureaucratic class divisions, no hierarchical family organization. Man, in Feuerbach, rarely has political or familial as distinct from human and sexual feelings.[42] Thus we find nowhere in Feuerbach a concrete presaging of Freud's account of religion, of his linking of religious attitudes, especially in Christianity, with familial attitudes and problems. Neither do we find in Feuerbach, apart from the material on Israel, the clear conception of a tribal emotion, used by Emile Durkheim in his *The Elementary Forms of the Religious Life*. There Durkheim develops the striking view (though many of his empirical claims about totemism and its historical place in the development of religious beliefs have not stood up to empirical investigation) that the *mana* of the totemic religions was a projection of the frenzy that seized men in the celebration of the tribal dance, that the transcendence ascribed to the divine and sacred (God and the flag) is the transcendence of society and of social activities and of the feelings they engender in relation to the individual. But the point is that all these lines of investigation are Feuerbachian in spirit and method – it was he who laid the foundations and established the guide lines for the complex task of analysing religion as an important but completely human phenomenon.[43]

The task of analysing religion is indeed a complex one – much more complex, no doubt, than Feuerbach realized. We have become increasingly suspicious of the view that a complex social phenomenon can be reduced to a simple set of essential characteristics – the modern social theorist is not so much inclined to choose between theories like Feuerbach's, Freud's and Durkheim's as to combine them. They are approaches or 'models', each of which helps to illuminate certain facets of religious development while proving irrelevant or misleading in relation to other facets. What I have in mind here has been reiterated by Professor Alex Inkeles in a recent address:[44]

. . . most social scientists approach the subject they are studying with some kind of conceptual scheme which we may call
a model. These models play an enormously important rôle in
deciding what is taken into consideration and what is left out,
what weight is assigned to one factor as against another, which
set of interrelationships are assumed to exist and which will
go largely unnoticed. There is a great deal of debate about
models, most of which deals with the question of whether or
not a particular model is right or wrong. In my opinion there
is no such thing as a right or wrong sociological model. There
are richer and poorer ones. There are the more sensitive and
the less sensitive. There are those which are more appropriate
to one time or place than another. All have a piece of truth,
but it is rare that any *one* model is really adequate to the
analysis of a highly complex concrete historical case.

Let us leave out of consideration here the philosophical problems
raised by Professor Inkeles' general looseness of expression and
his denial that models are right or wrong in any sense, surely
contradicted by his suggestion that they all have 'a piece of truth',
as well as the different kinds of procedural rules and generalizations
of which particular models may be composed. The word 'model'
does stand in need of further analysis – but not, I think, for our
purpose. What I want to suggest here is that Feuerbach has combined criticism and analysis of religion in such a way as to indicate
clearly, and in my opinion correctly, the *type* of approach that
would have to be used in analysing religion, and that this approach
(like any other 'model') does involve recognizing certain *features* of
the subject-matter itself. There can be many useful 'models' not
because none is 'true', but because the features of a particular
subject-matter, the connections and regularities within it, can
never be fully exhausted. Models are thus similar, in logical form,
to *questions* – they do assert something to be true, they provide a
sentence-frame (a propositional function) with an unfilled-in
variable which the hearer is invited to fill in, they say 'there is an X
which . . .; *what* is the X?'. Just as we can ask many questions about
an activity, or institution or thing, without contradicting ourselves,
so it is possible to have a number of models which are not mutually
inconsistent. Feuerbach's primary model, indeed, is one of very
great generality, which in Feuerbach's own work suggests a

number of sub-models (or sub-questions) and which can, without contradiction, be supplemented with the Freudian and the Durkheimian approach to religion, if these approaches are not interpreted as excluding other questions. Marxists, themselves far more rigid than Feuerbach, have added another assertion which they consider by far the most important – the assertion that human dependence is primarily social dependence evoked by class oppression and more generally by the impersonal laws that bind all classes in a class society. They often talk as though this is the *only* point to be made about religion; but this they need not do. I should be quite prepared to concede that this is another facet of religions that could in principle be taken seriously. It seems to me as a matter of fact, however, that is has played only a limited rôle in the development of religious consciousness. Bolshevik 'Marxist' discussion too frequently leads us back to the conspiratorial view of religion that Feuerbach was striving to overcome. Orthodox Marxists have not produced any analysis that can be regarded as an advance on Feuerbach's – on the contrary, they have in many respects (especially until very recently) regressed to eighteenth-century Enlightenment conspiratorial views as a result of their anxiety to *discredit* religion in the eyes of the vulgar.[45]

Feuerbach's analysis of religion, even taken at its most general, has two components, however, just as the Freudian analysis of dreams has two components. The content of religion, according to Feuerbach, is always to be found in human experience; the arrangement and selection of that content is guided by human strivings, especially by the attempt to overcome a recognized dependence. The latter side has been especially emphasized by Marxists, who argue that religion *must* disappear as social dependence disappears. This assertion may be regarded untestable in any direct way because social dependence is the sort of thing that does not disappear. There is, however, at least some support for the assertion – an assertion which in its general form is certainly Feuerbachian. Whole areas of human life do cease to be prominent in religious thought as the feeling of utter dependence, and especially of unpredictable dependence, is assuaged by the development of technology or of theoretical knowledge. It might also be argued that religious revivals, such as the revival after the Second World War, take place at times when the human belief in the rationality and controllability of human arrangements and human beings is most shaken. It should certainly be said, however, that the emotional drive behind religion is much harder to isolate or to indicate in general terms than the content of religious conceptions. Here, perhaps, one would have to recognize that in religion, as in all other areas of social life, there are many drives at work. One of the strongest – the search for security, for comfort and consolation, which Feuerbach repeatedly emphasized – comes into constant conflict with the recognition of reality, to which religious thinkers and leaders are also not immune. In religion, as in dreams, anxieties will break through to shatter a wish-fulfilment. These anxieties are quite often rational. To the modern reader – especially perhaps to those familiar with anthropological and sociological work on religion, work that is in itself grounded in the Feuerbachian view – it will be striking that Feuerbach pays very little regard to the *positive* social effects of religion. No doubt this was natural in an age in which the dominant tone of religion was reactionary in relation to the leading social and intellectual movements of the time. Take the definition of religion given by one contemporary anthropologist:

> Religion is a system of symbols which acts to establish powerful, pervasive and long-lasting moods and motivations in man by formulating conceptions of a general order of existence and clothing those conceptions with such an aura of factuality that the moods and motivations seem uniquely realistic.[46]

This is entirely in the spirit of Feuerbach's empirical analysis; it is in fact a restatement of his views. But more strongly than Feuerbach's work, this definition emphasizes the social rôle of religion in a positive way, it emphasizes that religion is not only an escape from reality, but a method of dealing with it. Religion, to an anthropologist like Geertz, is a culture pattern. Culture patterns are both models *of* and models *for* –

> they give meaning, i.e., objective conceptual form, to social and psychological reality both by shaping themselves to it and by shaping it to themselves . . . whether one sees the conception of a personal guardian spirit, a family tutelary or an immanent god as synoptic formulations of the character of reality or as templates for producing reality with such a character seems largely arbitrary, a matter of which aspect, the model

of or model *for*, one wants for the moment to bring into focus. The concrete symbols involved . . . point in either direction. They both express the world's climate and shape it.[47]

Geertz is in part expressing an attitude that has come more to the fore in the twentieth century and especially perhaps since the horrors of the Second World War – the belief that man acquires emotional comfort not only by simple fantasy, but by shaping the whole of his knowledge into an ordered scheme built on presumptions and using concepts and regulative ideas that are at the least untestable and are often patent fictions.[48] This was emphasized by Susan Langer in a passage quoted by Geertz:[49]

Man can adapt himself somehow to anything his imagination can cope with; but he cannot deal with Chaos. Because his characteristic function and highest asset is conception, his greatest fright is to meet what he cannot construe – the 'uncanny', as it is popularly called. It need not be a new object; we do meet new things, and 'understand' them promptly, if tentatively, by the nearest analogy, when our minds are functioning freely; but under mental stress even perfectly familiar things may become suddenly disorganized and give us the horrors. Therefore our most important assets are always the symbols of our general *orientation* in nature, on the earth, in society, and in what we are doing: the symbols of our *Weltanschauung* and *Lebensanschauung*. Consequently, in a primitive society, a daily ritual is incorporated in common activities, in eating, washing, fire-making, etc., as well as in pure ceremonial; because the need of reasserting the tribal morale and recognizing its cosmic conditions is constantly felt. In Christian Europe the Church brought men daily (in some orders even hourly) to their knees, to enact if not to contemplate their assent to the ultimate concepts.

There are, Geertz argues, three points where chaos as a tumult of events – events which do not only lack interpretation but seem to lack interpretability in principle – breaks in. This is when a man is at the limit of his analytical capabilities, when he is at the limit of his powers of endurance, and when he is at the limit of his moral insight. In these situations a challenge is thrown down which religion takes up. Or as Feuerbach would have said, and as Malinowski did say, the function of religion here is to relieve intolerable stress, to overcome the feeling of helplessness.

The discussion of religion in contemporary non-religious work is very much more sophisticated than the pioneering efforts of Feuerbach. It takes account of more complexities; it covers a much broader range of religious phenomena (Feuerbach almost completely ignored Islam, which did not fit his historical pattern well, and he knew little that was reliable of Asian or non-classical 'primitive' and pagan religions); it has rejected the simple evolutionism which (under the influence of Hegel and, in part, of Feuerbach) dominated nineteenth-century discussions of social phenomena. It has also achieved a detachment which helps it to avoid Feuerbach's frequent errors of over-emphasis. But its general conclusions seem to me only to confirm the chief lines of the Feuerbachian analysis: the *sine qua non* of religion is helplessness or the feeling of helplessness, whether in the form of bafflement or of suffering, and the alleviation of helplessness, by knowledge, by technological development and by social and emotional security is, as Feuerbach saw, the chief enemy and destroyer of religious belief and of the social importance of religion. Feuerbach's optimism about the complete disappearance of religion rested on a false foundation – on the belief that human feelings of helplessness and dependence could be overcome, comparatively simply, by a democratic political order and further scientific progress. We know now that alienation does not simply disappear: those very phenomena that alleviate or remove alienation and suffering in one sphere impose it in others. But Feuerbach's general position *is* confirmed, I would say, by an attentive examination of the shifts of emphasis and concern in religious development. As man ceases to feel helpless in a particular field that field ceases to be of special concern to religion. Thus, as man has conquered nature but has failed to 'conquer' his own society, religion has moved more and more into social concerns; as his feeling of helplessness is before evil, rather than before tempest and lightning, religion comes to be interpreted as primarily moral, in advanced industrial societies if (significantly) still not by the villagers of Mexico or southern Italy.

4. Ludwig Feuerbach's critique of philosophy

When the young Ludwig Feuerbach entered the University of Berlin in a 'highly divided, unhappy, undecided state', this obviously reflected an internal religious crisis, a disillusionment with theology which was probably accompanied by a loss of religious faith in general. Nothing that Feuerbach writes or does from that time (1824) onward indicates any belief in God or in the doctrines of the Christian religion. Formally enrolled as a student of theology in the first semester, he devoted himself almost entirely to philosophy. He attended Hegel's lectures on logic, metaphysics and the philosophy of religion; at the end of the academic year, in 1825, he gave up theology and transferred to philosophy. By 1826, when he was completing a second year of Hegel's lectures, he had become an enthusiastic though not uncritical Hegelian. Hegel had given him a philosophy and a *Weltanschauung* to take the place of his shattered Christian belief. Through Hegel, he wrote later,[1]

I came to self-consciousness and to consciousness of the world. It was he whom I called my second father, just as I called Berlin my spiritual birthplace. He was the only man who let me feel and experience what a teacher is. . . . Yes, I stood in a more intimate relationship with Hegel, one more fraught with influence, than with any other of our spiritual forebears; for I knew him personally,[2] for two years I heard him, heard him with undivided attention, with rapture. I did not know what I wanted to do or what I ought to do . . . but I had hardly listened to him for half a year, when my heart and head were straightened out; I knew what I wanted to do and what I should do: not theology, but philosophy . . . not to exercise faith, but to think!

In 1824, Feuerbach had assured his father that, though excited by Hegel, he had no intention of becoming a Hegelian (W XII, 230); by 1826, there was no doubt that Feuerbach was one, prizing both the content of Hegelian philosophy and its method. In Hegelianism he saw the successful overcoming of the dualism in Descartes, Kant and traditional scholastic philosophy, the overcoming of the subjectivity of Fichte and of the thoughtless, mindless empiricism of Locke, Berkeley and Hume, who never could rise from the particular to the general, from the individual to the concrete universal. By 1827 and 1828, however, the reservations that Feuerbach had about Hegel had become doubts. In the *Philosophical Fragments*, under the heading '1826', Feuerbach wrote:

> Now I am finished with Hegel; with the exception of the aesthetics, I have heard all his lectures, I have even heard the logic twice. But Hegel's logic is also the *corpus juris*, the Pandects of philosophy; it contains the whole of philosophy, old as well as new, according to its principles of thinking; besides that, it is the exposition of a method. This is the most important thing, to acquire not only the content, but the method of a philosophy (W II, 362).

The next paragraph of the *Fragments*, headed '1827–8', carries the sub-heading 'Doubts':

> How is thinking related to being, how is logic related to nature? Do we have a basis for passing from the former to the latter? Where is the necessity, where is the principle on which this transition is grounded? We see within logic itself simple determinations, like being, nothingness, something, otherness, finite, infinite, essence, appearance, passing into one another and being dissolved and taken up [*aufgehoben*]; but these are in themselves abstract, one-sided, negative determinations (W II, 362–3).

How then, Feuerbach goes on to ask, can the Hegelian Idea, as the totality of things, overcome this one-sidedness, this 'negativity' of logic? How can it come to include within itself something *other* than logic, Nature?

How do you know that there is still *another* element? From
logic? Never; for it is precisely logic which knows from its
own resources only about itself, only about thinking. Therefore
that which is other than logic cannot be deduced from logic;
it cannot be deduced logically, but only non-logically. Logic,
in other words, passes over into Nature only because the thinking subject finds before it, independently of logic, an immediate being, Nature, which the subject's own unmediated,
natural standpoint forces it to recognize as such. If there were
no Nature, unspotted virgin Logic would never have succeeded
in bringing one forth from itself alone (W II, 363).

This is one of the principal lines in Feuerbach's critique of
idealism. A philosophy that begins with mind, spirit, thought and
treats only these as real, or necessary, or self-evident, can never get
to Nature, to the non-mental, the non-spiritual, to that which is
experience*d* and not experienc*ing*. ' "How can man arise out of
Nature, mind or spirit out of matter?" ,' Feuerbach asks, rhetori-
cally, in the *Fragments* (W II, 389). 'First answer me *this* question:
How can matter arise out of mind or spirit? If you find no answer, or
at least no reasonable answer, to this question, then you will see
that only the converse question will lead you to your end.' Against
the Fichtean and Cartesian presupposition of philosophy – the
allegedly self-certifying *cogito*, the knowing mind whose existence
cannot be consistently doubted by the mind itself – Feuerbach
insists on another beginning: the self-certifying nature of the
experience of the senses. Nature is as much given to man as his
own mental activity; his senses are as primary, as *a priori* (for him),
as his thinking. Thus Feuerbach levels against Hegelian philosophy
the objection which he holds to apply to the whole of modern
philosophy since Descartes and Spinoza – 'the objection that it
makes an unmediated break with sensory perception, that it
directly presupposes philosophy' (W II, 184). Feuerbach does not
mean by this that sense-perception or what it gives us are self-
sufficient ultimates; he believes that science *works over* materials
provided in experience and that criticism (philosophy) is necessary
to supplement and organize experience. Criticism, however, cannot produce experience out of itself. Feuerbach does not believe
that there is an ultimate criterion of truth such as Descartes sought.
For him there are no significant propositions which are *a priori* in

the sense of being self-evident, indubitable because their contra-
dictories would be self-contradictory. Feuerbach believes that
sense-experience is *a priori for man* because man has nothing else
to start from. If we deny sense-experience we deny everything, we
cut off man from everything that makes him a being of a certain
sort, in a certain place, with certain needs, characters and capacities. The Cartesian *cogito*, like the Fichtean *ego*, is empty; it has no
character, no content, it is not even *human*. From it *nothing* follows,
certainly not man. If man does not recognize Nature, he cannot
recognize himself.

Feuerbach himself believes that man is, in one sense, the basis
of all philosophy, but he distinguishes his sense sharply from
Fichte's. In his very interesting review of J. F. Reiff's *Ueber den
Anfang der Philosophie* (*Concerning the Starting-Point of Philosophy*), a book which attempts to go back to the first Fichtean
system, Feuerbach writes:

> It is true that one can also make the ego a universal premise
> for deduction – though in a different sense from the meaning
> which we attach to this concept or word 'ego' since Fichte.
> One can do this only on the following condition, however, that
> one discovers and demonstrates in the ego a non-ego, or
> distinctions and contradictions generally; for with the undifferen-
> tiated monotonous litany of ego = ego one can certainly do
> nothing. The ego from which musical tones issue forth is *quite
> a different* ego from the ego from which a logical category or a
> moral or juridical law springs forth. The science which pre-
> cedes all other sciences, the first universal science, then, is
> only psychology, which has no other task but that of declining
> the ego, in order to deduce from the various inner states of
> the ego various principles. But then it would be quite improper
> and out of place to make psychology, as Reiff does, a particular
> science and to derive from it only the abstract sciences, logic
> and metaphysics. For the most essential, the primary, opposite
> of the ego tied together with it is the *body*, the *flesh*. The
> conflict of flesh and spirit, that alone is the highest meta-
> physical principle, that alone is the secret of Creation, the basis
> of the world. Yes, the flesh, or if you prefer the body, has not
> only an empirical-psychological significance, a significance in
> natural history, it obviously has a metaphysical significance.

For what is the body but the passivity of the ego? And how
can you want to deduce both the will and sensation out of the
ego without a passive principle? We cannot think of the will
without something striving against the will; and in every
sensation, no matter how spiritual, there is no more activity
than suffering, no more mind than flesh, no more ego than
not-ego (W II, 214–15).

A philosophy that pretends to be 'pure', then, that pretends to
deduce nature and concrete knowledge from pure thought or pure
reason, can get out of its constructions only what it puts into them
secretly, illicitly. It may pretend to begin without presuppositions,
but its beginning is never arbitrary, never without significance. On
the contrary, the point of departure it selects is not only a presupposition, but one which is deliberately (if unconsciously) selected
in the light of what is to follow. If a philosopher begins with mind,
this is not because the existence of mind is self-evident and that of
the non-mental, of Nature, is not; it is because he is concerned to
elevate the mental, he wants to see the universe as mind or spirit,
and therefore *begins* with mind or spirit as the only certain, self-
evident form of being. He sets out by assuming what he will later
pretend to prove. Thus Fichte, far from beginning without
presuppositions, has not even the courage to doubt the existence
of his own ego. In beginning with his conception of the thinking
ego as 'self-evident' he is in fact beginning with the whole of the
Fichtean philosophy of the ego, as though *it* were self-evident.[3]
In Fichte we find no 'mediation' (*i.e.*, no argument from one
proposition to another), but only clarification (W II, 180) – i.e.
the explication of what is assumed in the first place. Because
Fichte begins by assuming that only the subjective is real enough
for philosophy, his philosophy remains subjective. Because his
ego is posited as being by its nature active, he can never get to its
passivity, to that which acts on it, to nature or to the body. For
Fichte nature is never real nature; it is merely the ego positing
itself as another. Schelling, it is true, began by attempting to take
a non-idealist path, by attempting to recognize the existence of
Nature as a primary, logically independent truth not to be deduced from the existence of consciousness, of the thinking ego.
But Schelling, though trying to overcome subjective idealism, was
far from being free of it. In order to relate Nature to the self, he

conceived Nature as *another self*; his Nature is not the nature of science, of sense-perception, but a construct of the imagination: he sees nature as a visible form or manifestation of imaginative understanding, in which distinctions and determinations have no objective reality but appear and dissolve like figures in a dream. Through Schelling,

> Philosophy now became *beautiful*, poetic, pleasant, romantic, but also transcendent, superstitious, *absolutely* uncritical. The primary condition of all criticism, the distinction between the subjective and the objective, had disappeared. Thinking as *discerning* and *determining* came to be seen as a finite, *negative* activity – no wonder that the Philosophy of Identity fell help-lessly into the arms of the mysticism of the Görlitzer shoemaker [Jacob Boehme]! (W II, 193).

Feuerbach concedes that Schelling was an important mediating link between Fichte and Hegel, but he lost what was positive about idealism, its conception of mental activity as rational activity. When Hegel begins with the Absolute, his Absolute has a certain positive content, the notion of objectivity, which is counterposed to the subjectivity of the Kantian-Fichtean philosophy. Schelling's philosophy, far from being the philosophy of the Absolute which its supporters took it to be, was only subjective idealism with another accent. The subjective idealist said to Nature: You are my *alter ego*, my other self. The subjective idealist stressed only the *ego*, so that Nature became an offshoot, a reflection of his own personality. The philosopher of Nature (Schelling) said the same, but he stressed the *alter*. Nature for him was an *ego*, but a different one, another and separate self (W II, 188). Because Schelling wanted an Absolute and a Philosophy of Identity, because he wanted to be both an idealist and a philosopher of Nature, he could reimpose unity between man and nature, between science and philosophy, only in the imagination – he had to become a mystic (W II, 192–3).

Hegel claimed that his philosophy was without presuppositions. He therefore began his *Logic* with Pure Being. Nothing, according to Hegel, could be less tendentious than this – a pure category which begs no question and implies no suspect content. But Hegel's deductions from this point on are purely formal, on paper;

they do not represent the real movement of his thought. For in reality, Hegel does not begin with Pure Being, but with the Absolute Idea, in which the totality and connection which he wants to establish are already assumed (W II, 181–2). While it is one of Hegel's merits that he brings distinction, variety, into his totality, it is never in Hegel real empirical variety, it is always the *thought* of empirical variety. Hegel's philosophy is able to triumph over sensory experience only because it never deals with it; when Hegel writes of the 'other-than-thought' he is not dealing with it, but with a mental conception, with the 'thought of the other-than-thought' (W II, 187). The contradictions that Hegel overcomes are never 'real contradictions', the being that he dissolves into the Idea is not real, empirical being, but the philosophical category 'being', the thought of being. 'The Hegelian philosophy is thus the culminating point of speculatively systematic philosophy' (W II, 175); everything 'demonstrates' itself, i.e., is 'posited' and connected in thought; nothing is concretely demonstrated from what actually happens, in the world. 'The Hegelian system is the *absolute self-alienation* of reason'; the logical demonstration, which should be a means, becomes an end in itself; the theatrical representation is mistaken for the reality and substituted for it. When Hegel, in the famous first chapter of the *Phenomenology*, wants to show the inadequacy of sensory perception by showing that there are no individuals, that there is no singular 'this, here, now', what does he do? He does not deal with what we experience, with 'this', but with the *concept of 'thisness'* and tries to show that we never experience particulars, but only universals. Characteristically, Hegel is not concerned with the tree that man experiences, leans against, falls over, comes up against as a fact limiting man's movements, but with the 'tree' which man fixes in his consciousness. Are we to conclude, from any discussion of the latter, that the former does not exist? If there were no trees, Feuerbach wants to suggest, there would be nothing for us to talk about or analyse in our consciousness. Speech, logic, philosophy are all ways of identifying and organizing an empirical reality coming to us through our senses; without this reality, there would be nothing to talk about. The 'concept' of a tree can neither establish nor disprove the existence of actual as opposed to conceptual trees. Idealist philosophy, on the one hand, needs actual trees in order to give content to its concepts; on the other hand, it needs to deny actual trees in order to 'posit' as the ultimate reality the mind or spirit which has these concepts.

> The philosophy which derives the finite from the infinite, the determinate from the indeterminate, *can never truly establish the finite and the determinate*. The finite is derived from the infinite – in other words, the infinite, the indeterminate, is made determinate, *is negated*. It is admitted that the infinite is nothing *without being determinate*, i.e., *that it is nothing unless it is finite*. The *reality* of the infinite is therefore posited as *finite*. But the negative non-Being of the Absolute continues to underlie the whole position; the finitude that has been posited therefore has to be dissolved again [*wieder aufgehoben*]. The *finite* is the *negation* of the *infinite* and again the *infinite* is the *negation* of the *finite*. The Philosophy of the Absolute is a *contradiction*,

Feuerbach wrote in the *Preliminary Theses for the Reform of Philosophy* (W II, 229).

> The beginning of philosophy is not God, not the Absolute, not Being as a predicate of the Absolute or of the Idea – the beginning of philosophy is the finite, the determinate, the *actual* [*wirklich*]. The infinite cannot even be thought *without* the finite. Can you think of a quality, define it, without thinking of a definite quality? Therefore not the indefinite, the indeterminate, but the definite, the determinate comes first. For the *definite* quality is nothing but the actual quality; the quality that is thought of is preceded by the actual. . . . The infinite is the *true essence* of the finite, the *true* finite. True speculation or philosophy is nothing but *true and universal empiricism* (W II, 230–1).

Here, then, we find emerging very clearly – as early as 1839 – Feuerbach's conception of philosophy as a second-order activity, as criticism of materials provided by the senses, and not as the theory of a self-constituting, self-certifying (mental) reality. Philosophy mediates the break between sensory perception and speculative philosophy, he writes (W II, 184n), 'by producing itself out of non-philosophy'; philosophy must always stand in the closest possible relation to empirical experience and to science, without roots in these it is nothing. (In the same way, Feuerbach had argued in his article 'Against the Dualism of Body and Soul, Flesh and the Spirit', that thought or mind without the body is nothing, for thought is a function of the body and cannot exist independently of it. 'The division of man into body and soul, into a sensory being and a non-sensory being, is purely theoretical; in practice, in life, we deny this division' – we treat man as a whole man, we do not sever the intellectual gifts that he has from the rest of his being, as though they were not part of him (W II, 345). 'Do you know when only you philosophize without presuppositions?' he asks in the *Fragments* (W II, 390). 'When you put the empirical before philosophy, sense-perception before thinking, but not just in the imagination, in an illusory way, as in speculative philosophy, but in truth and in deed.' In his review of Erdmann's *Geschichte der neueren Philosophie* [*History of Modern Philosophy*], a review published in 1838, Feuerbach had argued that both Greek and modern philosophy sprang out of philosophies of nature. Just as the history of Greek philosophy should not begin with Anaxagoras, so the history of modern philosophy should not begin with Descartes but with the philosopher of nature, Telesius, even though the latter only revived, in modern context, the Parmenidean philosophy of nature.[4] It should include men like Campanella (who was a Cartesian before Descartes), Bruno, and above all Bacon, who belongs to the history of philosophy as much as he belongs to the history of natural science. For Bacon was the *logician* of empiricism – he was no modest, servile empiricist gnawing at the outward peel of nature, but a man seeking its very core, a 'titanic spirit' recognizing no limits to enquiry. This is the mark of the true philosopher. In any case, every founder of a natural science is a philosopher, for every act of founding is a philosophical act (W II, 97–101).

The beginning of philosophy is the beginning of *knowledge in general*, it is not the beginning of philosophy *as a particular form of knowledge distinguished* from the knowledge of the empirical sciences. This is confirmed by history itself. Philosophy is the mother of the sciences. The first philosophers were scientists [*Naturforscher*], as in ancient so in modern times (W II, 206).

The task of philosophy is not to distinguish itself from the empirical sciences, but to maintain its close connections with them, to recognize that 'empirical activity is also philosophical activity, that *seeing* is also *thinking*, that the *sense-organs* are *organs of philosophy*. . . . We must philosophize under the guidance of the senses' (W II, 207).[5] In the *Preliminary Theses* these thoughts are repeated over and over again. 'Philosophy is the recognition of *what is*. To think of things and beings, to recognize them, *as they are* – this is the highest law, the highest task, of philosophy' (W II, 232). 'Philosophy must once more tie itself to natural science and natural science to philosophy. This tie, based on mutual need, on inner necessity, will be more durable, happier and more truthful than the *mesalliance* that has prevailed up to now between philosophy and theology' (W II, 244).

The *mesalliance* between philosophy and theology, which Feuerbach sees as specially evident in the history of German idealism, raises another important aspect of Feuerbach's critique of (speculative, idealist) philosophy. Christianity as a religion, Feuerbach believed, had been fundamentally and irrevocably negated in modern times – unconsciously, in modern science and modern life, in art and in industry, even if not consciously, at the theoretical level (W II, 218). Modern man may be a Christian theoretically, in practice he lives secularly, reserving for Christianity only the Sunday. The last bastion of the religious consciousness, of *theology*, is to be found in speculative philosophy, which does in theory what man no longer does in practice. The concept of God, routed in practical life, has passed over into speculative philosophy, where it reappears as Fichte's creative ego, as Schelling's organic, poetic Nature, as Hegel's Absolute Idea. 'Ordinary theology makes the standpoint of man God's standpoint; speculative theology on the other hand makes God's standpoint the standpoint of man, or rather of the thinker' (W II, 252). Speculative philosophy has thus torn philosophy out of its natural alliance with science and has subjected it to the religious impulse. Hegel had already recognized, quite correctly so far as his own philosophy was concerned, that the *content* of philosophy and religion was the same; only their form was different. Religion dealt in concrete images; philosophy dealt in concepts. With this Feuerbach agreed – at least, so far as speculative, idealist philosophy was concerned. But Hegel was wrong, according to Feuerbach, in thinking that the common *content* of religion and philosophy was knowledge. It was not knowledge; it was feeling. The content of religion was not nature, or the world, but man – man in his imaginative functions, in his will and his feelings – abstracting these mental capacities from himself and projecting them into a fantasy-reality. As Professor Hook has put it:[6]

> Feuerbach defined the religious phenomenon as such as the projection and hypostasis of some element of human experience into an object of worship. He attempted to show that the whole of traditional philosophy represented the same arbitrary isolation of a local and limited feature of experience from its context in social life, and its subsequent erection into an absolute principle whose validity was independent of all space, time and society. Traditional philosophy, then, was religion, too, both in its essential nature and in its process of construction. The difference for Feuerbach was merely that in religion the hypostasis found its expression in concrete objects of sense and imagination while in philosophy the hypostasis was abstract and conceptual.

Just as religion takes certain attributes of man, rips them out of their real context and projects them on to another being, whom it calls God, so idealist philosophy abstracts human functions (and real predicates generally) and converts them into self-supporting subjects, into metaphysical entities – the Will, in place of men willing, Reason, in place of men reasoning. In so far as speculative philosophy in its own way again intensifies the alienation and abstraction begun by ordinary religion, in so far as it raises predicates, functions or attributes to the level of substance, it is a form of *theology*, of religion raised to a higher level of confusion and alienation. Theology concentrates on that which is supposed to distinguish God from man, i.e. in reality on God as the Understanding, as Reason, distinguished from the God of love and flesh, who has contact with the empirical man. Theology uses the religious imagination to separate this God. God as intelligence or reason or understanding, from reason as such; it makes this God a separate being. The historical importance of idealist philosophy lay in its bridging of this gap, in its identification of God (as reason) with Reason itself (W II, 247). 'The essence of speculative philosophy is nothing but the *rationalized, realized essence of God, brought into our presence.* Speculative philosophy is the *true, consistent rational* theology' (W II, 246). What theology treats as an *object*, speculative philosophy makes into a *subject*; what theology contemplates and thinks of, speculative philosophy treats as the contemplative and thinking activity itself (W II, 249–50). The essential properties and predicates ascribed by theology to God, however, remain the essential properties or predicates of speculative philosophy (W II, 254); they are not converted into real, empirical, spatio-temporal properties and into predicates of real, empirical, spatio-temporal subjects. Just as religion must be led back to man and nature, as its elevation of subjectivity and fantasy must be overcome, so philosophy must be led back to man and nature, linked with empirical science, made objective, concrete and real, instead of being subjective and infinite and dwelling in a fantasy-world of abstractions. It was in this sense that Feuerbach proclaimed that

> he who does not give up Hegelian philosophy does not give up theology. The Hegelian teaching that nature, reality, is *posited* by the Idea is only the rational expression of the theological teaching that nature is created by God, that a material being is created by an immaterial, i.e., abstract, being (W II, 239).

While the pantheism of a Spinoza or a Hegel overcomes the *principle* of theology (its theoretical aspect, the separation of God and the rest of reality), it does not overcome the *consequences* of theology (its abstraction and alienation of properties,[7] its practical aspect); only empiricism can overcome the latter (W II, 266). 'The subject of divinity is reason, but the subject of reason is man' (W II, 388); it is to the real ground of philosophy, man and nature, man and his sensations, that philosophy must return. If philosophy means abstraction, the study of concepts in themselves, then Feuerbach proclaims: '*No* religion is my religion; *no* philosophy is my philosophy' (W II, 391).

PART THREE

The 'Philosophy of the Future'

5. Feuerbach's 'Transformation of Philosophy'

For more than a half century after the French Revolution, philosophy in Germany played an intensely ideological rôle. It strove to determine man's place in the universe, to bridge the apparent gulf between man and nature, between knowing and willing, between 'ought' and 'is'. It transformed the categories of logic and the types of judgment into proclamations of the rights and duties of man; it gave a Constitution to the universe, and called on man to respect and obey its provisions, while living up to their promise. The appointment of Fichte as first Rector of the newly-founded University of Berlin and the calls that went out, first to Hegel, to prove that the actual is the real and rational, and then to Schelling, to justify Frederick William IV's retreat to conservative romanticism, were rightly seen as political-ideological acts. Rulers and rebels agreed that philosophy was neither neutral nor irrelevant: in German idealism philosophy, *Weltanschauung* and *Lebensanschauung* had become inextricably interwoven. It was thus not only in its content, but also in its intellectual, social and political rôle that Feuerbach, like Marx, could see German idealism continuing and consummating the work of religion.

At the same time, like religion, German idealism stood for the primacy of the spirit. It saw reality either *as* spirit or in spiritual-mental terms; it consciously or unconsciously made matter a projection of mind and patterned the movement of nature after the movement of thought. Feuerbach, rightly, saw this as the culmination of a *particular* tradition in philosophy and not as a fundamental truth of philosophy which all philosophers must accept. It was Descartes, as opposed to what Feuerbach calls 'the philosophers of nature', who put the problem of knowledge at the centre of philosophical enquiry and obscured its nature by treating consciousness as (unextended) *substance*, instead of seeing mind as a function of empirical, natural men. German idealism, in seeking to overcome the Cartesian dualism of extended matter and unextended, infinite, consciousness came down on the wrong side, brought everything within consciousness, made consciousness or spirit or mind the stuff of all things. Philosophy could fall into this error only by *abstracting* from real, practical life, by tearing out of their human and natural context specific functions and aspects of man, projecting them into an independent existence and then subordinating all other existence to them. For Feuerbach, philosophy in its idealist form had not only the social rôle of religion, but also the same origin: it projected man's functions outside man and then subordinated both real, empirical men and real, empirical nature to these functions.

Taking up (for literary effect) the Kantian notion that time is the form of the inner sense while space is the form of the outer sense, Feuerbach wants to argue that any genuine theory of reality must combine both space and time. It must recognize man's mental functioning and the external world apprehended through the senses as equal in status, as logically independent terms of a single situation. Feuerbach is rejecting completely the view that the universe is mind-dependent, whether that mind is seen as an individual human mind or as a divine mind. If the material, physical world did not exist independently of our mind and its workings, we would never get to a conception of a physical, material world or object. From spirit, mind or consciousness, seen as infinite and unextended, we could never get to the finite and extended. The mind by itself may give us time, but it cannot give us the notion of space. In Hegel, Feuerbach argues (W II, 159), this is precisely what we find: the form under which Hegel perceives reality is that of time, but not that of space. 'His system knows only subordination and succession, it knows nothing of co-ordination and co-existence.' Though Hegel pretends that each particular stage in his development is 'taken up' into the final culmination of the process, into a *totality*, Hegel's final stage and his final totality remain in fact particular. The particular totality cannot take up concrete individuals without robbing them of their independence and individuality. Because Hegel sees everything in time but not in space he cannot, in the end, tolerate real differences and distinctions, which can be genuinely co-ordinate only in space. Because Hegel's totality is particular, it cannot accommodate the true infinite variety that we find in the world. As Feuerbach puts it, time, the inner sense, is monarchical, despotic, subordinating everything to its requirements; only space, the outer sense, is tolerant, democratic, allowing each thing its independence and freedom. Knowing, for Feuerbach, is one of man's relationships to nature and these relations, Feuerbach insists, should not consist in mere egoistic impositions of the will, of force and rapine. Man has not only hands with which to master nature, but also eyes and ears with which to admire it for its own sake and in its own form.

> The horse, which the groom subdues with his buttocks, the painter elevates into an object of art, and the sable which is killed by the furrier in order to make its fur into an element of adornment for human vanity is preserved alive by natural science so that it may study the sable in all its aspects (W II, 160).

Feuerbach, then, is insisting on the continuity as well as the distinction between man and nature. The mental world and the physical world interact on the one logical and ontological plane – this, at any rate, is Feuerbach's view in the late 1830s and early 1840s. Unlike Descartes and Fichte and – for that matter – the British empiricists, Feuerbach simply rejects the question how to *prove* the existence of an external world. Though Feuerbach does not explicitly make these points he seems to have two points in mind: (1) The *problem* of knowledge, of relating mind and nature, arises only if we first erect a false dualism of mind and nature, if we tear mind out of the body and out of the physical world, where we originally find it. Only then do we find it hard to get back to the physical world. In fact, we become acquainted with mind as part of reality in general, and if we did not have a concept of the body, of nature, at the same time, we could not have a concept of the mind. (2) Propositions do not certify themselves. Descartes and Fichte thought that one could doubt everything except the thinking mind only because they *began by assuming* the thinking mind. Having assumed it, they could not at the same time not assume it, doubt it. But they might just as well have begun by assuming the existence of a man, Descartes, or Fichte, and found that they could not doubt his (material) existence. Here Feuerbach sees clearly that proof is a relation between propositions, a relation in which premises prove a conclusion. The conclusion proved by such premises can never contain terms not contained in the premises; if we do not include the material world in our premises, we can never get to it in our conclusion. If we begin by including only mind in our premises it is not surprising that we are left with only mind in our conclusion. If we begin with nothing but mind, we will never get to anything but mind. This in itself is enough to show that we must begin with more. If we want to get to the material world, then we must begin with it. It is as much 'given' for us as our mind.

In a very important sense, then, Feuerbach's critique of idealism has ended with an anti-Promethean, naturalistic view of man. Ontologically, man is not the Lord of Creation or its First Cause. On the contrary, he is a part of nature and a natural product.

> 'Man cannot be derived from nature.' No! But the man who sprang directly from nature was indeed, at first, a purely primitive natural being, not a man. Man is a product of man, of culture, of history. Even many plants and animals have changed so much under the care of the human hand that we can no longer trace their original forms in nature. Do you want to take recourse to a *Deus ex machina* in order to explain their origin? ... 'Man is the highest being in nature: therefore I must begin with the nature of man, seize hold of it, if I want to make clear to myself the origin and cause of nature.' Quite true; but it is precisely in man that 'understanding comes with age', that matter comes before spirit, lack of consciousness before consciousness, lack of purpose before purpose, sensuality before reason, suffering before the will (W II, 388–9).

Man has to be understood as acted upon and not only as acting, as physical as well as mental, as feeling as well as reasoning. Nature, further, must be recognized as having a certain integrity of her own. 'Whence stem the lacunae and limitations of our knowledge of nature? From the fact that knowledge is neither the basis nor the goal of nature' (W II, 389). It is only the idealist, who treats nature as a mental creation, Feuerbach is suggesting, who would expect nature to be wholly transparent to human enquiry.

Infinity, we have seen Feuerbach arguing in the *Essence of*

Christianity, is a matter of quantity, not of quality, of extension (as the logicians put it) and not of intension. There can be no question, therefore, of converting the genuine, extensional, spatial infinity of nature into a *particular* but allegedly qualitative infinite totality having the character of 'allness'. Just as *one man* cannot express the infinity of the species, so a *particular* totality cannot express the infinity of nature. For the infinity of nature is the infinity of a series or collection; it is made up of an infinite (i.e. endless) number of *finite* things.

> Whatever enters into space and time must accommodate itself
> to the laws of space and time. The god of boundaries is the
> guardian standing at the gateway to the world. Self-limitation
> is the condition of entry. Whatever becomes real or actual, can
> only become real or actual as a specific thing. The incarnation
> of a species in all its fullness within a single individual would
> be an absolute miracle, a forcible dissolution of all the laws and
> principles of reality – it would in fact be the *destruction of the
> world* (W II, 162).

Thus, according to Feuerbach (W II, 163), when divinity tries to enter the actual world or history, the world or history have to be destroyed. The religious belief in a Messianic coming *requires* the destruction of the empirical world which is supposed to precede that coming; only thus can it make room for divinity. Similarly, the Hegelian philosophy (which encourages the belief of its disciples that it is the *ultimate* philosophy, the *culmination* of all thought) has to destroy time; philosophy and history are temporal before Hegel, but not after him. The ultimate, the culmination, cannot develop further.[1]

Philosophy, we have said, is for Feuerbach a second-order activity; it is *criticism*. 'Philosophy should awaken, awaken thought, not make our understanding a prisoner to a spoken or written word' (W II, 173–4); the task of philosophy is not to dominate, but to convey. It cannot construct the universe, it can only explicate it. After his retirement to Bruckberg, Feuerbach was wont to be very scathing indeed of the professional philosopher, who buries himself in concepts instead of looking at reality. There was in this, no doubt, a certain element of pique. But Feuerbach does also want to say, quite seriously, that only absurdly narrow professionalization, only the blinding effects of a division of labour, can make philosophers mistake their abstractions for living reality, can make them blind themselves to all those things that do not fit into their system, or to the fact that their system can only be understood in reference to a wider whole. It is as though critics of literature or art had begun to write solely about the concepts of other critics, and had forgotten the actual literary or artistic productions that were the subject of criticism, the source of these concepts.

Philosophy, as criticism, is for Feuerbach a *practical* activity, i.e., it is part of man's dealing with the world around him, part of *life* itself and cannot be simply divorced from it. Theory and practice as conventionally distinguished are both part of man's activity as an organism, as a living being, part of his grappling with reality. They are thus continuous with each other and mutually supporting.

> 'Science does not solve the riddle of life.' If you like; but what follows from that? That you should run to faith? That would be jumping out of the frying-pan into the fire. You must go over to life, to praxis. The doubts which theory cannot resolve, are resolved by praxis (W II, 389).

The significance of the senses, for Feuerbach, is that they provide the material for both theory and practice, that they are the foundation on which man's dealings with nature and with other men rest.

In 1842, almost immediately after finishing the *Essence of Christianity*, Feuerbach began to issue a series of calls for a radical transformation of philosophy. In his article 'Notwendigkeit einer Reform der Philosophie' ('The Necessity of a Reform in Philosophy'), he linked this transformation not merely with his logical critique of idealism, but with the historical development of mankind. 'The periods of humanity,' he writes (W II, 216), 'are distinguished from one another by religious changes.' Humanity has just gone through another religious revolution, comparable to, and presaged by, the Lutheran revolution that brought God out of heaven into the soul and consciousness of man. So far, men have lived in the Protestant Middle Ages, only half-emancipated from the Roman Church, from Roman law (W II, 221), from the external subjugation of man by religious and moral conceptions that he himself created. During this period, the *unconscious* negation of Christianity has proceeded apace – Christianity has been negated 'in heart and in mind, in science and in life, in art and industry, in a thorough-going way, leaving nothing to salvage or recall, because men have appropriated for themselves the true, the human, the anti-holy, so that Christianity has lost all power of opposition' (W II, 218). In practical life, man has recognized his own powers, has become self-reliant, has worked on his own behalf, has overcome (unconsciously, without fully knowing it) his previous alienation. In theoretical life, however, the alienation of man, the abstraction of his qualities from himself, has been continued in philosophy. Now the time has come for the freeing of man from both religious and philosophical alienation, the time for man to take back consciously, into himself, his own powers: to become a man instead of a Christian. The idealist philosophy has exhausted its capacities; it has nothing more to tell us. It has been unable to solve the contradiction between contemporary man's life and thought and the forms of religious consciousness, for idealist philosophy has itself kept the *forms* of religious thinking while proving itself incapable of fulfilling the positive functions of religion.

The new age, then, is one in which man strives for political freedom, for the untrammelled exercise of his own capacities, and he now recognizes Christianity as having become a hindrance to this exercise. The new age, therefore, requires a new philosophy – a philosophy that can become a satisfactory substitute for religion, a basis for life, a means for the reconciliation of feeling and reason, of theory and practice. Religion, Feuerbach had argued, was an art of life, man's way of dealing with reality. But in religion man realized his own potentialities and mastered nature only in the imagination. The same was true of idealist philosophy. The new philosophy, the philosophy of the future, must provide the basis for the conscious, real, practical vindication of man. It must be both realistic and atheistic. In rejecting a God set over and above man (or a Reason fulfilling God-like functions) man accepts himself and through himself the nature in which he lives and of which he is part.

The outline which Feuerbach gives of the 'philosophy of the future' – in his *Preliminary Theses for the Reform of Philosophy* (1842) and his *Basic Propositions of the Philosophy of the Future*

(1843) – adds almost nothing of significance to this and to the passages already quoted above (Chapter 4). Characteristically, Feuerbach sets out his position in a long series of aphorisms which emphasize, in various ways, the theological character of German idealist philosophy, the human content of religion, and the need for vindicating man by making him politically free and empirically inclined in his dealing with nature. Politics, Feuerbach often stresses, should be the new religion of mankind: the State (as a republican, democratic state representing men) is the new expression of humanity (W II, 220, 244). The philosophy of the future, in other words, is philosophical naturalism coupled with political republicanism. (Feuerbach feels, and not implausibly, that the two support each other – philosophical hierarchies lead to political hierarchies and vice versa; the God of religion and the Spirit or Absolute of the philosophers both have monarchical pretensions.) Beyond this Feuerbach does not go in any systematic way. It is not clear whether the philosophy of the future is a continuation and development of the naturalistic, empirical tradition in past philosophy, or a dissolution of philosophy as a specific discipline altogether. (Feuerbach obviously vacillates between these two positions or, rather, proclaims each in different aphorisms.) While Feuerbach had devoted a great deal of attention to the positive content of religion, he has vacillated – as we have seen – between its emotive and its cognitive roots, amalgamating the two when he should have distinguished them. In philosophy, he does not get that far. Most of the traditional problems of philosophy are simply not discussed by Feuerbach; one of the central problems, the nature of logic, is hardly touched upon at all. At best, one might say that Feuerbach sketched a few fundamental principles of philosophical enquiry; one could not even call it a programme because it is not clear whether Feuerbach thinks philosophy can have any specifically philosophical programme. At worst, one might say that Feuerbach proclaimed a few slogans, at times suggestive and not ineffective in criticism of certain positions, but not really helping to solve any genuine problems. (The young Marx was behaving in a very Feuerbachian way when he suggested that all the problems – 'contradictions' – of economic science and economic life would be resolved once economists stopped reifying economic categories and made man – the whole, complete living man – the basis of economic science and the master

of the economic process.) Nevertheless, while Feuerbach's thin-
ness at this vital point in his development as a public figure explains why he was not able to retain leadership of the movement
he founded, and why he has never been taken seriously by those
who see philosophy as above all systematic in character, the
principles he suggested were quite fundamental. Let us examine
them in more detail, as involving a method, a naturalistic ontology
and theory of knowledge and a (somewhat contradictory) concept
of man. After that, we shall turn to the concerns of his final
years, ethics.

6. Feuerbach's method

The most important, the foundation-laying propositions of the philosophy of Feuerbach arise as antitheses to the Hegelian philosophy [the disciple of Feuerbach's later years, Friedrich Jodl wrote at the beginning of his study of Feuerbach's thought,[1] adding with characteristic but excessive enthusiasm], yes, the whole historical position of Feuerbach may perhaps be characterized in the shortest and most apposite way by saying that he brings about a revolution in the philosophy of Hegel like that which Copernicus brought about in the Ptolemaic astronomy: that which was the centre of everything, the Absolute Spirit, he pushes to the periphery as a mere projection; Nature, which was there [in Hegelian philosophy] self-alienation of the spirit, becomes the central concept and the carrier of the spiritual or mental life.

The suggestion that Feuerbach may be compared, in the history of philosophy, with Copernicus in astronomy, or with that Copernican revolutionary in philosophy, Immanuel Kant, will only seem amusing to modern ears. Yet to Feuerbach's own contemporaries (or at least, to the young and radical among his contemporaries) this was precisely how it seemed. Feuerbach, with one book and a few articles, had destroyed the very foundations of Christian belief and had shown up the theological character of the Hegelian system. His importance, even to his contemporaries, was primarily negative: Feuerbach had exposed the illusions that hold man in thraldom; the very act of exposure was a fundamental, world-historical act of liberation. Man had been shown his own nature, as it really was. Now man himself could carry on. Feuerbach, in his 1842 article 'Toward the Evaluation of the Work: The Essence of Christianity', emphasized that his philosophy of religion and his thought generally could only be understood and evaluated as arising in opposition to the Hegelian philosophy (W VII, 265–6, 267). At the foundation of his opposition to the Hegelian philosophy and to theology generally, and thus at the very foundation of all his achievements, Feuerbach thought, lay a method, an approach to philosophy and to religion which had indeed yielded results as startling and yet as simple as those of Copernicus.

In the later years of his life Feuerbach liked to emphasize that he was the philosopher of the common man. But as Hook puts it,[2] 'It would be truer to say that Feuerbach attempted to do justice to the nature of *common experience* – a common experience born of practical activity and accessible to all human beings with the possible exception of professional philosophers.' In 1839 Feuerbach thought that this common experience, which reflected the fusion of feeling and reason, perception and thought, involved a philosophy and a philosophical method which overcame and reconciled the one-sidedness, the narrow-mindedness, found in both materialism and idealism. In a letter to C. Riedel, commenting on a newspaper suggestion that Feuerbach's talent would shine even more brightly if he were to become active in spheres nearer to life and art instead of writing, as he had then been doing, almost solely on the history of philosophy, Feuerbach insisted that his writing was in fact practical:

The practical tendency (in the higher sense of the term) of my literary activity is expressed in its very method. The method consists in this: that it aims to achieve a continuous unification of the noble with the apparently common, of the distant with the *near-at-hand*, of the *abstract* with the *concrete*, of the *speculative* with the *empirical*, of *philosophy* with *life*. . . . In speculative philosophy I miss the element of empiricism and in empiricism the element of speculation. My method therefore is to unite both, not as two different materials but as different principles, i.e. empirical *activity* and speculative *activity*. And for me the mediating link between these real, not abstract, opposites is *scepticism* or *criticism* of what is *only* speculative as well as of what is *only* empirical (W II, 398, 400).[3]

Two years later Feuerbach was to announce that his method was simply this: to reduce everything to man, to show that philosophy is Anthropology. Yet, as Feuerbach himself was to realize a few years after that, these phrases were not particularly happy ones. Feuerbach, as we have seen, reduced philosophy and religion to 'man' only in a very extended sense, he reduced them to what Hook rightly calls 'common experience', i.e. to man and to 'nature' as perceived by and known to man.

The foundation of Feuerbach's method, on the cognitive side, then, is not philosophical anthropology but 'empiricism', or the 'scientific attitude'. Sensory experience, human sensory experience, not logic or reason, is the only criterion of existence available to man. We can pass from being to essence (from real, actual, i.e. experienced processes or things to concepts); we cannot pass from essence to being (from logical categories, concepts to actual, experienced processes or things). The first principle of philosophical method is that all philosophical statements must have their origin and real content in the facts of sensory experience. In a 'healthy', self-reliant state man's activities, including his thinking, *are practical*, do relate to his sensory experience and seek to deal with it. Only when man feels helpless, when he has recourse to fantasy (and thus to self-alienation), does he abstract and distort concepts originally grounded in reality and build up a fantasy-world or a fantasy-philosophy from them. Between the way of science and the way of dreams (whether religious or philosophical) there can be no reconciliation and no third path. 'Philosophy has Cuvier's eye,' Feuerbach writes to Christian Kapp in 1840 (W XIII, 35). 'From the splinter it can recognize the skeleton of the whole.' But it must begin with a splinter. 'No law of metaphysics is valid for me if I cannot establish it as a law of natural science,' he writes to Kapp again. Many years later, in a letter to Bolin, he still insists that the basis of his philosophy is natural science 'to which alone belongs past, present and future, while philosophy, at least the kind which appropriates the name, can only claim that past which contains the *peracti labores* or rather the *errores* of mankind'.[4]

Feuerbach's insistence that all knowledge and all speculation must be traced back to experience leads him to what he calls his 'genetic-critical' method. This consists simply in tracing conceptions and beliefs back to their origin in the experience and attitudes of men. But Feuerbach himself makes it clear that this method must always begin with the analysis of the conception or belief itself – there is absolutely no warrant in Feuerbach for the Stalinist vulgarity of dismissing a philosophy because of the 'class origin' of a philosopher.

Where does man spring from? Ask first: *What* is man? If his essence or nature is clear to you, then his origin will be clear to you as well. What? asks the man; where from? asks the child (W II, 388). What does my 'method' consist in, then? It consists in the fact that I reduce everything supernatural, through man, to nature and everything superhuman, through nature, to man; but I do so always only on the basis of observable, historical, empirical facts and examples (W II, 390).

'I lack one talent,' Feuerbach wrote to Christian Kapp in 1840 (W XIII, 50), 'the formal-philosophical, the systematic, the en-cyclopaedic-methodical, or at least I have not cultivated it, I have placed least value upon it in the current state of philosophy and science.' Feuerbach was right in noting this lack, but he was probably also right in the reason he gave for it. Feuerbach's proclamation of an empirical, scientific method in philosophy and of a controlled genetic-critical approach to *error* (illusions, fantasies, etc.) was both perfectly sound and extremely apposite in the intellectual climate of his day. No doubt, Feuerbach of the early 1840s was inclined to exaggerate its result, to think of it as removing problems instead of seeing it as enabling us to tackle problems in the appropriate manner and the appropriate context. In philo-sophy, indeed, Feuerbach simply side-steps some of the central problems of the subject. As we shall see in discussing his theory of perception, he does not tackle seriously the question of precisely what is given or implied in 'experience' and he does not examine the relation, in science or in practice, between what he calls the speculative and the empirical. Yet this after all has been one of the central problems agitating philosophers. The difficulties of this problem account for the constructions of Kant and even of Hegel at least as much as the influence of religious conceptions.[5] Feuerbach, though at one stage aware of the positive content of the Hegelian and even more of the Kantian critical philosophy, of their concern with the logical structure of our 'experience', simply leaves this content out of account. He does not tackle the problem of logic and to that (very great) extent he does not tackle the prob-lem of philosophy. In over-reacting against the 'abstractions' of the idealists, Feuerbach failed to isolate specific issues as specific-ally philosophical issues. To say that logic cannot and does not tell the whole story, and that it cannot talk to itself and of itself, is not to remove the problem of deciding what story logic does tell.

Another problem arises from Feuerbach's constant emphasis on the *essential* nature of a being, process or thing and his tendency to identify its *Wesen* or nature with the *sine qua non* of the being, process or thing. Max Stirner, in his onslaught on Feuerbach, accused him of retaining a theological concept of *Wesen* as far as man was concerned, of setting up an alienated and fantasy-concept of *human nature* that had no roots in the actual behaviour of empirical men. In so far as Stirner was upholding a logical individualism and treating each man as a pure particular, Feuerbach was able to reply (in spite of his own vestigial nominalism) that it was Stirner's solitary, particular, egoistic man who was a construct, a figment of the imagination. Real men *were* members of a species, did have common characteristics with other men, and had their nature shaped in *relationships* in which they recognized the importance of others, in which they felt love, gratitude, sympathy, etc. It was no use saying that man strove only to vindicate his self, when his self was not solitary, not alone, not cut off and opposed, by its nature, to all other selves, not the product of its own, self-contained history. In so far as Feuerbach's use of *Wesen* emphasizes the common characteristics of a class as opposed to individual variations, it does not involve any logically vicious 'essentialism'. Neither is Feuerbach wrong in arguing that any science, from botany and zoology to anatomy and history and 'the philosophy of the future', will treat certain characteristics as more fundamental than others, as forming part of a coherent group of related characteristics. A zoologist can write about the 'nature' of mammals, while he cannot write about the 'nature' of grey animals; there is a group of characteristics that goes with being a mammal, while there is no group of characteristics that goes with being grey. Feuerbach, in using the word *Wesen*, meant to imply no more than this; what he wanted, in the case of religion, and of man, was to bring out characteristics that are 'part of the concept', that are not mere disparate or individual characteristics found here or there, but that stand in connected relationships with other characteristics and thus help to create and define the class. Here, too, there is no theoretical viciousness – if one proceeds with care.

Unfortunately, Feuerbach did not always proceed with sufficient care. He tended to see the 'nature' of a thing in excessively simple terms, and his genetic-critical method rather encouraged him in this. It led him, all too often, to find the 'secret' of its nature in its *sine qua non* and then to make that *sine qua non* the whole of its 'nature': 'Religion *is* dependence', 'man *is* the sensory'. As a new *sine qua non* came up – for one and the same thing may have several conditions necessary for its existence – the second term in the identity changed. The internal structure of the *Wesen* Feuerbach rarely examined, except in the case of religion – in his treatment of man, humanity or human nature is presented in far too coherent and simple a fashion. The recognition, as a matter of principle and method, of *complexity* is conspicuously missing from Feuerbach's work, as it is in statements of general principle, though not in detailed examinations, from Marx's. The result is a looseness of language possibly only to those who have not a constant eye on the difficulty of the border-line case or the need to account for what seem to be disconfirming instances: Feuerbach, to a far, far greater extent than Marx, lacked the caution of a precise and systematic thinker. We should not blame this entirely on his method, or use his personal weakness to discredit that method. What we can say, rather, is that his method provided no in-built checks against this weakness. In emphasizing the *function* of theories, beliefs, institutions, it too frequently leaves one with the impression that they have just *one*, coherent function.

7. Feuerbach's theory of knowledge and his 'materialism'

Among the labels that Feuerbach attached to his own philosophy, 'sensualism' (*Sinnlichkeit* or *Sensualismus*) was one of the most frequent. Feuerbach, characteristically, used the word in a wide and imprecise sense to bring together several logically distinct parts of his doctrine. It is through the senses, we have seen him arguing, that man comes into contact with the objective reality around him; he cannot deduce, create or describe this reality 'out of his head'. The senses are thus the beginning of all knowledge. In the preface to the second edition of the *Essence of Christianity* (EC xxxiv; W VII, 281), Feuerbach wrote:

> I unconditionally repudiate *absolute*, immaterial, self-sufficing speculation, that speculation which draws its material from within. I differ *toto coelo* from those philosophers who pluck out their eyes that they may see better; for *my* thoughts I require the senses, especially sight; I found my ideas on materials which can be appropriated only through the activity of the senses. I do not generate the object from the thought, but the thought from the object; and I hold *that* alone to be an object which has an existence beyond one's own brain.

'Only the senses, not thought, give us an object or thing in the true sense,' he wrote elsewhere.[1] 'The secret of immediate knowledge is sensualism.' In the rather sloganish form in which Feuerbach set down his proposals and propositions for the reform of philosophy, Feuerbach often stretched this primacy of 'sensualism' to convey another aspect of his philosophy, very much to the fore in the *Essence of Christianity* – the notion that man is a *sensual* creature rather than a reasoning or a thinking machine or a mere passive receptacle. The confusion of sights, sounds, pressures and tastes that beat in upon man produce and interact with feelings, fears, hopes and passions, without which man cannot be understood and without which his beliefs cannot be explained.

Feuerbach did not develop this latter aspect of his epistemology in any systematic way. After 1848 especially, he often slipped into statements closer to the passive 'materialist' conception of knowledge of a Condillac and Helvétius. Nevertheless, parts of Feuerbach's work hint at a dynamic theory of knowledge akin to the Freudian one in place of the passive receptivity of earlier empiricists and materialists. For Feuerbach, implicitly at least, knowing is a *practical* activity, a transaction between man and his surroundings. It is an activity involving the whole man: not only man's senses and his understanding and reason, but his interests, his passions, his fears and his hopes. Errors, illusion and fantasy can thus be explained, in principle, by saying that feelings, fears and desires, participate actively in the knowing process. What knows, Feuerbach does say specifically, is not the senses, or the understanding, but the whole man:

The maxim hitherto adopted by speculative philosophy: All that is mine I carry with me, the old *omnia mea mecum porto*, I cannot, alas, appropriate. I have many things outside myself, which I cannot convey either in my pocket or my head, but which nevertheless I look upon as belonging to me, not indeed as a mere man – a view not now in question – but as a philosopher. I am nothing but a *natural philosopher in the domain of mind* and the natural philosopher can do nothing without instruments, without material means. In this character I have written the present work, which consequently contains nothing else than the principles of a new philosophy verified practically, *i.e.*, *in concreto*, in application to a special object, but an object which has a universal significance: namely, to religion, in which this principle is exhibited, developed, and thoroughly carried out. This philosophy is essentially distinguished from the systems hitherto prevalent, in that it corresponds to the real, complete nature of man; but for that very reason it is antagonistic to minds perverted and crippled by a superhuman, *i.e.*, anti-human, anti-natural religion and speculation. It does not, as I have already said elsewhere, regard the *pen* as the only fit organ for the revelation of truth, but the eye and ear, the hand and foot; it does not identify the *idea* of the fact with the fact itself, so as to reduce real existence to an existence on paper, but it separates the two, and precisely by this separation attains to the *fact itself*; it recognizes as the true thing, not the thing as it is an object of the abstract reason, but as it is an object of the real, complete man, and hence as it is itself a real, complete thing. This philosophy does not rest on an Understanding *per se*, on an absolute, nameless understanding, belonging one knows not to whom, but on the understanding of man; – though not, I grant, on that of man enervated by speculation and dogma; – and it speaks the language of men, not an empty, unknown tongue. Yes, both in substance and in speech, it places philosophy in the *negation of philosophy*, *i.e.*, it declares *that* alone to be the true philosophy which is converted *in succum et sanguinem*, which is incarnate in Man; and hence it finds its highest triumph in the fact that to all dull and pedantic minds, which place the *essence* of philosophy in the *show* of philosophy, it appears to be no philosophy at all (EC xxxiv–xxxv; W VII, 281–3).

Although Feuerbach did not much develop this side of his thought, we may take it to be one of Feuerbach's contributions to the theory of knowledge that he declined to treat the knower as a logical simple – as a disembodied mind or as a particular mental faculty, as consciousness or that whose nature it is to know. In Feuerbach, the knower was as historical, as much subject to conflict, influence and related to other activities, as the known. His theory at least suggested that consciousness or the act of knowing was not logically discontinuous from man's other activities and states. (In his later ethical writings, examined in Chapter 9, he reinforced this view by what seems to me a sound attack on the concept of moral freedom, on the notion that moral consciousness is ahistorical and discontinuous with man's strivings, fears, and condition.)

Feuerbach's contribution to epistemology proper, to the philosophical discussion of the nature, scope and reliability of knowledge, is much more questionable. However, he did make a number of points, but he did not pull them together into a coherent theory and he did not examine their implications and difficulties with the care expected of a serious philosopher. One of his points, not put precisely in this form, was that the very conception of knowing implied and required an objective reality, existing independently of the knower. Accepting the traditional Kantian–Hegelian hierarchy of knowledge as comprising the levels of sense-perception, 'contemplation' or 'intuition' (*Anschauung*) 'understanding (*Verstand*) and reason (*Vernunft*), Feuerbach agreed that we get a material content or thing from sense-perception, a concept from the understanding and logical principles or logical relations from reason.[2] According to Feuerbach, however, the whole of this hierarchy could not get started without the material content; sense-perception could not be distinguished from the other faculties or forms of knowledge except by reference to an objective reality implied by such contents. He had argued, as we have seen, that we could never arrive at a material content, at the notion of qualitative distinctions and of an external world, by starting from logic or even from concepts – if objectivity, materiality and qualitative distinctions were not 'given' to man, he could never come to believe in them. They are thus objective at least in the sense that they are *a priori* for man; he cannot explain the structure of his thought and being without them. Further, man's sense-perception gives him knowledge of other sentient beings. He thus has a check against the subjectivity of his own sensory reactions by observing the reactions of others. He can guard against the broader 'subjectivity' of man as a species by observing the reactions of animals, to light, for instance (W II, 251). More frequently, however, Feuerbach referred to the check on subjectivity in the narrower sense provided by man's relation with other men – another aspect of his insistence on the I-Thou, on man's character as a species-being whose knowledge becomes species-knowledge. Here Feuerbach vacillated between the view that common human agreement was a *check* on truth or objectivity and the quite different view that it *constituted* truth or objectivity. When Feuerbach wrote 'what I see myself I doubt, only that is certain which another also sees', he was still using agreement as a mere *test* of truth, but in his repeated view that 'man is the measure of reason', that 'the measure of the species is the absolute measure, law and criterion of man' (EC 16; W VI, 20), he went beyond this to the proclamation that the conventional, the socially accepted, *is* truth:

That is true in which another agrees with me – agreement is the first criterion of truth; but only because the species is the

ultimate measure of truth. That which I think only according to
the standard of my individuality is not binding on another, it
can be conceived otherwise, it is an accidental, merely subjective, view. But that which I think according to the standard
of the species, I think as man in general only can think, and
consequently as every individual must think if he thinks
normally, in accordance with law, and therefore, truly. That is
true which agrees with the nature of the species, that is false
which contradicts it. There is no other rule of truth (EC 158;
W VI, 191).

The main difficulty, and the logical root that accounts for
Feuerbach's vacillation or imprecision, is his conflation (in the
notion of truth as objectivity) of different senses of the word
'objective'.[3] We may say that a statement or conception is objective in the sense that it accurately conveys what is actually the
case 'in reality'; the statement or conception *coincides* with the
'external' fact. We may also say that a statement or conception is
objective in the sense that it is not an individual idiosyncrasy; it
agrees with the common opinion of man's fellows, or it is what all
of them think, or it is what any man, because of his nature and
situation, *must* think, even if we have no way of knowing whether
it corresponds to an external reality or not. Feuerbach conflated
all these senses; he failed to take seriously the important distinctions between them and to bring out precisely which was his view.
There was frequently an element of punning in his discussion of
objectivity, an element that comes out clearly in a passage already
cited where he writes that his philosophy 'recognizes as the true
thing, not the thing as it is an object of the abstract reason, but
as it is an object of the real, complete man, and *hence*, as it is itself
a real, complete thing' (italics added).

In fact, when it came to the question of discussing the content
of our knowledge, the relation of things known to things in themselves, Feuerbach vacillated between a number of different views –
views that might be characterized, respectively, as *realism*,
nominalism, and *agnosticism*. Feuerbach did emphasize that there
was not a primary logical distinction between 'man' and 'the
external world' so far as epistemology was concerned. Man was
as much the object of his own knowledge as the subject, and was
therefore himself also 'external':

Not only 'external' things are objects of the *senses. Man* is *given
to himself only through the senses* – he is an object for himself as
an object of the senses. The *identity* of *subject and object*, which
is only an *abstract thought* in *self-consciousness*, is *truth* and
reality only in the *sensory contemplation of man* by *man*
(W II, 303–4).

To say that man can be both the object and the subject of knowledge, of course, is not to show 'the identity of subject and object' –
in any particular relation of knowing, the knower and what is
known must be logically distinct. Is what is known the thing in
itself, or is the object of our knowledge some intermediate 'object'
which is neither the thing in itself nor our thought in itself? There
are passages in Feuerbach to suggest that he thought that we know
things directly, in the sense that the 'objects' of our knowledge are
the things themselves; certainly Feuerbach thought that we know
things directly in the sense that they act causally upon our organs
of perception. Often, he conflated the two senses, as in the Preface
to the second edition of the *Essence of Christianity*, when he wrote
(EC xxxv; W VII, 283) that his philosophy 'generates thought
from the *opposite* of thought, from Matter, from existence, from
the senses; it has relation to its object first through the senses,
i.e., passively, before defining it in thought', leaving it unclear
whether matter and matter as known to the senses are identical.
Similarly, when he wrote in the *Basic Propositions* (W II, 296)
that 'the real *in its reality* or as *real* is the real as an *object of the
senses*, as the *sensory*', he was concerned to distinguish the objects
of the senses (as real) from the objects of thought; he did not make
it clear whether he also meant that man could only speak of
reality *as reality for man*, as that which he found in his senses.
Certainly, we do find a strong strain of realism in his work.
He insisted, at times, that 'philosophy is the recognition of what
is', of things as they are, and that space and time are the forms in
which all things exist (W II, 232). He occasionally spoke of man's
thoughts as 'copies' of things (W II, 257); in his review of F.
Dorguth's *Critique of Idealism*,[4] he praised 'the great thought of
Spinoza' that 'the connection and order of psychic events is the
same as the order and connection of things' (W II, 139n). In his
supplementary critical remarks to the *Basic Propositions of the
Philosophy of the Future*, he wrote:

'With our senses,' I once wrote, 'we read the Book of Nature:
but we do not understand it through them.' Correct! But the
Book of Nature is not composed of a chaos of letters strewn
helter-skelter so that the understanding must first introduce
order and connection into the chaos. The relations in which
they are expressed in a meaningful proposition would then
become the subjective and arbitrary creations of the understanding. No, we distinguish and unify things through our
understanding on the basis of certain signs [Merkmale] of unity
and difference given to our senses. We separate what Nature
has separated; we tie together what she has related; we classify
natural phenomena in categories of ground and consequence,
cause and effect because factually, sensibly, objectively things
really stand in such a relation to each other (W II, 322–3).[5]

Another strain in Feuerbach's work, however, reflects that
belief in the inadequacy of philosophical (British) empiricism which
he inherited from Hegel and which remained as an unworked-out
assumption in much of his later work. In his critique of Dorguth,
he argued that the senses gave us only pictures; things in themselves could only be given us by thought. 'The thought is the thing
as it is; sensory representation is the thing as it *appears*' (W II,
135). Only philosophy converts appearance into things. Earlier,
in 1835, in his review of Bachmann's *Anti-Hegel*, Feuerbach had
argued that the agnostic upshot of the Kantian philosophy was
characteristically 'the upshot of empiricism, namely that true
knowledge is limited to the field of the object found in sensory
experience' (W II, 45) – though he thought that Kant went
beyond empiricism in recognizing that these objects of experience
were mere appearances.[6] In the critique of Dorgurth, Feuerbach
again emphasized that empiricism, the senses, cannot distinguish
appearance from reality – only thought can do that. He hailed the
Copernican system as 'the most glorious victory which idealism
has won over empiricism, reason over the senses' (W II, 136),
since it is only thought and not the senses that can tell us that we
move around the sun and not *vice versa*.[7] In the passage we have
seen him later half-repudiating, he portrayed the inadequacy of
the senses alone by using the comparison of reading Plato: seeing
the letters on the page is not yet reading, and reading is not yet
understanding. Understanding has to make sense of the signs and

symbols given us in a volume of Plato or in the Book of Nature.

> We read the Book of Nature with the senses, but we do not
> understand it through the senses. The understanding is an act
> through itself, an absolutely independent act. What the
> understanding grasps it grasps only in and through itself, only
> that which is consonant with the understanding is an object
> which can be understood. The understanding is its own
> measure, its own principle; it is *causa sui*, the absolute in man.
> ... The senses give us riddles, but they do not give us the
> solution, understanding (W II, 144).

In a later essay, as Hook has reminded us,[8] Feuerbach actually
defined the task of science as consisting in 'making a scientific
object of that which is not an object' but merely an appearance
given in sense-experience. In his critique of Hegel's discussion of
this and *that* in the *Phenomenology* (W II, 184–7), one of Feuerbach's lines is clearly nominalistic: sense-experience gives us only
particulars, which we group into classes and fix in our consciousness by employing concepts or names. Here Feuerbach's con-
ventionalist theory of truth comes in; naming is a human,
conventional activity, determined – as Feuerbach would put it –
by the species. However, its only significance, ultimately, is that it
enables us to find individuals, particulars. For sense-perception,
words and concepts are mere signs enabling it to reach the individual thing which is the only thing 'we know as a truth sealed with
our blood' (W II, 185).

In other parts of his work Feuerbach treated what is given in
sense-perception as itself only a *sign* of reality and not reality
itself. This was the so-called Feuerbachian theory of knowledge
developed – without any particular insight or skill – by Plekhanov
as the 'hieroglyphic' theory of knowledge.[9] What is known to
sensory experience, according to this theory, is not the object or
process in itself, but the causal effects of this thing or process.
These effects act as signs or hieroglyphs of the actual thing or
process, enabling us to deduce connections and distinctions and
to deal with the things signified. All this, however, is not developed
in Feuerbach in any satisfactory or even interesting way. His
contribution to the theory of knowledge lay on the critical side in
his clear realization that we could never pass from concepts or

thoughts also to an objective reality, that idealism could only create an illusory world, and that consciousness could not be divorced logically from the carrier of consciousness, from man as a physical and emotional animal. On the positive side, he rightly emphasized the logical unity of the senses and the character of knowing as a practical activity, as involving interests and social and natural interaction. He also saw that we could not *begin* epistemology by 'criticizing the instrument', by seeking a criterion of certainty that would logically precede the analysis of knowing. But he did not look closely enough at the actual process of knowing, whether through the senses, the understanding, or 'reason' to make any further contribution and he vacillated in a manner characteristic of the dilettante in this – or any other – field.

> What is thinking? [Feuerbach asked at the beginning of his review of Dorguth.] How does it behave in itself, in relation to the object, in relation to the being or essence of nature, in relation to the being or nature of man, in relation to the organism? These questions belong to the most important and most difficult of the questions of philosophy. The difficulty lies in the fact that precisely that which is nearest to us is everywhere that which we know least and which is furthest away from us, in so far as thinking is externally the most *invisible*, the most modest, silent, gaseous, ungraspable and therefore for us the least substantial activity in the world. The importance, however, lies in the fact that the question whether we can know truth, the problem of the origin of ideas, of the independence of the spirit and of the reality of idealism,[10] are all tied to the questions we have raised, not to mention the fact that philosophy legitimizes itself as philosophy only through the investigation of the nature of thinking and thus distinguishes itself, to its advantage, from speculative mysticism ... (W II, 131).

Dorguth's materialism, Feuerbach argued, was a consistent decided empiricism (W II, 131). Empiricists in the past had loosely thought of thinking as *dependent* on the brain (Feuerbach evidently had in mind the early French medical materialism of Cabanis, and La Mettrie presumably); but if mind is truly dependent, always passive and never active, then, according to

Feuerbach, it cannot have any independent quality or character of its own. A consistent materialism requires precisely the view proclaimed by Dorguth – the view that everything is body and that thinking is only brain activity. In 1838, Feuerbach had no doubt that such 'absolute materialism' was false.

Feuerbach marshalled a number of arguments against absolute (or reductive) materialism, arguments that took their departure from his insistence on the specific, irreducible, qualitative nature of thought and its power to react back on bodily states, as well as the fact that thought, unlike physical processes, involved truth-claims. Feuerbach had no doubt, even by 1838, that thinking was a product of physical processes, but he was insistent that the product could not be reduced to its cause or *sine qua non*; having been produced, it became an independent thing, functioning in its own right.

The most interesting, though imprecise, of his arguments may be an adumbration of Professor Gilbert Ryle's conception of category-mistakes. One cannot say that thinking is brain activity, Feuerbach argued (W II, 133), because in making such a statement we would be combining a subject and a predicate which do not belong to a common species. Feuerbach seemed to have in mind the suggestion that saying 'thinking is brain activity' is like saying 'gravitation is green' or 'Saturday is in bed': it is applying predicates that belong to one class of things to another class to which they simply do not belong. It should be noted, however, that this argument may lead further than Feuerbach would have wanted it to lead. It does not merely suggest that thinking has an irreducible quality, that it is more than brain activity, or that it is in vital respects other than brain activity. The argument suggests that thinking and brain activity belong to what some philosophers today would call different 'universes of discourse', which Feuerbach would have taken to imply different ontological and logical statuses. It points towards dualism and Feuerbach's thorough-going rejection of such dualism is, at any rate in 1838, not clear. He obscured the issue by speaking of *species (Gattung)*, with its suggestion of nothing more than natural kinds; yet the argument would not hold, there would be no objection to combining in one proposition subject and predicate belonging to different 'species', unless 'species' were used to indicate more fundamental logical discontinuities. In the rest of the passage, indeed, Feuerbach suggested rather that thought could not be *identified* with brain

activity because the essential quality of thought ('sense', as Feuerbach called it) was lacking from brain activity. Thinking produced
processes belonging to its own 'species' – it produced thoughts.
'An activity can only recognized by what it does, by its product, its
objects. It *is* what it does. . . . By their fruits shall ye know them'
(W II, 133).

Another argument that Feuerbach used was the following: If
thoughts were mere modifications of the brain they could not be
wrong. Truth and error would have the same ontological status,
they would both be 'true' in the sense that they would both be
actual, existing states of the brain. Idealism would merely be a
different brain activity from materialism; it would not make sense
to say that one was false and the other true (W II, 135). Further,
according to Feuerbach, we could not have our knowledge of the
material world if it were not for the independent, creative power
of thought. (This argument, that understanding *provides* concepts
and connections that are not given, Feuerbach – as we have seen –
was later to reject, though never with complete decisiveness.)
In a passage we have already cited, Feuerbach argued that understanding and science (*i.e.* thought) must go beyond what is given
to the senses, that the Copernican system *e.g.*, was a triumph of the
understanding over sense-perception. If thinking then, goes
beyond the senses, it must be a suprasensual, independent activity
(W II, 138). What is true in relation to nature – that thought has
the capacity to surmount what is given to it by nature – is also
true in relation to the body. Man's ability to commit suicide, in
fundamental violation of the natural drives and aspirations of his
body, is evidence of the power of thought to react back on the
body, to subdue it to its will (W II, 139). Further, if we did not
have a concept of the mind, we would have no concept of matter,
for the concept of matter arises through distinguishing it from
that of mind.

Intelligence, or thought, or mind, according to Feuerbach, then,
cannot be reduced to the physical, psychology cannot be reduced
to physiology. It is true that there can be no mind without a body –
already in 1838 Feuerbach was strongly insistent on this – but the
body acts as a vehicle for an activity that is higher than itself. Not
the body, but only the understanding, can distinguish the body
from the non-body. Where there are no 'pictures' (or representations given by the senses) there is no impetus to think, but without

the understanding we cannot recognize sensory representations as mere appearances. 'Brain activity is picture-making activity, the culminating point of brain activity is imagination; brain activity can go no further' (W II, 141).

We can now understand, I think, why Feuerbach proclaimed *man*, and not mind or matter, to be the basis of all philosophy. The concept of man in Feuerbach's philosophy represents Feuerbach's attempt to overcome the traditional dualisms of metaphysical philosophy – the dualism of mind and matter, of the knower and the known, of theoretical and practical reason. Man is both matter and mind, man has both understanding and will, sensation and passion. Man is the locale in which the knower and the known came together; he is both of nature and outside it, both active and passive. He is the ground and focal point of what Feuerbach sees as a dialectical unity, a logical interdependence, of the subject and object of knowledge. Feuerbach does believe with Protagoras that *man is the measure of all things* – though he also believes that things exist independently of man and that we cannot consider one without the other. Here, of course, is a source of much unexamined difficulty, reflected in the imprecision of Feuerbach's discussion of the relation between 'man' and 'nature', just as it was reflected in the imprecision of his discussion of the relation between thought and body, and of the relation between understanding and sense-experience. 'By "nature",' Feuerbach said in the *Lectures on the Essence of Religion* (W VIII, 113), 'I understand the totality of all forces, things and beings known to the senses which man distinguishes from himself as non-human'; 'Nature,' he had written in a footnote to the *Essence of Religion* in 1845 (W VII, 433n), 'is nothing more for me . . . than a *general* word for indicating those beings, things, objects which man distinguishes from himself and his products and pulls together under the common name nature; it is not for me a *universal*, personified and mystified being abstracted and separated from real things'. What Feuerbach thinks of as 'real things' are always things as known to man. They are not created by man or totally subsumed to his interests (as Feuerbach took idealism to treat things); they can impede man's interests, frustrate his desires, limit his actions. But man cannot speak or think of things except as they come into contact with him, directly or indirectly. If we speak of the *objectivity* of things, it is because *man* experiences this objectivity, this intractability, because *man* finds that he is not only an active but also a passive, a suffering, creature. To go beyond this, to ask what things are 'really' like 'in themselves', Feuerbach ultimately seems to hold, is to go beyond what is possible to man. Man can never eliminate himself entirely from the process of knowing, can never achieve the known outside its relation to the knower. In a certain sense, Feuerbach suggests, nature *is* intractable to human knowledge, for man can only know what comes under the laws of *his* being, *his* thinking. Feuerbach, as we have seen, remains in some indecision whether the laws of thought (logic) are also the laws of being, though much in his position would require him to hold this. But there are overtones in Feuerbach, as in Marx, of Vico's famous *verum factum*, of the view that man can know completely and with certainty only that which he has fashioned himself. Idealism, indeed, tried to make nature transparent by making it a product of mind. If we recognize that nature was not a product of mind, was not man-dependent, then it must remain to some extent always outside perfect understanding. The weakness of Feuerbach's epistemology, however, remains in the fact that he cannot decide with any consistency just what the relation of knowing is and just what sort of understanding we do have of 'nature'. These issues he was able to skirt because of his unsystematic and unprofessional way of writing. His reduction of philosophy to man, in epistemology especially, obscured as many issues as it illuminated. It pointed the way to a similar obscurantism in the modern philosophy of existentialism, which takes its departure from one aspect of Feuerbach's thought – the alleged centrality of the subject-object problem in philosophy – and like Feuerbach, sees man as the foundation of all philosophy.

In 1850, in his notorious review of Moleschott's *Lehre der Nahrungsmittel* [*The Science of Foodstuffs*] under the title 'Natural Science and the Revolution' (W X, 3–24), Feuerbach appeared to go overboard for the most reductive of materialisms. Moleschott's book, he announced, dealt only with eating and drinking, but it was in fact of the highest philosophical significance:

Yes, I go further and maintain that only it [Moleschott's book] contains the true *Basic Propositions of the Philosophy of the Future* and of the present, that we find solved in it the most difficult problems of philosophy. How philosophers have racked

their brains over the problem of the link between body and soul!
Now we know from science, what the common people long
knew from experience, that eating and drinking hold body and
soul together, that food is the link we have been searching for.
How people have quarrelled whether ideas are innate or
acquired and how contemptuously they have looked at those
who derive the origin of ideas from the senses. Now it is just as
impossible for us to speak of innate ideas as to speak of innate
meals or innate heat, which once indeed played a leading part
in natural science under the name *calor innatus*. Now we know
that respiration is the main source of heat, that air is an essential part of ourselves, that we pump everything from outside,
that we have nothing of our own, that we come into the world
as pure ragamuffins and Communists, that there is nothing
within us which does not exist outside us, that we are ultimately made up only of oxygen, nitrogen, carbon and hydrogen,
of these few substances, simple and yet capable of infinitely
different variations. . . .

How the concept of substance has vexed philosophers! What
is it? Self or not-Self, Spirit or Nature, or the unity of both.
Yes, the unity. But what does that mean? Only sustenance is
substance. Sustenance is the identity of spirit and nature.
Where there is no fat, there is no flesh, no brain, no spirit. But
fat comes only from sustenance . . . Everything depends on
eating and drinking. Difference in nature is but difference in
food. . . .

The brain cannot be formed without phosporus-bearing fat
. . . Without phosphorus, no thought . . . (W X, 12–5).

The argument culminated in a passage that was to become the
butt of endless jokes:

From this we can see immediately how much *ethical* and
political significance the science of foodstuffs has for the nation.
Food becomes blood, blood becomes heart and brain, the stuff
of thoughts and attitudes. Human sustenance is the basis of
human education and attitudes. If you want to improve the
people then give it, in place of exhortations against sin, better
food. *Man is what he eats* (W X, 22).

The remainder of the article became almost a parody of medical materialism – the English worker, reared on roast beef, is superior to the Italian, whose laziness derives from his predominantly vegetable diet. Feuerbach cited with approval Moleschott's suggestion that the 'undecided will and cowardly surrender of independence' by the Indians was to be explained by the fact that they lived almost solely on vegetables; he went on to suggest that the failure of the 1848 revolution in Germany was due to the sluggish potato blood produced by the German potato diet:

> Shall we, then, therefore despair? Is there no other foodstuff which can replace potatoes even among the poorer classes and at the same time nurture them to manly vigour and a manly disposition? Yes, there is such a foodstuff, a foodstuff which is the pledge of a better future, which contains the seeds of a slower and more gradual, but also of a more thorough, revolution: it is beans. (W X, 23.)

This 'degenerate sensationalism', this 'most "vulgar" of "vulgar" materialisms', as Hook calls it,[11] has been the butt of enough gibes. They are deserved by the – not uncharacteristic – extravagance of Feurerbach's style rather than by the point he was concerned to make. Feuerbach was over-reacting against the idealist view of man as determined by ideas, mental attitudes, spiritual traditions and intellectual education alone. He wanted to show that ideas were not independent: he moved over, in the process, from his earlier view that thought was a product of physical processes, entering upon its own subsequent history, to the view that thought was a function of physical processes, not only needing to be constantly sustained by them but having, it seems, no independent history. But Feuerbach worked out in detail neither his former nor his later view: he was not so much a non-reductive materialist at one stage and a reductive materialist at another, as a confused interactionist all the way through, over-emphasizing various aspects at various times. In 1858, in his review of Knapp's (materialist) *System der Rechtsphilosophie* [*System of Legal Philosophy*], Feuerbach was arguing (W X, 25–6) – in flat contradiction to his views in 1838 – that body and soul could be related only if they were equally 'material' (belonged to the one physical order), but that material or flesh did not have to be all of one sort.

What is more interesting about the style of 'Natural Science and Revolution' is the way in which Feuerbach's reduction of philosophy to foodstuff parallels his reduction, a few years earlier, of philosophy to man and contains the same confusion. In each case, the argument moves from the suggestion that X (man in 1841, foodstuffs in 1850) is the *sine qua non* of everything that matters to the suggestion that X is the stuff of everything, or the term through which everything is to be understood, or the ultimate determinant of everything. Feuerbach's reductive materialism in the Moleschott review is no more logically vicious or confused than his earlier 'anthropology'; it simply has the misfortune of working with a much more specific and definite fundamental, which makes the extravagance of the reduction much more evident. At the same time, just as Feuerbach's anthropology had a cutting edge when directed against despotism and illusion, so his reductive materialism helped to emphasize that man was part of nature, and that thinking was as much historical, and influenced by physical processes and conditions,[12] as man's wants and desires. Fundamentally, the movement from his position in 1838 to his position in 1850 reflected an underlying ambiguity (or at least tension) in his view of man. This we shall now go on to examine.

8. Feuerbach's concept of man

'The task confronting the modern period,' Feuerbach proclaimed in the opening proposition of his *Basic Propositions of the Philosophy of the Future* (W II, 245), 'was to make God real and human, to transform and dissolve theology by making it anthropology.' The philosophy of the future, he had written in the Preface to the Swiss edition of the work (W II, 245n), therefore 'had the task of leading philosophy from the realm of "departed souls" back into the realm of living souls, of pulling it down from the divine blessedness of thought which knows no needs into human misery. For this purpose it needs nothing more than a human understanding and human speech. But to think, speak and act in a purely and truthfully human way is granted only to the coming generations. At present, our task is not yet to explicate man, but to pull him out of the morass into which he has sunk.'

The morass into which man had sunk was for Feuerbach, at least between 1840 and 1848, primarily that of *alienation*. Man had severed from himself those powers and capacities which were at least potentially his; he had projected them into a God or fetish. He had thus made himself a slave to one of his own creations. This is why Feuerbach saw the critique of religion as the *sine qua non* of human emancipation, for in religion, he believed, he had found the 'secret' or paradigm of the process of alienation. Alienation, for Feuerbach, was a form of intellectual error, a fantasy which could be cured by showing how it arose and what its real content was. Religion, indeed, was not only the intellectual model of all other alienation-fantasies, it was also their necessary material support. The Protestant, in announcing that the Pope had no more authority than any other believer, in recognizing that the Pope was a man just like others, was also making it clear that the King had no special authority, was in the same way a man. 'The Protestant is a *religious* republican. Therefore, when Protestantism is dissolved, when its religious content disappears, i.e., when this content is exposed to view, unveiled, it leads to *political* republicanism'

(W II, 222). It is not fair, I think, to regard Feuerbach as a man who was never able to get to grips with political realities, who criticized alienation only in the realm of ideas. It is not that Marx grasped the overwhelming importance of a 'material weapon' in making a revolution, while Feuerbach did not. The two men simply had fundamentally different conceptions of the process of political emancipation, of the nature and function of revolutions in social life. Marx, at least in 1848, tended to see political emancipation as a bitter struggle for power between two *armies* and a reactionary government as primarily dependent on cannon and bayonets for its social authority. Feuerbach was basically a democrat who believed that government could not go on for long without the consent of the governed. He saw the reactionary governments of his own time and of the past as resting, in a manner vital to their continuance, on the illusions of the governed. Religion, he believed, was the most important of these illusions; it made man servile. When it was destroyed, when man recognized his own capacities, a democratic republican frame of mind followed. *In the long run* political despotism could not resist the consequences of the exposure of religious illusions and the servility based upon them. (In this, of course, the despots themselves – from Charles II of England and Frederick William III and IV of Prussia to Nicholas I of Russia – agreed with Feuerbach.)

What distinguishes man from the animal, Feuerbach wrote (W II, 315–16), is not just consciousness, but the fact that man is a universal being.[1]

> Man is not a particular being, like the animal, but a *universal* being, therefore not limited and unfree, but unhemmed-in and free, for universality, lack of limitation, freedom are indivisible. And this freedom does not exist in a *particular* capacity, in the *will*, just as the universality does not lie in a particular capacity of the *power to think*, in reason – this freedom, this universality stretches over the *whole* being of man. The senses of the animal, it is true, are sharper than those of man, but only in relation to specific things necessarily connected with the needs of the animal, and they are sharper precisely because of this condition, because of their exclusive limitation to particular interests. Man does not have the sense of smell of a hound or of a raven, but only because his sense of smell takes in all kinds of smells,

and is therefore free, indifferent to particular smells. Where a
sense raises itself above the limitation of particularity and above
being tied to need, it raises itself to *independent* and *theoretical*
significance and dignity; the *universal* sense is *understanding*,
universal sensualism is *intellectualism*. Even the lowest
senses, smell and taste, raise themselves in man to the level of
intellectual, scientific acts (W II, 315–16).

When man surrenders to particular desires, when he wants only
to gorge his stomach, we speak of him as having become, or behaving like, an animal. In the opening chapter of the *Essence of
Christianity*, entitled 'The Essential Nature of Man', Feuerbach
had made the same point. Man was distinguished from animals by
having *religion*; but religion, in its positive content, was consciousness of infinity, and this consciousness was consciousness
of man's own infinity. Man was therefore distinguished from
animals by his infinity, his universality:

> A really finite being has not even the faintest adumbration, still
> less consciousness, of an infinite being, for the limit of the being's
> nature is also the limit of its consciousness. The consciousness
> of the caterpillar, whose life is confined to a particular species
> of plant, does not extend itself beyond this narrow domain.
> It does, indeed, discriminate between this plant and other
> plants, but more it knows not. A consciousness so limited,
> but on account of that very limitation so infallible, we do not
> call consciousness, but instinct. Consciousness, in the strict
> or proper sense, is identical with consciousness of the infinite;
> a limited consciousness is no consciousness; consciousness is
> essentially infinite in its nature. The consciousness of the in-
> finite is nothing else than the consciousness of the infinity of
> the consciousness; or, in the consciousness of the infinite, the
> conscious subject has for his object the infinity of his own
> nature.
>   What, then *is* the nature of man, of which he is conscious,
> or what constitutes the specific distinction, the proper humanity
> of man? Reason, Will, Affection. To a complete man belong the
> power of thought, the power of will, the power of affection.
> The power of thought is the light of the intellect, the power of
> will is energy of character, the power of affection is love.

Reason, love, force of will, are perfections – the perfections of
the human being – nay, more, they are absolute perfections of
being. To will, to love, to think, are the highest powers, are the
absolute nature of man as man, and the basis of his existence.
Man exists to think, to love, to will. Now that which is the end,
the ultimate aim, is also the true basis and principle of a being.
But what is the end of reason? Reason. Of love? Love. Of will?
Freedom of the will. We think for the sake of thinking; love
for the sake of loving; will for the sale of willing – *i.e.*, that
we may be free. True existence is thinking, loving, willing
existence. That alone is true, perfect, divine, which exists for
its own sake. But such is love, such is reason, such is will. The
divine trinity in man, above the individual man, is the unity of
reason, love, will. Reason, Will, Love, are not powers which
man possesses, for he is nothing without them, he is what he is
only by them; they are the constituent elements of his nature,
which he neither has nor makes, the animating, determining,
governing powers – divine, absolute powers – to which he can
oppose no resistance (EC 2–3; W VI, 2–3).

It was on behalf of the Feuerbachian conception of the free
man, and on behalf of Feuerbach's programme of 'anthropotheism' that Ruge, Marx and Bakunin joined in 1843 to plan the
radical *Deutsch-französische Jahrbücher* of 1844, in which Marx
launched himself on the path from Feuerbach to Marxism. It was
with perfect understanding of what Feuerbach had been doing in
the *Essence of Christianity* and in the writing for the reform of
philosophy that Marx wrote:

The criticism of religion ends in the teaching that *man is the
highest being for man*, it ends, *i.e.*, with the categorical imperative to overthrow all conditions in which man is a debased,
forsaken, contemptible being forced into servitude, conditions
which cannot be better portrayed than in the exclamation of a
Frenchman at hearing of a projected tax on dogs: Poor dogs!
They want to treat you like men![2]
Every emancipation consists of leading the human world and
human relationship back to man himself. . . . Human emancipation will be complete only when the actual existing individual
man takes back into himself the abstract citizen, when, as

individual man, he has become a species-being [*Gattungs-wesen*] in his everyday life, in his individual work and in his individual relations, when man has recognized and organized his own forces [*forces propres*] as social powers, and thus no longer severs this social power from himself in the shape of political power.[3]

Man's self-esteem, freedom, must be awakened once more in the heart of these men. Only this feeling, which disappeared from the world with the Greeks and from the blue mists of heaven with Christianity, can once more make from a society a fellowship of men working for their highest purposes, a democratic State.[4]

The *Economico-Philosophical Manuscripts* that Marx jotted down in Paris in 1844 still take their departure from the Feuerbachian conception of man.[5] Modern bourgeois society dehumanizes man, it makes him an animal, by severing his capacities from him and through deprivation forcing him into servitude to the most elemental, narrow, animal needs. The dogmas of the theoretical economists set up as 'objective categories' human powers and capacities, human functions and relations, and permit them to dominate man. Economics, in bourgeois theory and bourgeois society, has become a form of fetishism. This fetishism can be overcome only by leading economics back to its presupposition or ground, man himself.

The social principles of Christianity [Marx wrote angrily in the *Deutsche-Brüsseler Zeitung* in 1847[6]], preach cowardice, self-contempt, debasement, subjugation, humility, in short, all the properties of the *canaille*, and the proletariat, which does not want to be treated as *canaille*, needs its courage, its consciousness of self, its pride and its independence, far more than its bread.

Six years later Marx was writing in the *New York Daily Tribune*[7] on the village communities of India:

We must not forget that these little communites were con-taminated by distinctions of caste and by slavery, that they subjugated man to external circumstances instead of elevating man to be the sovereign of circumstances, that they transformed a self-developing social state into never-changing natural destiny, and thus brought about a brutalizing worship of nature exhibiting its degradation in the fact that man, the sovereign of nature, fell down on his knees in adoration of *Kanuman*, the monkey, and *Sabbala*, the cow.

Twenty years after that, when one of his daughters handed him a Victorian questionnaire asking him, *inter alia*, to state the vice he detested most, he wrote: 'Servility'.

All this is entirely in the Feuerbachian spirit and consciously derived from his work. 'We must fashion what we want to become into a highest principle, a highest word: only thus can we sanctify our life and provide a firm basis for the tendencies of our period,' Feuerbach wrote (W II, 219). Religion has substituted the religious tie for the social tie; we must make politics our religion and substitute the practical self-realization of man in the political State, the political community, for his illusory self-realization in religion (W II, 219–20). 'The spirit of the times or of the future is *realism*' (W II, 221); as long as we do not make man the highest principle of all his activities, we necessarily make man dependent on some other principle, and fail to achieve inner unity and universality. '*Existence, life* is the highest good, the highest essence, the original God of man,' Feuerbach wrote in the addenda and explications to his *Essence of Religion* (W VII, 391). In his reply to Max Stirner's attack on him in *The Ego and Its Own*, Feuerbach insisted (W VII, 304–5) that on passing from pupilage to manhood, from slavery to freedom, man cried out – 'only now am I a man', meaning by this that only now was he realizing his capacities, expressing his nature, becoming a complete and full human being. Such a being, according to Feuerbach, could not be abstracted, divided against itself, split into contradictory parts, seen as inadequate or incapable. The principle of Feuerbach's reform of philosophy, *atheism*, meant for Feuerbach the giving up of everything above and beyond man, everything in the name of which man could be dominated.

The complete, full, *true man*, according to Feuerbach, was a *universal* being. His universality lay in the fact that he was not, by nature and being, an isolated monad, an egoistic individual as portrayed by Stirner. Man's being went beyond his individual self and could not be understood without going beyond it. It went beyond the self in two directions: towards nature or the objective physical world through the senses, and towards other men through reason and love.

> The new philosophy makes *man, including nature* as the basis of man, the *sole universal and highest object* of philosophy – it therefore makes *anthropology, including physiology*, the *universal science. Art, religion, philosophy* or *science* are only appearances or revelations of the *true human nature or essence*. Man, complete true man, is only he who has *aesthetic* or *artistic, religious* or *moral* or *philosophical* or *scientific* sense – only he is man who *excludes nothing that is essentially human from himself. Homo sum, humani nihil a me alienum puto* – this proposition, taken in its *most universal and highest significance*, is the *slogan* of the *new philosopher*.

Thus Feuerbach wrote in paragraphs 54 and 55 of the *Basic Propositions of the Philosophy of the Future* (W II, 317). Love and sense-perception take man out of himself (W II, 297–9). Only in art and science, in recognizing the objectivity of the external, does man get beyond the human and so help to define it. Only in his relations with other men, and in his recognition of himself as part of a species, does man satisfy his drives, perfect his nature, realize his infinity. Man cannot know everything by himself; only the species can do that, at least in principle (W II, 259). In his 'Contribution to the Critique of Hegelian Philosophy' Feuerbach had quoted approvingly from Goethe's correspondence with Schiller: '"Only *a number of* men," says Goethe, "recognize Nature, only *a number of* men live the human life" ' (W II, 162).

Feuerbach in the 1840s, then, is fundamentally in line with the Promethean ethic, with the conception of man as the ultimate subject, as *ego agens* by his very nature. Feuerbach himself sees his philosophy as the culmination of the idealist tradition – substitute *man* for self-consciousness, he writes (W II, 242), and you translate the old philosophy into the new. If we recognize the concept of God as embodying the capacities and potentialities of man, as portraying that which man is striving towards, then we can see how pantheism was the necessary logical and historical consequence of theism, while atheism was the necessary logical and historical consequence of pantheism (W II, 223). The disintegration of religious dualism was begun by Protestantism, which brought God back into the heart of man, and was strengthened by the increasing practicality and scientific and industrial confidence of modern man; it cannot now be halted. Man now knows his own powers: sooner or later, he will use them, in politics as in industry. Not the Hegelian philosophy, but the democratic society based on humanism and empiricism, is the expression of a consummated self-consciousness, of the return of man and his spirit to himself.

The function of *sensualism*, of empiricism, in liberating mankind seems to have been twofold for Feuerbach. First, in focusing man's attention on objective reality, on nature, it makes man practical, helps him to exercise his powers in an effective and realistic way. It overcomes fear of nature and dependence on nature. It also overcomes a fantasy-isolation from nature, or a fantasy-subjugation of nature in the mind, which leaves man constantly threatened by the breaking into his consciousness of a reality outside his control. Industry and science are *the* enemies of religion and alienation because they substitute real gratifications for fantasy-gratifications. Secondly, the senses are democrats: they treat reality, man and nature, the knower and the known, as all belonging to one level of existence. Empiricism and science reject the fictions and authorities and hierarchies erected by law and the State: 'Science knows no distinction between a noble and a bourgeois stomach; it knows of only one origin common and equal among all men' (W X, 7). The scientist, like Copernicus, is a genuine 'overthrower' who can turn the highest into the lowest and free man from the magic of religion and superstition (W X, 10).

Feuerbach's insistence that man is a species-being, that he contained the I-Thou, is perhaps one of the best known parts of Feuerbach's doctrine. It was unquestionably important as a corrective to the epistemological individualism of the Cartesian tradition in philosophy and to the logical individualism of Hobbes and the French materialists. It pointed directly to Marx's conception of man as a social being. Characteristically, Feuerbach ran together a number of conceptions. His main argument was that the essential or typical human properties – love, reason and will – could not be understood or accounted for in terms of a single individual: they required a minimum of two, an I and a Thou. Love was a relation between people, especially between sexes; it could not be made into the human characteristic of one single solitary individual. Thought, for Feuerbach, depended upon language and language was a relation between people, based on common agreement and common perceptions. If we imagine a man reared in complete isolation from any other human beings, utterly unaware of the existence of other human beings, we would be quite unable to imagine this man as human, as having the properties that are characteristic of our species. Man shapes himself and understands himself in his relation to other men. From time to time, Feuerbach attempted to reinforce this empirical point with a logical one – an individual man could not recognize himself to be a man, see himself as the bearer of common properties or as a member of a class, if he could not compare himself and contrast himself with other men. He would not know what was essential (human, common to the species) and what was accidental (irrelevant to his humanity). Further, the elevation of man and his capacities (which we find in concealed form in the religious concept of God) is possible only if we recognize the capacities of the species as the real content. Science, art and industry are universal because they have a continuing tradition, because each practitioner can build on the achievements of those who preceded him, because mankind can do what one man cannot possibly do. Thus Feuerbach saw language as fundamental in human culture and human emancipation, because it made possible the division and organization of labour, made possible collective effort and collective achievement, even over generations or centuries.

Feuerbach's concept of man, it will have been noted, serves a normative function. There is such a thing as a 'true man' – one who has realized, or is realizing, the capacities, wants and enjoyments that characterize men as men, that constitute the specifically human. Feuerbach thus attempts to assimilate the alienation (and subjugation) of man to error: it rests on *false* conceptions of man's nature, it necessarily involves confusions, errors, dualisms, fantasies. It denies to man what is man's not only in a moral sense, but in a straightforward descriptive sense. Political despotism requires illusion and falsehood, in the same way as religious belief requires illusion and falsehood. Only humanist, atheist republican democracy treats men as they (really) are. Only it accepts the principle of science – that each thing be treated according to its nature, its own principles – as the principle of politics. What Feuerbach does not seriously examine – just as the young Marx did not seriously examine – is the assumed internal coherence of Feuerbachian man. Human servility, illusion, conflict and domination are taken to rest on an artificial bifurcation or on external domination: the human essence itself, once free to work for self-expression and self-realization, is taken to be fundamentally coherent and to imply a coherent set of principles.

Feuerbach, however, was not by temperament the romantic revolutionary and thoroughgoing Promethean that the young Marx was and that the older Marx never quite ceased being. Marx, in order to make man the absolute subject of history, had to rob nature of all independence *vis-à-vis* man. This is why he put such emphasis on practice as the revolutionary transformation of nature and why we find in Marx no coherent position on natural science. Feuerbach, in insisting on both man and nature, in writing that man must be seen as both passive and active (W II, 213), recognized the activity of nature as well as that of man. Philosophy, he wrote (W II, 235–6), must become Franco-German, combine the active man (the active consciousness) of German idealism with the naturally-conditioned man of French materialism. Feuerbach thus did not see history as culminating in a simple glorious leap from the realm of necessity into the realm of freedom; in his later years, especially in his ethics, he put more and more emphasis on the continuity between man and nature, between anthropology and physiology. He was closer to the humanism of the rank-and-file German social democrat, of the English Fabians and utilitarians and of the old Rationalist Associations (now Humanists), than he was to the Prometheanism of a Marx or a Nietzsche – much as he may have done, in his writings of the 1840s, to propel these two thinkers along the paths they were to take.

9. Feuerbach's ethics

Feuerbach's philosophy, we have seen, is an attempt to work out, or rather to exemplify, certain fundamental themes – his anthropology or anthropocentrism, his increasingly but never fully reductionist naturalism or materialism, and his 'tuism' or proclamation of the 'I-Thou'. These are also the fundamental themes of his ethics. Feuerbach devoted far less systematic attention to ethics than he did to religion and the manner in which he attempts to give his general principles content and body in his ethical writings is often embarrassing in its lack of attention to logical analysis. Nevertheless, at other times it is interesting and not unimpressive. For Feuerbach, ethics must first of all be human – i.e., man-centred and man-determined, grounded both logically and empirically in man's nature and man's desires. It must derive moral principles from man and not man from moral principles. It must, in other words, be an anthropological or anthropocentric ethic. Man, however, is logically continuous with nature: his needs, wants and beliefs are natural phenomena, determined by his natural, empirical character and his natural, empirical circumstances. There is no noumenal will, conscience or moral faculty that stands above and outside the empirical world (including man), that can be divorced from the empirical nature of man and that can be understood without reference to this nature. An ethical theory, therefore, must be naturalistic or materialist as well as anthropocentric. The human being who is the subject and not merely the object of ethics, who determines its nature and content, is the empirical human being given to us and to himself by sensation: he is not the abstract, unempirical, characterless ego, will, soul or mind elevated above man by religious theology and philosophical idealism. 'Morality', Feuerbach proclaimed in one of his last essays on ethics (W X, 288), 'is as much an empirical science as medicine.' Kant, it is true, wrote his ethics not only for man but for all possible rational creatures (W X, 291). However, apart from Professors of Philosophy, who are professionally concerned to pretend that they are not men but reasoning machines, there are no rational creatures without heart and blood, feelings and sensations that determine their strivings and beliefs, including their moral strivings and beliefs. Finally, for Feuerbach, man must be understood as embodying not only the 'I' but also the 'Thou'. Just as it requires two – a man and a woman – to produce a human being physically, so it requires at least two to produce and satisfy the emotional, linguistic and even reasoning powers of man. The least intelligible unit to which the human race can be reduced is the 'I-Thou'. The individual, as pure individual, is not human: it is only as a member of a species conscious of his species-membership that he *is* human.[1] Both individual man and the ethics grounded in man require the existence and recognition of relationship with others; they require the 'I-Thou'.

Feuerbach's ethical opinions nevertheless have to be treated as falling into two periods – the Promethean-anthropological of the late 1830s and 1840s and the materialist-hedonist of the post-1850s. These reflect the general movement in his philosophy, greatly intensified after his becoming acquainted with Moleschott and medical materialism, towards an ever more reductive and empirically concrete materialism which brought him closer, in intellectual style, to Holbach and Helvétius than to the Kant, Fichte and Hegel on whom he was reared. In the 1830s and 1840s, concerned with the criticism of religion and of theologizing idealism, he is defending human dignity and spontaneity against the religious and the political debasing of man. His work here expresses a set of ethical prejudices, having some foundation in his general philosophic views; it does not set out a systematic ethical theory. In the 1860s, between 1863 and 1869, he set down on paper, for the first time, his comparatively connected thoughts on the nature of ethics. Here we have Feuerbach's later ethic – a universalized eudaemonism based on a critical working over of Holbach's *La Système de la Nature*.

The works that established a world-wide reputation for Feuerbach in the 1840s – the *Preliminary Theses for the Reform of Philosophy*, the *Basic Propositions of the Philosophy of the Future* and the *Essence of Christianity* – were written in the period of growing romanticism and of revolutionary élan, of resistance against the Prussian police state and of the *Vormärz* of 1848. Their enormous impact, in Germany and outside, rested on their unequivocal commitment to the freedom and dignity of man. Feuerbach's ethic, at this stage, stood for human dignity: he was maintaining the Kantian and Fichtean autonomy of ethics, and of the human spirit, against the heteronomy thrust upon it in the name of theological imperativism, working hand-in-glove with the gendarmes of Europe. The chief targets of Feuerbach's moral criticism are *fetishism* and *servility*. The moral crime of religion is that it demeans man, treats him as a base and spiritless creature dependent on a creator. It takes away from man his productive powers and his independence; it ascribes them to another whom it calls God and in whose name it then threatens and humiliates man. Since religion is an illusion, a *human* fantasy, this abasement is in the final analysis self-abasement, servility. Religious servility, Feuerbach believed, necessarily spilled over into political life: the man who abases himself before God will also abase himself before kings. Democracy is the true religion of man, his truly human morality.

In Feuerbach's earlier work the moral autonomy of man is clearly not presented as an *egoistic* autonomy. Feuerbach's man has nothing in common with the solitary self-seeking individual of Max Stirner's *The Ego and Its Own*: contemporary critics (like J. Schaller[2]) who accused Feuerbach of inevitably leading the reader to egoism and the demoralization of the spirit were talking nonsense.

> The individual man by himself, whether as a moral being or as a thinking one [Feuerbach wrote in the *Basic Propositions* (W II, 318)], does not contain in himself the nature of man. The nature of man is contained only in community, in the unity of man with man – a unity, however, that rests only on the reality of the distinction between I and Thou. Isolation is finiteness and limitation; community is freedom and infinity. Man by himself is but man; man with man, the unity of I and Thou, is God.

Throughout the *Essence of Christianity* and the writings leading up to it, the denial of humanity and its practical consequence, egoism, are represented as the moral core of theological Christianity, which sees man only as an individual, which gives no religious significance to marriage and the family, which preaches an individual God and an individual salvation. The Christian, for Feuerbach, in the last analysis cares only for himself, for his *own* soul, which in Christianity is an isolated monad only externally related to others. The Christian loves other men not for their own sake, but for Christ's – i.e., in order to return God's love and thus ensure his own salvation:

But in him [the believer] good works do not proceed from essentially virtuous dispositions. It is not love, not the object of love, man, the basis of all morality, which is the motive of his good works. No! he does good not for the sake of goodness itself, not for the sake of man, but for the sake of God; – out of gratitude to God, who has done all for him, and for whom therefore he must on his side do all that lies in his power. He forsakes sin, because it wounds God, his Saviour, his Benefactor. The idea of virtue is here the idea of compensatory sacrifice. God has sacrificed himself for man; therefore man must sacrifice himself to God. The greater the sacrifice the better the deed. The more anything contradicts man and Nature, the greater the abnegation, the greater is the virtue. This merely negative idea of goodness has been especially realized and developed by Catholicism. Its highest moral idea is that of sacrifice; hence the high significance attached to the denial of sexual love, – to virginity. Chastity, or rather, virginity, is the characteristic virtue of the Catholic faith, – for this reason, that it has no basis in Nature. It is the most fanatical, transcendental, fantastical virtue, the virtue of supernaturalistic faith; – to faith, the highest virtue, but in itself no virtue at all. Thus faith makes that a virtue which intrinsically, substantially, is no virtue: it has therefore no sense of virtue; it must necessarily depreciate true virtue because it so exalts a merely apparent virtue, because it is guided by no idea but that of the negation, the contradiction of human nature (EC 260–1; W VI, 316–17).

It is a logical consequence of the whole trend of Feuerbach's earlier work, then, and not an inconsistency in it, that Feuerbach should proclaim in the *Basic Propositions* (W II, 319) that 'the highest and ultimate principle of philosophy is the unity of man with men. All essential conditions – the principles of the various sciences or branches of knowledge – are only different forms and aspects of such unity.' The positive description and analysis of this 'unity' in non-metaphysical terms is entirely absent in the early Feuerbach. To be moral, Feuerbach is saying, man must recognize himself as a member of a species, as a species-being and not as a particular individual. The highest expression of man and of his unity with man is *love*. This love Feuerbach often describes in hyperbolic and metaphysical terms. Critics[3] are not entirely unfair in singling out, as indicative of Feuerbach's treatment of love, the following notorious passage from the *Essence of Christianity*:

> Love is the middle term, the substantial bond, the principle of reconciliation between the perfect and the imperfect, the sinless and sinful being, the universal and the individual, the divine and the human. Love is God himself and apart from it there is no God. Love makes man God, and God man. Love strengthens the weak, and weakens the strong, abases the high, and raises the lowly, idealizes matter and materializes spirit. Love is the true unity of God and man, of spirit and nature. In love common nature is spirit, and the pre-eminent spirit is nature. . . . Love is materialism; immaterial love is a chimera. In the longing of love after the distant object, the abstract idealist involuntarily confirms the truth of sensuousness. But love is also the idealism of nature, love is also spirit, *esprit*. Love alone makes the nightingale a songstress; love alone gives the plant its corolla. And what wonders does not love work in our social life! What faith, creed, opinion separates, love unites (EC 47; W VI, 59).

The last sentence, indeed, represents the main theme of the well-known twenty-sixth chapter[4] of the *Essence of Christianity*, entitled 'The Contradiction of Faith and Love'. Faith, on Feuerbach's view, divides men, sets one against the other, narrows and particularizes; love, however, brings men together, makes them conscious of the common unity of the species, widens and universalizes. 'A loving heart is the heart of the species throbbing in the individual,' Feuerbach writes (EC 266; W VI, 324). Faith, for Feuerbach, treats man as an object, as a means; love treats man as a subject, as an end in himself.[5]

In the ethical writings of the 1860s, Feuerbach's approach to the question of ethics has become somewhat more systematic and concretely empirical, certainly much less rhetorical. The notion of man as a *loving* being is no longer flung at us in extravagant and metaphysical terms. The centre of Feuerbach's concern now is a much more concrete and empirical man – a man who eats and drinks, who feels cold and hunger, who seeks to satisfy his drives, and who *also* loves and feels sympathy for his fellow-men. Feuerbach begins negatively, by criticizing theological morals in their philosophic guise, i.e., by rejecting the Kantian morality of the (non-empirical) good will. The will, Feuerbach argues, is neither timeless nor undetermined; there is, in fact, no will – there are only men willing.

> The will is no wizard or miracle-worker, no talent or capacity ready to perform any little trick one happens to want at any time or place; the will, like man generally – for what indeed is the will, but man willing? – is tied to time and place . . . A neutral, indeterminate will striving in the abstract, in thought, toward all things, even if they be quite contradictory, is in reality no-thing, *ein Unding* (W X, 100–1).

What I willed yesterday, I can no longer will today, and vice-versa. F. H. Jacobi, Fichte and Hegel all treat suicide as an example of the freedom of the abstract will, capable of destroying even life itself. In truth, suicide is not the result of freedom at all, but of 'sad necessity' (W X, 94). The man who commits suicide cannot go on living; he does not *abstract* from life, but he is unable to abstract from life, he cannot bear to live in a certain way. His organism is so constituted that certain sufferings become unbearable; his choice to die is determined and not free. This is shown by the fact that the act of suicide which he could not carry out a year earlier he cannot shrink from now.

'The will', then, like man, is a creature of time and place. Even in language, the verb 'to will' has all the finite determinations of tense and mood; it is past or present, conditional, etc. 'The will' seeks specific objects and it cannot be described except in relation to the object it seeks[6] (there is no 'will', there is only a 'will to . . .', which can and does conflict with other wills in one and the same person). Morality cannot be based on a 'pure' will because there is no 'pure', detached will seeking nothing: the moral law as an

KP

expression of the pure will or of practical reason untouched by desire has no *content* and cannot produce one out of itself. Kant's effort to create a morality logically independent of desire is thus a fundamentally mistaken effort. It can produce only the juggling of empty abstractions; it must go to desires, to concrete men with concrete wants, in order to give its abstractions content.

The content of morality, according to Feuerbach, then, can be derived only from the positive, committed desires of man, i.e., from the empirical nature of man, and not from an abstract, unempirical will.

> Where there is no drive, there is no will, but where there is no drive to happiness, there is no drive at all. The drive to happiness is the drive of drives. . . . Even the drive to know-ledge is only the drive to happiness satisfying itself by means of the understanding, just as later in the development of culture, when the drive to knowledge becomes an independent one, it satisfies itself within the understanding (W X, 108).

I will [want] means I will [want] to be happy; 'where there is no drive to happiness there is no will, or at most a Schopenhauerian will, a will that wants nothing' (W X, 110). The drive to happiness, Feuerbach takes Holbach's *Système de la Nature* to have shown, is of the essence of man, since man is so constituted as to avoid suffering and to seek various satisfactions. 'The drive to happiness is the first and basic drive of all that which lives and loves, which is and wants to be, which breathes and does not take into itself – with 'absolute indifference' – carbonic acid and nitrogen in place of oxygen, deadly air in place of life-giving air' (W X, 230–1). 'Yes, man necessarily strives for *bienêtre*, well-being' (W X, 112). Kant, in his moral philosophy, distinguished two totally different kinds of judgment – the judgment of whether an action is good or evil and the judgment of whether an action is conducive to our weal or woe. But this distinction, Feuerbach argues (W X, 115), arises only when we think in relation to ourselves. If we think only in egoistic terms, then, in calling an action good we have to take account of the weal or woe of others and we recognize this as distinct from our own weal or woe. Such a distinction does not arise, however, when we think of others, of man in general. In relation to all men, we do not feel a distinction between what is good for them and what is conducive to their well-being or happiness. Morality cannot be abstracted from the drive for happiness in general and then counterposed to it; it can only be counterposed to my drive for *my* happiness at the expense of another's. If men felt neither satisfaction nor dissatisfaction, morality would make no sense. 'Where there is no difference between happiness and unhappiness, between weal and woe, there is no difference between good and bad either. Good is the affirmation, bad is the denial, of the drive to happiness' (W X, 114).[7] The conflict between duty and the desire for pleasure is nothing but the conflict of two competing desires for pleasure – my own and that of other people, or my own now and my own in the long-run.[8]

> Personal happiness is not the aim and purpose of morality, but its foundation, its presupposition. He who gives this happiness no place in morality, he who throws it out, opens the door to devilish arbitrariness, for only from the experience of my own drive to happiness do I know what good or bad, what life or death, what love and hate are and how they act (W X, 275–6).[9]

Only my own drive to happiness teaches me that it is inappropriate to give a stone to the starving – the 'pure will' could never teach me that.

Morality, then, in Feuerbach's view, is the universalization of happiness. Its *content* is given by personal experience of pleasure and of pain, of satisfaction and of dissatisfaction. Its *form* is given by the principle of universality, which says that another's happiness counts as much as my own. Morality consists in using the same yardstick for myself and for others – *the Golden Rule thus provides both the form and the content of ethics*. It is *not* immoral to seek pleasure, to eat caviar daily if you have the means to do so and do not thereby neglect other duties and tasks, but

> it is immoral to take away from others, or not to allow others, the good you allow yourself, to recognize your own drive to happiness as counting, practically and theoretically, but not to recognize that of others, not to take the misfortunes of others to heart as an injury to your own drive to happiness. Active participation in the fortune and misfortune of others, being

happy with the happy and unhappy with the unhappy – but
only, of course, in order to help remove misfortune where
possible – that and only that is *morality*. We have no other
source for our duties toward others, no other source from
which we can derive what is good or bad, we have no other
material and no other yardstick, but that which we use for the
duties relating to ourselves. Good is what accords with the
human drive to happiness; bad what consciously and deliberately
contradicts it (W X, 275–6).

The voice of conscience, therefore, is not something in principle
opposed to the voice of happiness.

The I outside me, the empirical Thou, is the origin of the
allegedly 'super-empirical' conscience in me. My conscience is
nothing but my I putting itself in the place of the injured
Thou, nothing but the agent or representative of another's
happiness acting on the basis and at the behest of my own
drive to happiness (W X, 279–80).

Truly, *Gewissen ist Mitwissen*, 'conscience' is 'con-scientia',
knowing with one another. He who has no drive to happiness, he
who does not know or feel what misfortune is and therefore has no
sympathy for others, has no conscience. In the case of the 'good
conscience', of course, we are scarcely aware of having it because
it is so closely identified with satisfaction or happiness. We are
aware of the bad conscience, but the bad conscience is only some-
one else's drive to happiness digging about and disturbing ours.
'Conscience is nothing but another's cry of woe or vengeance
against me, or, in reference to the man himself, nothing but the
cry of woe or vengeance of an injured or suppressed drive against
its suppressor' (W X, 284).[10]

Those who seek to make an egoistic psychological hedonism the
basis of ethics notoriously land themselves in a series of difficulties.
They begin with egoistic psychological hedonism – each man as a
matter of fact seeks his own pleasure or happiness. They end with
universal moralistic hedonism or 'utilitarianism' – each man ought,
as a matter of moral duty, to seek the happiness of all men, counting
all other men's happiness as he would his own. They cannot show
how they pass logically from my concern for my own happiness to

my duty to be concerned for others. Yet they cannot account for moral language and the moral life (the conflict of duty and inclination, the use of 'good' to recommend unwelcome courses, etc.) except by making this passage from descriptive egoistic hedonism to prescriptive universal benevolence. Has Feuerbach not committed the same error, in a very crude form? Certainly, Feuerbach uses a great deal of highly-charged moral language to put conventional moral positions – e.g., the wickedness of deliberately and consciously causing suffering to others – and he does not plausibly derive either the wickedness of causing suffering to *others* or the relevance of deliberation and consciousness from his individual drive to happiness.[11] But Feuerbach *does* attempt to give a naturalistic account of benevolence as flowing out of the nature of man and he *does* insist, in spite of his lapses into the language of moral imperativism, that 'true' morality does not issue commands, does not rest on imposed 'oughts'. Like benevolence, it issues out of the nature of man and his relations with others. It is not founded on an ultimate irreducible imperative, but on men's empirical longings and demands. To ask 'why must I be moral?', or 'what is the ultimate justification of a moral view?', he probably would have said, is like asking 'how can I be *certain* my beliefs are true?', it is to get caught in a vicious infinite regress instead of getting to work on the materials man *must* accept because he has and can have no others.

True morality, for Feuerbach, then, is not a theological imperativist structure of rights and duties, but a habit, a way of living that comes spontaneously or not at all. 'Morality is nothing but the true, complete, healthy nature of man, and error, depravity . . . are nothing but a distortion, imperfection, abnormality, often a true abortion of human nature. The truly moral man is not moral because of duty, because he wills it – this would be creating morality out of nothing. He is moral by and out of his nature' (W X, 289). People, Feuerbach insists, do act morally out of inclination and not out of duty. Sanctions can produce the semblance of benevolence, and can prevent men from overtly harming others – but they can do so only to a limited extent and they can never produce true benevolence. Thus, the criminal law, in wishing to enforce the moral injunction 'thou shalt not steal', has to abolish (hang) the thief in order to abolish theft (W X, 135).

How does the universal *form* of morality, the principle of

benevolence or of concern for the happiness of others, flow out of the individual drive to happiness? Here Feuerbach returns to his 'tuism', to his insistence on the 'I-Thou' as an essential part of human nature. If this 'I-Thou' were not part of human nature, there would in fact be no morality. Morality cannot arise out of the mere 'I' or out of mere reason without the senses; it can arise only out of the consciousness of the 'I-Thou', out of the consciousness of man as a species-being, which is itself given by the senses. Just as two people – a man and a woman – are needed to explain the appearance of man, so two beings are needed to explain the appearance of morality (W X, 270). Morality for an individual conceived as solitary is an empty fiction. 'Where there is no Thou as well as an I, no other person, there one does not speak of morality; only social man is a man. I am I only through Thee and with Thee' (W X, 269). 'We can speak of morality only where the relationship of man to man, of one to another, of I and Thou are in question' (W X, 270).[12]

How then, does a man come from his egoistic drive to happiness to the recognition of duties towards others? Nature solved this problem, Feuerbach argues (W X, 271), by creating a *mutual* drive to happiness – a drive which one cannot satisfy oneself, but for which one needs other people, even if only the family circle of parents, brothers and sisters. Together with life the young child suckles into itself the elements of morality, the feeling of belonging to a fellowship. It learns to limit the infinite autocracy of its own drive to happiness. If it does not learn unconsciously, then the blows of its brothers and the pinches of its sisters will teach it to do so consciously.

Feuerbach's general position here again has much similarity to Hume's. Morality and moral attitudes grow up naturally on the basis of men's seeking happiness and avoiding suffering, coupled with their 'sympathy' or ability to imagine and understand and participate in other people's sufferings. They are reinforced by man's emotional need of contact with others and by his vulnerability to their displeasure. The foundations of life are thus also the foundations of morality.[13] 'Custom is the secret of virtue' (W X, 267). Love is moral and has a special position in morality because in it your happiness and that of another coincide. 'Love is not made moral by my abstracting from the drive to happiness, by my living out of duty, but only through the fact that in making

myself happy I make another happy and that is what I *seek* to do'
(W X, 116). Feuerbach would like to believe that most human
intercourse is, or without interference, would be, of this kind.
There is a natural *Gemeinschaft* or community in which people find
that the happiness of each is dependent on the happiness of
others and conducive to it. But Feuerbach concedes that there are
also divisions. He speaks of mutually rewarding competition
(emulation), but he recognizes mutually destructive competition.
The disparity between my own happiness and the things others do
produces the moral *wish*: 'Would that others were happy without
interfering with each other's happiness or my own.' Virtue is that
happiness of one's own which feels happy only when tied together
with other's happiness. It is prepared to sacrifice itself, but only
when this sacrifice is a sad necessity, when it is necessary to ensure
a happiness that the doer himself feels to be more important than
his own (W X, 287–8). The lack of virtue, the lack of concern for
the happiness of others, arises out of desperate individual need.
It does not arise out of undetermined, sell-explanatory moral
viciousness resulting from the failure to heed moral injunctions.[14]
Not the good will of the moral philosopher, not reason intervening
in the nick of time to safeguard man against weakness and tempta-
tion, but happiness, ordinary plebeian happiness content with
relative necessities – that is what stops men from embarking on
crime. 'Everything that contradicts the happiness man needs –
which is identical with living – all this is an obstacle to virtue
and stands in contradiction to it' (W X, 268). 'The will is not
capable of anything without the support of material, corporal
means,' Feuerbach says elsewhere (W X, 153) and adds, with the
over-emphasis of his new enthusiasm for medical materialism,
'morality can do nothing without gymnastics and dietetics'.
Descartes had been right to recognize the dependence of the mind
on the body and to think that the means to make men wiser and
more clever would be found only in medicine. 'The freedom from
evil – and only this is freedom – is no direct property of the will;
no, it is determined and brought about by the knowledge and use of
natural, material and sensuous remedies' (W X, 150).

Morality, then, is a set of rules and attitudes that arise in the
course of man's pursuit of happiness as a member of a species,
bound to others of the same species, requiring their happiness
for his and capable of sharing their suffering. Even when an

individual's drive for happiness is confronted by the most brutal sanctions, these sanctions have their origin only in the drive for happiness of another. Penal measures stand in contradiction to the happiness of the sufferer, but not to the happiness of the inflicters (W X, 272). *Anthropology*, the analysis of the natural foundations of morality, transforms the imperative of morals into an optative. '*The arrogant categorical imperative is impressive when viewed from the standpoint of abstract philosophy, but from the standpoint of nature it is a very humble pious wish*' (W X, 289; italics added).

Moral judgments for Feuerbach, then, are *wishes* – 'would that everyone behaved in a certain way'.[15] The content of these wishes is given by human drives and needs; the universality of address by human interdependence, love and natural sympathy; the force of these wishes in relation to ourselves where virtue has not become simple habit by our consciousness of interdependence, by our sympathy for another's suffering and by our fear of his revenge. Law is nothing but a wish made sacred by the highest authority. 'Thou shalt not steal' is the wish that there would be no stealing, accompanied by sanctions. It is the wish expressed in imperative form: '*It ought to be* or *it ought not to be* is nothing but a wished being and not-being. 'I wish', says man as a private person; "I want no theft, therefore I believe that one cannot steal", says man as an empowered legislator. *Volo, ergo cogito.*' I want to make theft impossible through law. I do believe that the thief is free to steal without law, but to stop him, I arrogantly decide that all he needs is the consciousness of law and that my consciousness of it is enough to justify taking his life to do away with his theft. Just as law is not interested in the connection between the thief and the man, so man is not interested in the connection between an action and its determining circumstances. That which offends my drive to happiness must not and cannot be. Man is not interested in whether something arises out of the circumstances or not – if it wounds his drive to happiness, he wants it not to be. Thus men attribute to free will what they do not like – even inanimate objects are treated as 'contrary', as 'doing it deliberately', when they interfere with our pleasure[16] (W X, 135–7). On the other hand, 'law as rational, just law,' according to Feuerbach (W X, 108), 'and not as arbitrary, aristocratic or despotic law is nothing but my drive to happiness co-ordinated and set in harmony with other people's drive to happiness.'[17]

But what is this 'drive to happiness'? The fundamental criticism normally made of egoistic and of universal psychological hedonism is that both fail to provide an adequate analysis of the notion of 'happiness'. They vacillate between the tautological 'all men seek the satisfaction of their desires' (where a desire is merely that which strives to attain an object and is satisfied in attaining it) to the significant but highly dubious proposition 'all men seek a positive state called pleasure', as though the two propositions were equivalent in meaning and empirically obvious. When we analyse these statements all sorts of difficulties pile up. The notion of 'pleasure' is at best confused, at worst systematically ambiguous, as is brought out, in part, when we try to consider the position of the masochist. We ask whether he is seeking 'pleasure' or 'pain', and in having to give the preliminary answer 'both at once' bring out that 'pleasure' and 'pain' are not true opposites as we initially pretended. The satisfaction of desires, the achievement of happiness, is treated far too readily on the mechanical model of the relaxation of tension – as though men never found 'satisfaction' in continued activity, in grappling with difficulties or problems rather than in achieving their removal or solution. The universalistic hedonist, besides, often assumes that 'happiness' or 'pleasure' can be reduced to a common measure or yardstick – so much (such and such a quantity) of my pleasure must, in this case, be set against so much (such and such a quantity) of his pain and a balance drawn up – and that in seeking 'happiness' or 'pleasure' all men seek the same thing.

Now, the doctrine that all desire is desire for pleasure, as Professor Nowell-Smith has reminded us,[18] has not been held nearly as often as its opponents suppose. Feuerbach specifically repudiates the proposition that the drive for happiness is a distinct and separate drive. With some vacillation he implicitly comes down *against* the proposition that drives do not aim at food, sexual objects, understanding, etc., but 'really' only at happiness. 'Happiness or bliss', he writes (W X, 231), 'is nothing but the healthy, normal condition of a being, the condition of well-being or being well, the condition in which a being can and does in fact satisfy without impediment the needs or drives belonging to its individual, characteristic life and being.' Generally, in speaking of 'happiness' or 'well-being', Feuerbach treats both of these as the absence of misery or suffering, i.e., as the satisfaction of various human drives.

Every drive is a drive to happiness in the sense that it seeks objects which promote man's well-being. 'Aversion, aversion to distress and pain, abhorrence is the first will, the will with which a sensitive being begins its existence and maintains it. The will is not free but it seeks to be free, free from misery and evil, from dissatis-faction of drives' (W X, 231-2). What I want is always to remove a load, state of misery, to be happy. 'To satisfy a drive means to become free of it, even if only momentarily' (W X, 123). This does not mean, Feuerbach insists (quoting the *Investigations into the Human Will by* the contemporary critic of Kant, Feder of Göttingen), that

> some sort of *idea* of happiness or of only pleasure even causes
> the first manifestation of the human power of willing, or
> [that] every subsequent mood or even every involuntary action
> [is] provoked by this abstract idea. All that is being main-
> tained is that the immediate objects of the human will are
> such inner conditions as in the individual case are called well-
> being and which once they reach a certain quantity are called
> happiness; that the will of man is so fashioned that in virtue
> of its essential direction and exertions the drive to pleasure,
> to happiness and self-love must be imputed to it, at least as
> its main predisposition (W X, 233).

Professor Ryle, in his well-known paper on 'Pleasure',[19] seeks to show by a series of important (though not, I think, wholly decisive) arguments that 'a pleasure' is not a recordable occurrence in the sense in which a flash of lightning or even a stab of pain are. 'Doing X' and 'enjoying doing X' are therefore not different or distinct events in the sense that lightning and thunder are different and distinct events. Feuerbach, I think, has seen this point. Though he frequently speaks loosely of the will to happiness, it is clear that he does not regard seeking 'pleasure' or 'happiness' as distinct from seeking the specific things that drives aim at. Feuerbach holds, I should argue, that man has certain (changing and in principle endless) requirements. Satisfaction of these is happiness, non-satisfaction of these is misery, evil.[20] The drive to happiness is thus simply the drive(s) to satisfy these requirements (W X, 236-7). It is true that Feuerbach writes 'Will is will to happiness' (W X, 230) and 'The drive to happiness is the original and basic drive of all that lives and loves, that is and wants to be' (W X, 230–1). But he also insists that man has many desires; man is not like a hose or barrel the whole nature of which consists in holding liquid (W X, 122–3). He writes, 'It is often overlooked that the drive to happiness is not a simple and particular drive, but that rather . . . every drive is a drive to happiness' (W X, 234–5); he insists that 'happiness' is subjective and cannot be separated from the subject's individuality (W X, 262), not distinguishing here between a 'state' of happiness and that which causes it; he dismisses, as we have seen, the notion that drives aim at an 'abstract idea of happiness' and seems to be saying merely that drives aim at those objects that give men satisfaction, so that attaining the object and gaining satisfaction fuse into one concept. The drive in which this is not so is a sick drive, Feuerbach implies in an afterthought. Happiness thus consists in

> everything that life consists in, for life (naturally defectless, healthy, normal life) and happiness are in themselves originally one. All, or at least all healthy, drives are, as we said, drives to happiness;[21] all, or at least the necessary and not superfluous or useless, members and organs of life or of the body are organs of happiness; but they are not of the same importance or of the same value (W X, 239).

Different people, however, find their happiness in different ways. 'Man, together with his drive to happiness, is a natural creature, just as his body and soul, his head and his heart are constituted and determined by nature, so his happiness is constituted and determined' (W X, 251). The hero has his happiness and the coward his – but both can find it. Even in the particular individual, the value of things is not fixed, but rises and falls like a barometer – as fundamental a good or form of happiness as health is trivial to the healthy (W X, 240). Cultural conditions and cultural progress produce new drives and new satisfactions. 'Every pore newly opened to the influence of air and light through the soap of culture is also a new source of virtue and happiness' (W X, 264). But while men find happiness in different ways, while tastes vary, those variations, Feuerbach believes, become important only at the level of luxury. In morality, as in food, he writes, taste becomes subjective when you reach the caviar (W X, 275). The basic needs seem to Feuerbach clearly universal, just as it seems to him obvious that there is a hierarchy of satisfactions, that some are connected with 'higher' and more lasting drives and some with 'lower' and more transient ones (W X, 256).[22]

All this, however, will still hardly satisfy the contemporary, especially the Anglo-Saxon, moral philosopher. Is Feuerbach laying down an ethical principle of conduct or a psychological one? Is he providing a logical foundation for morality in the shape of a basic norm, or is he writing a natural history of morality, which leaves its fundamental logical problems untouched? Or worse still, is Feuerbach – according to the common custom of his country and his time – failing to recognize the distinction between these tasks?

Feuerbach is not, I think, failing to recognize the distinction so much as rejecting it. The sharp logical distinction between 'ought' and 'is', he would have argued, arises only if we think of the *ought* as expressing a categorical imperative. But there are, according to Feuerbach, no categorical imperatives – all imperatives, including those of morality, are hypothetical. The hypothetical imperative gains its force from the acceptance of certain ends. Such ends, Feuerbach believes, are built not only into the nature of man but into the theoretical structure of every science or body of knowledge. Feuerbach, already in his earlier period, had put it in this way: In the body of every science we find both 'laws' (*Gesetze*) and 'principles' (*Prinzipien*). The laws lay down what occurs to a given thing or activity in given conditions. The principles delimit the sphere of applicability of the basic concepts used in the science. That which violates the principles of the science belongs outside it, to some other sphere; that which violates the laws cannot occur at all. Every science has a conception of what is essential and what is accidental or unimportant *in the context of that science*; in the same way, every science has a conception of what is normal and of what is by contrast abnormal, of what is stunted, perverted, and therefore, for that science, uninteresting. The abnormal can and does occur, and can be scientifically interesting, of course. At a certain point of deviation, however, it becomes – *from the point of view of a particular science* – an abortion or a monster to be excluded from the subject-matter of *that* science *as an abnormality*. In general, the more developed a science, the more specific its principles become, the more definite is its conception of what is to be excluded from that science. Only in the beginning of their career do sciences collect facts 'impartially', without discriminating at all sharply between the relevant and the irrelevant, the normal and the abnormal. The conception of the monster or the perversion is a sophisticated scientific conception.

We are now in a position to see how Feuerbach would have attempted to systematize his ethics. Psychological hedonism provides the *laws* of the subject: all action is the outcome of drives seeking satisfaction and is determined by them. The immoral action is as much determined by drives as the moral action, the infliction of pain (even on oneself) as much as the pursuit of bodily pleasure. But morality as a subject or science has *principles* as well as laws: it has a concept of man and a conception of typically human behaviour, just as medicine has a concept of health and of the normally functioning body. Without such principles, neither medicine nor morality can lay claim to the status of a fully-developed science. The *principles* of morality enable us to distinguish moral actions from those that fall outside morality, that are immoral, just as the principles of zoology enable us to decide what is not a normal animal, what is a 'monster'. Such principles, of course, are *prescriptive*, but not arbitrarily so – in moral science they arise out of the empirical data about men, out of empirically-based conceptions of normalcy and out of the logical need to make the data coherent.

The fundamental problem of ethics – a problem that has not been removed or overcome by the contemporary logical analysis of the language of morals – is the continuing uncertainty about the nature of the subject, the confusion of aims and concerns that can be descried in traditional and modern ethical theory. Ethics has been variously seen as concerned with the 'welfare' (desires and satisfactions) of the individual, with the conditions of co-operation between individuals, and with certain 'values' – truth, beauty, etc. – taken to be 'good' or 'desirable' in themselves. It might well be argued that a certain common core can be found for the two latter concerns in the concepts of *co-operation* and *communication* and that the subject-matter of ethics can be clarified by looking at it in this way.[23] We could then take ethical theory to have been concerned, though often in a confused and uncertain way, with the character and conditions of co-operation and communication. Its

difficulties have been linked with vacillation between theories of
spontaneous or natural co-operation, relying on 'virtues', 'sympathy' and other habits of mind and social activities, and 'imperativist' conceptions of morality as a system of rules enforcing
co-operation from above. In either case, the moral theorist has had
difficulty in linking his conception of ethics with the desires and
drives of the individual. He has felt impelled to do so in order to
elicit consent; like the politician, he has sought to argue that the
good is directly or indirectly what the individual himself 'really'
wants. This political appeal has unquestionably done a great deal to
retard the clarification and systematization of ethical theory. If
ethics is concerned with what individuals want, then it may well
not be a coherent subject at all – then its ambiguities and imprecisions are as necessary to maintain the illusion of coherence as
ambiguities and imprecisions are necessary parts of a political
platform for a party that wants to win. The clarification of ethics,
like the clarification of political theory, may in fact require the
rejection of the concept of the individual as the ultimate logical
unit; it may require the recognition that there are conflicting
drives (both 'vices' and 'virtues') within individuals and that there
is no question of being able to construct an ethical theory without
making ethical distinctions *within* individuals.

Feuerbach, in the concept of love and in the concept of sympathy,
does seem to be trying to set up a paradigm of natural and spontaneous co-operation and communication and to see these as
fundamentally ethical. In love, he believes, the conflict between
individuals and their desires disappears: in it my well-being and
yours fuse into one. Nevertheless, a certain tension between
egoistic hedonism (the individual drives) and universalistic
hedonism (benevolence and concern for the happiness of others)
keeps breaking out in Feuerbach's (later) ethic. Much of his work
suggests a concern to *subordinate* individual 'happiness' to the
common weal. In relation to oneself, he writes (W X, 291), one
cannot be sufficiently 'idealist' (i.e., abstracting from one's own
material desires); in relation to others one cannot be sufficiently
'materialist'. Stoic in relation to oneself, Epicurean in relation to
others – that is the motto Feuerbach recommends to the moral
man. Feuerbach, as we have striven to bring out, does believe
that man's concern with others is a spontaneous concern flowing
out of the individual's nature and he thinks that such concern

becomes spontaneously greater as men are freed from need and oppression. 'Happiness. No, justice! But justice is simply mutual or reciprocal happiness in contrast with the one-sided, egoistic or sectional happiness of the old world' (W X, 292). Feuerbach betrays a certain uneasiness about the spontaneity and sufficiency of benevolence, however. When he writes of conscience as the echo of the cry of woe or vengeance of an injured other, he is replacing the morality of sympathy (or at least reinforcing it) with fear of another's wrath; when he bases the moral education of the child not only on its need for love, but also on the blows of its brothers and the pinches of its sisters, he shows a similar awareness of tension and conflict between the individual and his fellow 'species-being', not fully resolved by love. The proposition that might (if true) solve this difficulty – 'love evokes love; hate breeds hate' – is not in fact put forward or examined in Feuerbach's work. It would have required him to distinguish *between* drives instead of seeking to satisfy them all 'if natural'.

A similar half-hearted appeal to the normative may be found in Feuerbach's attempt to assimilate ethics to medicine and to derive norms from the 'nature' of man. The parallel between the immoral action and the monster (the two-headed calf) is not a convincing one and Feuerbach's obvious difficulty is that 'normal' men have 'immoral' drives. True, Feuerbach would have denied that we have a right to ask for a clear indication of the nature of man and the principles it sets for conduct before we embark on ethical enquiry. Ethics, he would have replied, is not to be deduced from a finished basic norm any more than medicine is to be deduced from a finished basic norm. The concept of 'health' is given ever-increasing content and precision only in the course of developing medical science, and not before such science is begun. Similarly, the physical-intellectual concept of well-being, with which morality is concerned, is given content and precision only in the *course of development* of moral science. It is not to be laid down at the beginning of enquiry as morality's abstract and abstracted postulate. Neither should moral science be thought of as something to be framed in the manner of a decalogue of precise prohibitions and commands: it is a flexible system of rules just as medicine is a flexible system of rules of health.

Precisely because Feuerbach does not succeed in bringing the concrete man and his drives or demands into convincing relation with his ethic of natural co-operation, Feuerbach falls into a characteristically *political* treatment of ethics, with its attempt to gloss over disagreement by the use of imprecise and loaded terms. Much that he says is best understood as a political programme, as a loose expression of that individualistic ethic coupled with a sense of social responsibility and social inter-connection which has become the basis of social democratic thought. The parallels between Feuerbach's view of ethics and the social democrat's view of society are indeed extremely striking. The conception of 'happiness' is used by Feuerbach as the social democrat uses the conception of 'welfare' – to provide a vague socio-ethical goal that will give direction to social and human striving without simply suppressing or denying the conflict of interests within such strivings. Feuerbach's drives and his varying and changing satisfactions are the competing interests recognized by democratic theory – each entitled to the maximum satisfaction consonant with affording similar satisfactions to others. Love and benevolence play the rôle in Feuerbach's ethic that the recognition of social and individual interdependence play in democratic social theory. Like the social democrat, or Fabian, Feuerbach passes lightly over the bitterness that conflicts of interests can create, over the extent to which they can threaten the whole conception of a social fabric or of a common humanity. Like the social democrat, or Fabian, Feuerbach is inclined to think that such conflicts become destructive when the most important primary needs are not fulfilled: the higher the level of satisfactions, the higher, as we would say, the general standard of living, the less deep and serious the conflicts between individuals and social groups, the less need or desire for the individual to satisfy himself at the expense of others.

Feuerbach, then, does not make any great contribution to clarifying the issues involved in moral philosophy or the concepts employed in the ethics of social democracy. His energy was still largely taken up with combating moralities that seek to bind man in the name of something other than his own, concrete, spiritual and material well-being. His argument is at its strongest not when he is analysing, but when he is telling us what we cannot ignore. The argument that morality cannot be got going without a concept of suffering will seem to many a powerful one: what Feuerbach is doing most successfully is to remind us that a moral philosophy cannot ignore this concept – it must make it morally relevant or show it to confuse different issues. Here, as in so many other places, Feuerbach points the way, without going any significant distance along it.

One other contribution of Feuerbach's is at least equally important. This is his analysis of moral or ethical judgments as *wishes*. There is, it seems to me, a most fruitful line for development here. The view that the moral judgment is a wish – like the view that the moral judgment is an imperative – enables us to show why moral imperatives as such are *not* issues about the truth or falsity of moral judgments. The 'immoral' action does not tell a lie or rest on a mistake; it interferes with certain of the moralist's wishes. The analysis of moral judgments in terms of wishes seems to me in certain ways superior to the analysis of moral judgments as imperatives – though wishes obviously have a prescriptive or imperative function. First, we can wish about the past (make moral judgments about it), where commanding the past seems odd. Second, by treating moral judgments as wishes we tend to set moral judgments in a social and psychological context, while treating them as imperatives tend to divorce moral judgments from such a context, to present them as abstracted prescriptions, floating about in a world of 'ultimate' unanalysable principles.

This is not to say that Feuerbach's analysis of wishing is close enough or thorough-going enough to *settle* the problems of analysing moral judgments. Neither does Feuerbach show in detail how he would distinguish the moral wish from other wishes. One strain in his work suggests that he would distinguish moral wishes from ordinary wishes by their universality, along the lines that R. M. Hare followed in distinguishing moral prescriptions from simple imperatives.[24] Another suggests that he would distinguish the moral wish from other wishes by also referring to the essential or common nature of man, to his basic, fundamental, 'truly human' requirements.[25] Neither strain is adequately worked out, though Feuerbach makes it clear that human requirements are both complex and variable. Both strains, however, suggest continuing themes in moral philosophy that cannot be ignored. The third strain – the positive distinction in ways of working suggested by Feuerbach's distinction between love and faith – is not concretely developed in his ethical theory at all. It would have come into conflict with his individualism, and made the relation between democratic republicanism and culture a much more complex one than Feuerbach, or Marx, recognized.

LP

Postscript

10. In place of a conclusion

Philosophy, Feuerbach wrote, should awaken thought instead of constraining it; it should make us look at life, investigate nature and society, instead of tying us to books and concepts. Feuerbach saw himself as a man standing on the threshold of a new secular, democratic, scientific culture, beckoning others to leave their idols and their scholastic manuals and to follow him into the new age. He saw himself as a liberator and not as a Constitution-maker; he invited people to use their eyes, he did not tell them what to see.

Feuerbach's influence on subsequent generations has thus understandably been primarily that of an *Anreger*, an exciter of thoughts and ideas, and not that of a systematic teacher, producing a Feuerbachian school in the history of ideas. (Those who tried to create a Feuerbachian school and to preach a systematic Feuerbachian philosophy, as we have argued, did their master's reputation more harm than good – the creation of a philosophical system was not where Feuerbach's talents were ever employed.) One tends to think of those who were influenced by him as 'fastening on' to aspects of his thought, using and developing his insights for their own purposes. One might say of Feuerbach, as Savigny said of a far greater thinker, Vico, that his thought was like a series of lightning-flashes on a dark night, illuminating for those who already had some conception of the way but only blinding and confusing for those who had not. Those who did see had to find the rest of the way for themselves.

It is therefore not easy and not, I think, very useful, to end with an 'appraisal' of Feuerbach's thought. Feuerbach was the kind of candidate that leaves examiners unconfident about the principles they use in marking. He was capable of great insight and logical acuteness, he had an original and imaginative mind; he was loose, careless, unsystematic and could confuse or gloss over problems in the most shameless way. Yet constantly, he leaves one with the feeling that he could have done philosophy in the conventional way and at a more than respectable level if he had only cared to do

so. He did not; his character and work, in many respects, suffered
in consequence. His imagination and insight survived. He has
appealed, on the whole, to original thinkers, to those searching for
insights and illumination rather than finished solutions or systems;
he has also appealed, less fortunately, to the dilettante and to the
man searching for a simple method or key that will straddle a
number of disciplines. Marx found in the Feuerbachian analysis
of religion, and in Feuerbach's critique of Hegel's reversal of the
subject-predicate relation, a model for the Marxian analysis of
society and the Marxian critique of ideologies. Feuerbach's concept of the *Gattungswesen*, the species-being, was the seed-bed of
Marx's conception of 'pre-historical' man as an ensemble of social
relations and of the free man as necessarily co-operative. For those
seriously concerned with the evolution and meaning of Marx's
thought, an understanding of Feuerbach is indispensable. Others,
like Chernyshevsky in his *magister*'s thesis, have tried to use
Feuerbach's 'anthropological principle' as a basis for aesthetics.
The influence of Feuerbach on Nietzsche is as patent as it was
fundamental; his influence on Kierkegaard, if less obvious, is
equally important. Theologians for many decades either ignored
Feuerbach or showered him with inept 'refutations', but it is now
being widely recognized that Feuerbach was probably the most
significant *theological* thinker in the nineteenth century, whose
importance has finally become evident in the twentieth. Feuerbach
referred to himself, on more than one occasion, as Luther II; we
can now see that he was right. The systole/diastole that he saw as
lying at the heart of religion has become the dominant issue in
theological thinking in the twentieth century. On the one hand, we
have precisely that secularization, humanization and moralization
of religion which Feuerbach predicted. On the other hand, we have
the Barthian school arguing that Feuerbach was indeed the logical
and inevitable consequence of the Lutheran Christology and of the
Lutheran Doctrine of the Last Supper and therefore urging the
'Calvinist corrective' – the recognition of the complete sinfulness
of man and of the consequent *impossibility* of making the divine
predicates human predicates in the way that Feuerbach and the
new theology seek to do. It is around Feuerbach that this argument
basically revolves. Feuerbach's concept of man, and especially his
concept of the I-Thou, have again moved to the forefront of
philosophic consciousness since they were taken up by Max

Scheler, Karl Löwith, Berdyaev, the young Martin Buber and others and passed into the stream of subsequent existentialist thinking. In recent times – in the work of Althusser, for example, not to speak of Sartre – this has happened in France as much as it did earlier in Germany. At present, indeed, when young intellectuals or pseudo-intellectuals are passing through a stage of romantic Promethean revolt against industry and the rationalities of social science and economics, comparable to the Left Hegelian revolt against Prussian conservatism, religion and idealist philosophy, the Feuerbachian concept of man lurks behind much of the socialist humanism and existentialist Marxism proclaimed by the middle-class revolutionaries of our day. It is perhaps an appropriate time to go back to Feuerbach and to consider the weaknesses as well as the strengths of that concept.

One aspect of Feuerbach's thought, his empiricism, which was so needed in Germany,[1] is unlikely to make any great impact on the English reader. Feuerbach's emphasis on science had been absorbed and understood in England even before Feuerbach wrote. As Rawidowicz puts it, Feuerbach's empiricism made no impression in England (while his critique of religion made at least some), because the English did not need it. The English reader is much more likely to be aware of the way in which Feuerbach, in his attempt to overcome the division of labour and the 'abstraction' of problems, fails to recognize *specific* intellectual problems or puzzles. This comes out especially strongly in his theory of knowledge and in his treatment of the mind–body problem. It prevents him from making any real contribution in these fields.

'Philosophy has gone beyond Feuerbach,' Rawidowicz wrote in the final paragraph of his study, 'and it had to do that. Many philosophers thought they could pass Feuerbach by completely, but in this they were not justified. If passing by Feuerbach is inadmissible, so on the other hand is going back to Feuerbach at least equally impossible. Neither past Feuerbach nor back to Feuerbach, but through Feuerbach and with him to a new understanding of German philosophy of the last century, of the philosophy of Hegel and his school.' Thirty years later, Feuerbach's significance once again stretches beyond the history of German philosophy. But his significance lay in the suggestiveness of his thought, not in his capacity for careful, systematic, philosophical thinking. The reader will have more chance of appreciating the basis on which this significance rests from the kind of exposition and illustration attempted in the preceding pages than from any 'appraisal' that judges Feuerbach by criteria, and in relation to interests, that may not be the reader's own. The story of Feuerbach's actual historical influence, and the fate of his ideas in the hands of those stimulated by him, is another story. It has not been told here. The present work is a more modest attempt to provide the material for an understanding of Feuerbach himself.

NOTES

PREFACE

1. A highly abridged translation of Feuerbach's *Essence of Religion* by Alexander Loos was published in New York in 1873.
2. *Basic Propositions of the Philosophy of the Future*, transl. as *Principles of the Philosophy of the Future* by H. Vogel, Indianapolis, 1966; *The Essence of Faith According to Luther*, transl. by Melvin Cherno, New York, 1967; *Lectures on the Essence of Religion*, transl. by Ralph Manheim, New York, 1967. George Elliot's translation of the *Essence of Christianity* (London, 1854, reprinted in 1874) was reprinted again in 1957.

PART I. THE TIMES, THE MAN AND THE WORK

I. THE PROMETHEAN BACKGROUND

1. Herbert Marcuse, *Eros and Civilisation – A Philosophical Enquiry into Freud*, pp. 109–10.
2. Arthur O. Lovejoy, *The Great Chain of Being*, p. 200.
3. Alexander Pope, *Essay on Man*, I, lines 189–92.
4. Voltaire, *Remarks on M. Pascal's 'Thoughts'*, III, cited (in the William Fleming translation) from Leonard M. Marsak (ed.), *French Philosophers from Descartes to Sartre*, p. 181.
5. Georg Lukács, in *Goethe and His Age*, has argued – somewhat crudely – that Faust's restless striving is the restless striving of capitalism, its constant search for knowledge and mastery, its desire to encompass the world. For Goethe's extremely ambivalent attitude to this striving – which accounts for the contradictions in *Faust* – see Erich Heller, *The Disinherited Mind*, pp. 33–55.
6. While the French Revolution and the social and political tumult of the Napoleonic era occupied the minds of his German contemporaries, Goethe, as Arnulf Zweig has put it, 'calmly concentrated his attention on optics and plant morphology'. His lack of interest in the two great themes of the age, nationalism and democracy, led to a considerable slump in his reputation in the 1790s and early 1800s; his fundamental affinity, as we shall see, was with Spinoza and Leibniz rather than with Kant, Fichte, Herder, or the young Hegel and the young Schelling.
7. 'Saved from the Devil is the noble member of the spirit-world: him who strives incessantly we can redeem' – a quatrain in which the Faustian impulse is reduced to the virtues of the good housewife, who finds work for idle hands.
8. The seeming contradictions – maintained over a period of sixty years – that characterized Goethe's utterances about Christianity are to be resolved, as Karl Löwith emphasizes, by seeing in Goethe something

very close to what Nietzsche called the Dionysian justification of life. For Goethe, 'Christianity transcends ancient ways of sanctifying life because it includes positively within itself what appears to go contrary to life. It teaches us to view as divine even what is repugnant, odious, and loathsome: "Lowliness and poverty, scorn and contempt, disgrace and misery, suffering and death"; it even teaches us to love sin and crime as ways by which to go forward. It is like "nature" in *Satyros*: both *Urding* and *Unding* (primal matter and impossibility; everything and nothing), a comprehensive unity of contradictions. Life . . . is "its most beautiful invention", and death "its device to have much life". Birth and the grave are one eternal sea': Karl Löwith, *From Hegel to Nietzsche: The Revolution in Nineteenth-century Thought*, p. 23. It is nature, not man, that Goethe sees as ultimately divine: Man's task is not to rape Nature, but to live in harmony with its laws and in appreciation of its beauty, a beauty displayed even in death and suffering. What Goethe worshipped was not Man, but the productive power of the whole of Nature, against which war, plague, water and flame can have no effect. Goethe, then, is not Promethean precisely because he does not see the relation between man and nature as one of conflict, involving mastery and submission. The Faustian elevation of knowledge, and the Faustian spirit of striving and rebellion, in retrospect may seem important steps on the Promethean road, but for Goethe, the whole of Nature was animate (*beseelt*, as Leibniz put it), and human striving was but one manifestation of that universal striving that was for him a law of nature.

9. Radical contemporaries, indeed, treated Feuerbach's anthropology, and all other nineteenth-century deification of man, as the logical culmination and consummation of the German idealism that began with Fichte's elevation of the Ego. Thus a member of the revolutionary Petrashevskii circle in Russia, N. A. Speshnev, wrote to the Polish emigrant K. E. Chojecki *circa* 1847: 'You are right – all German idealism of the nineteenth century – the "great" German philosophy beginning with Fichte . . . drives only towards anthropotheism, to the point where, having reached its summit in the person of its latest standard-bearer and leading figure, Feuerbach, it calls things by their right name and exclaims with him: *Homo homini deus est* – man is God unto man.' N. A. Speshnev, *Pis'ma K. E. Khoetskomu*, in V. E. Evgrafova (ed.), *Filosofskie i obshchestvenno-politicheskie proizvedeniya petrashevtsev*, p. 494. Speshnev goes on to regard Proudhon (in his *Philosophy of Poverty*) and the Polish radical H. Kamienski (in his *Philosophy of Material Economy*) as having independently of Feuerbach reached the same anthropotheistic viewpoint, on the same Fichtean–Hegelian basis. (The dating of Speshnev's letter – 1847 – is conjectural.) As early as the 1820s, Fichte's philosophy had been taken up with enthusiasm in the Masonic lodges in Russia as a *revolutionary* philosophy and the historical progression of influences on the Russian radical intelligentsia was, indeed, Fichte, Schelling, Feuerbach, Marx (the latter two, in part, subsuming Hegel).

10. Marcuse, *op. cit.*, p. 115; the passage that follows is cited from the Baillie translation of the *Phenomenology*, as amended by Marcuse. 'Geist' can be translated either 'spirit' or 'mind'; by the end of the *Phenomenology* it is clearly no longer a human mind.

11. Heinrich Heine, 'Of Germany Since Luther', in *Revue des Deux-Mondes*, 1834, vol. 4, p. 408. I cite the English version given in Edith M. Riley's translation of Henri de Lubac, S. J., *The Drama of Atheist Humanism*, p. 21.

2. THE MAN AND HIS WORK

1. Sidney Hook, *From Hegel to Marx*, p. 220.

2. 'Retiring' might have been a better word than 'modest'. Feuerbach *was* a lonely figure, but his loneliness stemmed from the very opposite of modesty: it was the product of unsatisfied intellectual vanity, not of a feeling of unworthiness or of an inability to find satisfaction in intimate personal relationships. Feuerbach regarded himself as a philosopher of outstanding importance who had first been denied proper advancement in the academic sphere by the cowardice and servility of German universities and who had then been ignored by a fickle public that had proved itself incapable of sustaining the critical enthusiasm of the 1840s. Feuerbach's sense of grievance was in part justified, but it rested firmly on the intellectual arrogance of the man who is certain that he is better than his age. This arrogance did not carry over into personal relations – but it did lead Feuerbach to treat his own intellectual evolution as a matter of *public* importance.

3. [*The Essence of Christianity*], 1st edn. 1841.

4. Despite Strauss' acclaim of Feuerbach and the extent to which the two names were linked in the intellectual developments of their day, the two men met only once, in 1842, when Feuerbach was persuaded to interrupt a journey and visit Strauss at Heilbronn. The meeting was polite, but the two men patently did not hit it off (cf. Bolin's memoir W XII, 97, and Feuerbach's letter to Emilie Kapp of 9 January 1843, W XIII, 116–17.

5. D. F. Strauss, *Ausgewählte Briefe*, p. 184.

6. Ernest Renan, *Etudes d'histoire religieuse*, p. 404. Renan, however, was dubious of the value of Feuerbach's work – it seemed too Hegelian to him.

7. The leader of the circle, M. V. Butashevich-Petrashevskii (1821–66), had included a copy of the 2nd (Leipzig) edition of the *Essence of Christianity* in the library of banned books he organized in St Petersburg in 1845 (as was noted in the indictment at his trial for revolutionary activity in 1849). He also gave an account of the Feuerbachian critique of religion under the heading 'Naturalism' in the *Pocket Dictionary of Foreign Words* in 1846 – a device adopted in an unsuccessful attempt to get the material past the censor. The *Dictionary*, however, was seized by the censor and 1,599 copies of the edition of 2,000 were burnt in 1849, having lain for three years in the censor's office.

Another of Petrashevskii's associates, N. A. Speshnev (1821–82), also arrested in 1849, wrote to Chojecki, in a letter already cited, 'Instead of god-man we now have man-god.' A third member of the group, E.-F. G. Tol' (1823–67), also arrested with them, spent the early part of 1849 preparing a manuscript, in a quasi-Feuerbachian spirit, on the origins of religion. See E. V. Evgrafova (ed.), *Filosofskie i obshches-tvenno-politicheskie proizvedeniya petrashevtsev*, esp. pp. 742, 183–4, 751–2, 496, 699–702.

8. P. V. Annenkov, a member of the 'Westernizers', bears witness to this in his memoirs, and notes that Herzen's enormous Feuerbach enthusiasm was shared by Granovskii, but not to the point to which Herzen wished to take it, i.e. to creating a Feuerbachian sociopolitical philosophy. See Annenkov, *Literaturnye vospominaniya*, p. 431. Herzen worked on Feuerbach's book on Leibniz as early as 1844, as he noted in his *Diary* on 9 August 1844: cf. S. Rawidowicz, *Ludwig Feuerbachs Philosophie – Ursprung und Schicksal*, p. 480, and the other authorities there cited.

9. The general view was, and to a large extent remains, that Feuerbach had said everything of importance that he had to say by 1845, and that his subsequent work is either mere repetition or a falling-away into positions (such as 'vulgar materialism') which he had effectively criticized earlier. Thus the Russian radical writer Peter Lavrov, in his incomplete draft of a series of lectures on Feuerbach, written in 1868, when Feuerbach was 64, notes that the last three volumes of Feuerbach's collected works had contained nothing new. Lavrov quotes with approval a German reviewer writing in *Die Gegenwart* of 1849, who had said that in his *Essence of Religion* Feuerbach had apparently reached the heights made accessible to him by his intellectual gifts and his individual character, and that he was unlikely to produce another series of works matching this achievement in any new area: P. L. Lavrov, *Filosofiya i sotsiologiya – izbrannye proizvedeniya v dvukh tomakh*, vol. I, p. 641. Cf. Sidney Hook, *op. cit.*, p. 221: '[After 1850] Feuerbach relapses into positions which he had criticized earlier.'

10. N. A. Speshnev, *Pis'ma K. E. Khoetskomu (vtoroe pis'mo)*, circa 1847, in V. E. Evgrafova (ed.), *op. cit.*, pp. 497–8.

11. Karl Marx, 'Kritik der Hegelschen "Rechtsphilosophie"', written in 1843 and published in the *Deutsch-französische Jahrbücher* of 1844, here cited from *Marx–Engels Gesamtausgabe*, Section I, vol. I–i, pp. 614–15: cf. Eugene Kamenka, *The Ethical Foundations of Marxism*, p. 30 and, more generally, pp. 17–47.

12. W II, 410–11; I cite, however, the translation in Sidney Hook, *op. cit.*, pp. 222–3.

13. Many of these radicals emigrated to the United States after the defeat of the Revolution. Germans in America provided Feuerbach with the warmest (German) interest in his work in the 1850s and 1860s and with the first support in the economic difficulties of his later years.

14. Marxists, taking their cue from the later Engels, have honoured Feuerbach as the man who immediately preceded Marx and Engels in

the history of thought and laid one of the foundation stones on which Marxism was erected. It is no doubt through Marxists that Feuerbach's name has been kept before a large public in the last eighty years, even if only as the short title of a work by Engels. But Marxists have made no significant contribution (since Marx himself) to the *understanding* of Feuerbach's work or to the scholarly tracing of his thought. Since I am here concerned primarily with Feuerbach's own work and his own reputation, I have not especially emphasized Feuerbach's influence on later Marxist thinkers such as G. V. Plekhanov and his pupil, A. M. Deborin, whose interest in Feuerbach arose through Marx and Marxism. The Soviet literature on Feuerbach is surprisingly scant and makes no serious contribution to Feuerbach studies.

15. Anselm was born in Hainichen, a secluded village near Jena, on 14 November 1775, fifteen months before his parents' marriage in February 1777. He died, after a series of strokes, on 29 May 1833, when Ludwig was 28. The main primary sources for Anselm Feuerbach's life are the two volumes, containing the correspondence and papers left at his death, which were compiled by Ludwig Feuerbach as an act of filial piety entrusted to him by the family: *Anselm von Feuerbachs Leben und Wirken aus seinen ungedruckten Briefen usw* (1852). Ludwig issued a second, enlarged edition of this work in 1854 under the title *Anselm von Feuerbachs biographischer Nachlass*. The best general biography of Anselm, which also makes use of other primary sources, is Gustav Radbruch, *Paul Johann Anselm Feuerbach – ein Juristenleben*, published in 1934. One of the best studies of Feuerbach's legal work is Max Grünhut, *Anselm von Feuerbach und das Problem der strafrechtlichen Zurechnung* (1922).

16. *Philosophisch-juristische Untersuchung über das Verbrechen des Hochverrats*, 1798; *Revision der Grundsätze und Grundbegriffe des positiven peinlichen Rechts*, 1799. Anselm, on entering university, had a bitter quarrel with his father and refused to study law. Instead, he attended philosophy courses in Jena given by the Kantian Karl Leonhard Reinhold and took a doctorate in philosophy in 1795. In that year, and in 1796, he published two books on philosophical themes, setting out philosophical criticisms of natural law doctrine. He also published a few essays, Kantian in tendency, on the state of nature, the concept of the great man, and the concept of the cosmic. He entered the Law Faculty in the summer semester, 1796.

17. *Lehrbuch des gemeinen in Deutschland geltenden peinlichen Rechts*, 1801; further editions in Feuerbach's lifetime appeared in 1803, 1804, 1808, 1812, 1818, 1820, 1823, 1825, 1828, 1831.

18. The Feuerbach family tree, ascending upward from Anselm's grandson and Ludwig's nephew, the well-known German painter Anselm Feuerbach, is traced in Peter von Gebhard, 'Ahnentafel des Mahlers Anselm Feuerbach', in *Ahnentafel berühmter Deutschen*. See also Professor Schwinge, 'Zur Geschichte der Familie Feuerbach', *Heimatblätter fur Ansbach und Umgebung* (1933), nos 5–6.

19. Anselm and Wilhelmine had produced one other child before their marriage, Ernst Wilhelm, born in December 1796. He died early in July 1798; two weeks later his parents were married (Wilhelmine was pregnant again). The three daughters were Helen (baptized Rebekka Magdalene), born in 1808, who in 1826 married another lawyer, Freiherr Ludwig von Dobeneck, but had the marriage dissolved after three unhappy years, Leonore (Rosina Eleonora), born in 1809, and Elisa (Wilhelmina Theresa), the last child, born in 1813.

20. Bolin reports that a warm relationship grew up between the two boys and that Ludwig visited his Jewish friend in hospital when the latter was beaten up (as Jews all too often were) by a gang of boys (W XII, 8–9).

21. The standard, if over-adulatory and not at all scholarly, sketch of Ludwig Feuerbach's life (based primarily on the collection of his correspondence) is Bolin's biographical introduction to that correspondence, reprinted in W XII, 1–211. I have drawn on it here. Two biographies important as containing previously unpublished material are Karl Grün, *Ludwig Feuerbachs philosophische Charakterentwicklung, sein Briefwechsel und Nachlass* (1874) and A. Kohut, *Ludwig Feuerbach, sein Leben und seine Werke* (1909).

22. Cited in W. Bolin, *Ludwig Feuerbach, sein Wirken und seine Zeitgenossen*, pp. 12–13; cf. Bolin's memoir, W XII, 15–16.

23. The year 1827 was a specially bad year for the family Feuerbach; Karl, who had made a second attempt at suicide early in 1825 before being released from prison, had another severe attack of mental illness, almost on the same day as Anselm von Feuerbach's father died in Frankfurt. Karl had to give up his post as a mathematics teacher at the Court *Gymnasium*, was under treatment for a while, and then lived as a hermit, completely unkempt, until his death in 1834.

24. Bolin, both in his comments and in his adaptation of the dissertation into German, exaggerates the extent of the break with Hegel. For a detailed attempt to show how Hegelian much of the dissertation was, see Rawidowicz, *op. cit.*, pp. 15–33, though Rawidowicz seems determined to make the most of his case and is not always fair (or accurate) in his criticisms of Bolin and Jodl.

25. A list of Feuerbach's publications during his lifetime will be found in the bibliography at the end of this book, arranged in chronological order of publication. It supplements this sketch of his life and activity.

26. Later Feuerbach claimed, probably inaccurately, that he had left Berlin University saying to Hegel: Thank you very much, I have learnt all I can from you, now I go to study anatomy (W XII, 17). In the *Philosophical Fragments* under the heading 'Bruckberg 1836–41', he wrote: 'All abstract sciences stunt man; only natural science reinstates him as an integral being, makes use of all the capacities and senses of the whole man' (W II, 380). He did keep up an interest in anatomy, geology and the natural sciences generally for most of his life – but only in an amateur way.

27. Erdmann and Feuerbach began work on the history of philosophy simultaneously; Erdmann published a year or two later. Both Christian

Kapp and the Hegelian philosopher of law Eduard Gans praised
Feuerbach's history highly, Kapp saying that Erdmann had only
re-worked the material in a more pedestrian spirit. Erdmann himself,
like the other Hegelian historian of philosophy, Kuno Fischer, had a
high respect for Feuerbach's historical work (as did Hegel's bio-
grapher, R. Haym); both Erdmann and Fischer are often held to have
been influenced by Feuerbach's work in his Hegelian period.

28. In the article 'Luther als Schiedsrichter zwischen Strauss und Feuer-
bach', published anonymously and attributed to Marx by Riazanov:
Marx-Engels *Werke*, vol. 1, p. 27; *Marx-Engels Gesamtausgabe*,
Section I, vol. I–i, p. 174.

29. Feuerbach's reply, dated 25 October 1843, was recently published –
for the first time – in Werner Schuffenhauer, *Feuerbach und der junge
Marx*, p. 198. For some indication of the activities of Marx, Ruge,
Bakunin and others in this period, see Schuffenhauer, *passim* and
Kamenka, *op. cit.*, pp. 17–86, 121–31.

30. See Ruge's letter to Feuerbach from Halle on 4 December 1839
(W XIII, 22–3) and from Dresden on 10 December 1841 (W XIII, 81–2).
Feuerbach also rejected Ruge's plea that he move to a larger town, so
that he could play a part in editorial activity (W XIII, 7 and 21).

31. The police had searched the Feuerbach residence at Bruckberg in the
later half of 1842, when Feuerbach was being visited by Hermann
Kriege, a socialist journalist watched by the police. (Kriege, finally
threatened with arrest in 1844, fled from Germany to Belgium,
England and then the United States.) Feuerbach, who corresponded
with him for a period, burnt most of his letters when the police in
Dresden declared Kriege an undesirable person (*see* W XIII, 143).

32. The novelist Gottfried Keller also attended the lectures. He had
wrestled earnestly with Feuerbach's thought, as the famous discussion
of Feuerbach's doctrines in his novel *Der grüne Heinrich* shows,
having become acquainted with it through the activity of Ruge, Karl
Heinzen, Karl Grün and others in Zurich in the early 1840s, as well as
through the Swiss Feuerbachian, Wilhelm Marr. At that stage Keller
had been ambivalent, rejecting at least portions of Marr's (and
Feuerbach's) doctrines; at the lectures in Heidelberg he was converted. A personal friendship with Feuerbach sprang up and Feuerbach's thought became one of the most important influences on Keller,
especially on his aesthetics. See Rawidowicz, *op. cit.*, pp. 372–84, and
the works cited there.

PART II. THE CRITICAL PHILOSOPHY

3. LUDWIG FEUERBACH'S CRITIQUE OF RELIGION

1. Putting it even more minimally, one might say that Feuerbach is
what Professor Passmore has called an 'existence-monist', denying
that there are sorts, or levels, or orders of existence, insisting that the
'is' of existence has an invariant meaning: see John Passmore,

Philosophical Reasoning, pp. 38–9. Feuerbach, in part, rejects theology and idealist philosophy because they involve a dualistic treatment of existence, because they treat God or spirit as having an existence other than empirical existence. They counterpose an Absolute reality to 'mere' empirical reality (including man) and thus create both logical dualism and moral-political subjugation.

2. This criticism of Hegel, that he consistently reverses the true relation of subject and predicate, of cause (or ground) and effect, and thus deifies or personifies mere attributes, functions or relationships that cannot be understood in and through themselves alone, was enthusiastically taken over from Feuerbach by the young Marx: see Eugene Kamenka, *The Ethical Foundations of Marxism*, pp. 17–82, esp. pp. 20, 41, 71–2, and Shlomo Avineri, *The Social and Political Thought of Karl Marx*, pp. 8–40 (where Marx's use of what Avineri calls Feuerbach's 'transformative method' is very fully discussed). This Feuerbachian criticism of the relationship of subject and predicate in idealist philosophy lies at the root of Marx's critique of Hegel's political philosophy and of Marx's rejection and critique of alienation in intellectual work. The economists, Marx argued in his writings of 1843 and 1844, *reify* economic categories, treat them in abstraction from man, and thus make economics irrational, i.e., both contradictory and inhumane. Restoring the correct relation of subject and predicate in Hegel ('standing Hegel on his head', or rather on his feet), seeing the State as a predicate of society and not vice versa, led Marx to his 'materialist' conception of history. The Marxist conception of history, indeed, is an application to society of the Feuerbachian genetic-critical method of explaining religion.

3. Only when such analysis becomes a *substitute* for considering the truth or falsity of a belief does it become vicious. The two questions – 'why does a man have a certain belief?' and 'is that belief true?' are separate issues and must be kept distinct. If the distinction is maintained, however, then the first question is as legitimate as the second. In particular contexts (especially when the belief is patently false), this first question may be much more interesting and we may come to understand the nature of an error much more precisely by understanding how men are led into it.

4. Lange, *The History of Materialism*, vol. II, p. 247.

5. It also has, in such words as *Postwesen*, the post (office), the suggestion of a whole system that goes to make up an institution. Hegel thought it, for this reason, remarkably apposite for bringing out the real character of 'essences' as systems of predicates that are held together by a principle of development.

6. In the manuscript draft for his lectures on Feuerbach cited earlier: P. L. Lavrov, *Filosofiya i sotsiologiya – izbrannye proizvedeniya v dvukh tomakh*, vol. I, pp. 649–50.

7. Engels, *Ludwig Feuerbach and the End of Classical German Philosophy*, p. 29.

8. According to Bolin, portions of the *Theogony* were written down as

early as 1848; see W XIII, v–vi. There is no doubt that in the 1840s Feuerbach's work on religion betrays a growing, if still incomplete, emancipation from Hegelian language and the Hegelian cast of thought and a growing emphasis on the more concretely empirical. This is reflected in the changes that distinguish the second edition of the *Essence of Christianity* from the first, and the third from the second. It is Feuerbach's concern with the empirical, rather than the lingering Hegelianisms, that I stress in my account as constituting the most fruitful and significant part of Feuerbach's work, both for his time and in ours. For the contrary emphasis, see S. Rawidowicz, *Ludwig Feuerbachs Philosophie, passim,* but esp. pp. 9–232.

9. The third edition version given in the Bolin and Jodl edition ends at 'ground', omitting the reference to despair and rapture.

10. A. M. Deborin, *Ludvig Feierbakh,* p. 201.

11. Ludwig Feuerbach, *Sämtliche Werke* (1844–66 edn), vol. II, p. 180. In the earlier writings – *The Description and History of the Philosophy of Leibniz* (1837) and *Pierre Bayle* (1838), where Feuerbach is still only working towards the position he reached in the 1840s, he puts the matter somewhat differently. In philosophy, he says, universal man, man as humanity and human reason as the common characteristic of universal man or humanity, hold the place of authority; in religion man as an individual and practical necessities occupy the foreground. Science is universal and unconditional; theology is particular, conditional (W V, 136–7; AW IV, 30–1).

12. Feuerbach had heard Schleiermacher deliver both university lectures and Sunday sermons while Feuerbach was studying in Berlin. As an old man he still spoke enthusiastically of Schleiermacher's remarkable eloquence: see W I, 249, and Bolin's memoir, W XII, 176f. It has been argued, in current theology – by Karl Barth, among others – that Ludwig Feuerbach is the logically inevitable nemesis that overtakes Schleiermacher's (and Luther's) attempt to ground religion in feeling. Take that path, make God man-dependent even in the most restrictive sense, make religion man-centred, and Feuerbach follows. The reaction to Feuerbach can thus take the form of a retreat from 'religion' into 'theology', into proclaiming the complete 'otherness' of God and utter discontinuity between philosophy to theology. Feuerbach, of course, argues that this approach, while saving religion from *some* criticisms, destroys its function and point; a God who is wholly other is of no interest or significance to man.

13. This well-known Feuerbachian phrase stands in contradiction to the more interesting and more Hegelian line taken in his *Thoughts on Death and Immortality* (1830), where Feuerbach argued that the classical civilizations of Greece and Rome had no conception of the immortality of the individual soul because they placed no stress on the concept of the individual. These civilizations saw the individual as part of a human community which was already (comparatively, in relation to the individual) eternal. (W XI, 69–323, esp. pp. 77–81; cf. the subsequently revised version, W I, 1–262, esp. pp. 3–6.)

14. Professor Hook, recognizing this distinction, distinguishes Feuerbach's 'philosophy of religion' from his 'psychology of religion' – Hook, *From Hegel to Marx*, pp. 243–54. But the whole point of Feuerbach's work, of course, was to deny that a 'philosophy' of religion which ignores the psychology of religion could get to a real understanding of religious phenomena.

15. The Soviet writer I. P. Tsameryan correctly emphasizes that Feuerbach uses the word 'dependence' very broadly – man, according to Feuerbach, is dependent upon nature not only in the sense that it causes him suffering, but also in the sense that it brings him joy. The feeling of dependence can thus include gratitude, love and respect as well as fear, and the former feelings can also be reflected in the religious emotion: I. P. Tsameryan and others, *Osnovy nauchnogo ateizma*, p. 34.

16. C. A. van Peursen, *Body, Soul, Spirit: A Survey of the Body-Mind Problem*, p. 54.

17. Here Feuerbach, like Marx, remains under the influence of Hegel's *Phenomenology of Mind*, with its stages of development culminating in the mind's (spirit's) consciousness of itself. Man, for Feuerbach, 'comprehends' the universe and transcends all other species because he is not bound simply by the laws and forms of life governing a single species. Man can imaginatively apprehend and reconstruct all of nature: he can create according to the laws of other species. This point was taken over by Marx in a well-known passage of his *Economico-Philosophical Manuscripts* of 1844: see Kamenka, *op. cit.*, pp. 76–7. It forms a very important basis for the belief in the 'universality' of man and in his consequent at least potential rôle as lord of the universe, subjecting all things to his 'universal' will.

18. This, of course, would seem to conflict with the much stronger recognition in polytheism of the *community*, of man as a member of a social order, or of a social province, as opposed to the individualism connected with monotheism (and Platonic idealism). The division of history into stages rarely solves more problems than it raises.

19. Even in the *Essence of Christianity*, however, Feuerbach makes it clear that dependence on nature never ceases entirely. The two stages of religion, the physical and the moral, remain as 'moments' or aspects of the most developed monotheism. Thus, 'according to his physical properties, of which *power* is the most essential, God is the cause of physical beings, the basis of nature; according to his moral properties, of which *goodness* is the most essential, God is the cause of moral beings, of man.' In the *Essence of Christianity*, Feuerbach says, he had been concerned with God as a moral being (though in fact he certainly brings out the physical aspect as well), in the *Essence of Religion* he was concerned with God as a physical being. 'Just as I demonstrated in the *Essence of Christianity* that God according to his moral or spiritual qualities, God as a moral being, is nothing but the deified and objectified spiritual being [essence] of man – i.e., that *theology* in *reality*, in its ultimate ground and final upshot, is only

anthropology, so in the *Essence of Religion* I showed that the physical God, or God regarded as the cause of nature, the stars, trees, stones, animals and men in so far as they too are natural, physical beings, expresses nothing other than the deified and personified being [essence] of *nature*' (W VIII, 25–6; GW VI, 28). To the statement 'theology is anthropology', Feuerbach concludes, we must therefore add 'and physiology'.

20. If miracles were to be something other than acts of imagination, if they were to be empirical realities, 'sensuous facts', then, as Feuerbach had argued in *Pierre Bayle* (W V, 157–8; GW IV, 53–4), we would need to be shown *how* they were performed, *how* water became wine. Once we did see this, we would have an explanation (we would know *how*) and there would be no miracle. But as long as we have no such explanation, we do not know that water *became* wine; we know only that where water was previously, there is wine now. The 'miracle' is the typical imaginative substitution, not the (miraculous) practical transformation. The miracle, like the imagination, is not concerned with the means; it does not portray a *miraculous* causality, it portrays *no causality at all*.

21. Cf. the *Theogony* (W IX, 277–8), where Feuerbach stresses the projection of social dependence, of the social relation of master (*Herr*) and servant, in the notion of the lordship (*Herrschaft*) of God or the gods.

22. Compare, however, the opening sentences of Feuerbach's *History of Modern Philosophy from Bacon of Verulam to Benedict Spinoza*, where this aspect of Judaism is treated as generally characteristic of pagan religions: 'The essence of paganism was the unity of religion and politics, of spirit and nature, of God and man. But man as seen by paganism was not simply man, he was man in his national character – the Greek, the Roman, the Egyptian, the Jew; consequently his God was also a national, particular being, or essence opposed to the essence or God of other peoples' (W III, 1). Here the division between pagan and Christian cuts across the division between polytheism and monotheism.

23. This line of Feuerbach's, also suggested by Hegel, became one of the standbys of later nineteenth-century cultural anti-Semitism, being taken up in much anti-Semitic theological writing and in the work of Eugen Dühring (who combined it with a race-theory), Sombart, etc. Karl Marx took up the point in his review of Bauer's pamphlet on the emancipation of the Jews, arguing that the individual Jew could not be emancipated until society was freed from Judaism (i.e., practical egoism, commercial greed): see Eugene Kamenka, *op. cit.*, pp. 53, 60–2, 66. That Feuerbach himself was far from translating what he regarded as a historical matter of fact into a basis for prejudice is quite clear: on Marx's more ambiguous position (Marx was not free of *jüdischer Selbsthass* – Jewish self-hate), see Eugene Kamenka, 'The Baptism of Karl Marx' (1958), LVI, *Hibbert Journal*, pp. 340–51.

24. In *Pierre Bayle* Feuerbach argues that 'Christianity could come into the world only at the time at which it did appear, the time of the down-

fall of the ancient world . . . the time of the downfall of all national distinctions, of all national customary ties . . .' (W V, 154; GW IV, 50). Christianity, in other words, reflects the universalism of the Roman Empire – the emergence of a new and much wider conception of a polity.

25. The distinction between theology and religion, which, as we shall see, is very important for Feuerbach, is partly drawn by him in these terms – theology, which attempts to rationalize the products of the religious fantasy and to treat them as real existences, concentrates on that which is alleged to distinguish God from man; religion is concerned with the content and not the form of the fantasy and therefore emphasizes what is human and real in theistic belief.

26. In a special work, *Regarding the Essence of Faith in Luther's Sense* (1844), Feuerbach argues that it is precisely Luther who, in bringing out the Protestant conception of God, finally makes the true essence of religion manifest: 'Christ exists only in so far as he exists for us . . . God is a word whose meaning is only seen in man', says Luther. My work is as much for Luther as against him, Feuerbach later said of this essay; the contradiction lies in the subject itself (W II, 383).

27. Feuerbach does make it clear that this universalization of man, this transcending of the Old Testament limitations, involves loss as well as gain. The Jewish God, though nationally circumscribed, was worldly and political, the Christian God is unworldly and apolitical.

28. Feuerbach is here putting in genetic form what many philosophers, since Plato's *Euthryphro*, have recognized as a matter of logical analysis, that the phrase 'God is good', for instance, would be meaningless unless goodness could be recognized independently, in a logical sense, of God. Thus the seventeenth-century Cambridge Platonist Ralph Cudworth preached: 'Virtue and holiness in creatures . . . are not therefore good, because God loveth them, and will have them to be accounted such; but rather God therefore loveth them, because they are in themselves simply good' – *First Sermon*, reprinted in Ralph Cudworth's *The True Intellectual System of the Universe etc.*, vol. 4, p. 312, also cited in J. A. Passmore, *Ralph Cudworth*, pp. 83-4, where the source is mistakenly given as the 'Second Sermon'. Feuerbach argues specifically in *Pierre Bayle* (W V, 206-7; GW IV, 100) that God can provide no logical foundation for ethics *as God*; he can only do so as the bearer of an ethical predicate, as a being *that is good*. In that case we would be concerned solely with the predicate, the qualities or characteristics of *being good*; God as God (as the subject) would not enter into the argument at all. Feuerbach, of course, is also going beyond Plato and Cudworth to say we would have no conception of virtue if its elements were not found – empirically – among men, and we would not ascribe it to God if we did not first prize virtue for its own sake, or for man's. He also argues (*Pierre Bayle*, W V, 178-9; GW IV, 74-5) that a religion is not made good, sacred, divine by its religious form, by its projection of certain qualities into an allegedly supernatural person or realm; it is made good, sacred,

divine by the *content* which it projects, by the character it ascribes to God or the Gods. A religion can thus be evil – it could elevate and project vices.

29. Individuality for Feuerbach *is* suffering, the finite is necessarily that which is acted upon.

30. In this conception that the cognitive content of the notion of divinity lies in man's observation of the operation of his own mind, Feuerbach is following out and elaborating (completely unconsciously, it seems) some brilliant suggestions made a century earlier by David Hume. 'When we analyse our thought or ideas, however compounded or sublime, we always find that they resolve themselves into such simple ideas as were copied from a precedent feeling or sentiment. Even those ideas which, at first view, seem most wide of this origin, are found, upon a nearer scrutiny, to be derived from it. The idea of God, as meaning an infinitely intelligent, wise, and good Being, arises from reflecting on the operations of our own mind, and augmenting, without limit, those qualities of goodness and wisdom' – Hume, *Enquiry Concerning Human Understanding*, Section II, in *The Philosophical Works of David Hume*, edited by T. H. Green and T. H. Grose, vol. 4, p. 15. 'The mind rises gradually, from inferior to superior: By abstracting from what is imperfect, it forms an idea of perfection; And slowly distinguishing the nobler parts of its own frame from the grosser, it learns to transfer only the former, much elevated and refined, to its divinity' – Hume, *The Natural History of Religion*, in Green and Grose, vol. 4, p. 311.

31. Cf. Feuerbach writing more than twenty years later: 'Just as the divine being is only the human being thought of in the highest degree of generality and abstraction and therefore a nameless, concealed human being, so the divine will is only the secret, unnamed – but therefore true – will of man, for man confesses his true will only in secret, under the wing and protection of divine authority' (W X, 125).

32. Logically, of course, this does not follow, since Feuerbach has said nothing to show that the *stock* of properties is limited. What he is really relying on is the proclamation of a gulf between man and God, which prevents man from trying to be like God. On this issue, most religious thinkers wanted to have it both ways. Religion, in consequence, has both depressed and elevated man, told him to accept his fallen status and called on him to emulate God's capacity for love, charity, etc. (though never his omnipotence).

33. There is an echo here of Hegel's doctrine that God differs from a tree, in that a tree does not *need* to be known in order to be a tree, while God *needs* to be worshipped to be God. This doctrine, of course, stems back to Luther, as Feuerbach constantly emphasizes.

34. In one place, Feuerbach suggests that there is no truly Christian art precisely because Christianity contains this necessary ambiguity, that for it things are at once natural and divine. Art can portray only that which is true and unambiguous (W II, 228). This theme has been developed by a Soviet writer, E. P. Yakovlev, in his *Esteticheskoe*

chuvstvo i religioznoe perezhivanie (Aesthetic Feeling and Religious Experience).

35. It should be noted, however, that Feuerbach does not use the word *Wesen* in any strict, technical sense; the young Marx, having a much stronger logical bent, used it with far greater philosophical overtones. George Eliot translated it sometimes as 'essence' and sometimes as 'nature'; generally its meaning in Feuerbach is roughly that of 'true or fundamental nature' as opposed to the superficial characteristics, to the mere appearance in which the fundamental and the accidental, peripheral, temporary are not distinguished.

36. 'My work . . .,' Feuerbach writes in the preface to the second edition of the *Essence of Christianity* (EC xliii, W VII, 293), 'contains, and applies in the concrete, the principle of a new philosophy suited – not to the schools, but – to man. Yes, it contains that principle, but only by *evolving* it out of the very core of religion . . .' Feuerbach continually emphasized that his approach to religion was not external, that his principles and method did not precede his religious enquiries, but came to him from the subject-matter itself.

37. This issue is normally confused by such question-begging phrases as 'imperfect understanding'. An understanding can be 'imperfect' only by being partly understanding and partly misunderstanding, partly knowledge and partly error. What is it, in our 'imperfect understanding' of God, that is understanding, that is known 'perfectly', even if mixed with error? It cannot be that 'he' exists, for before we know *what* the 'he' is, we cannot determine whether it exists or not.

38. Here again Feuerbach is unconsciously echoing one of the basic positions put in Hume, which Feuerbach came close to probably indirectly, through the influence of French materialism: 'Nothing is more free than the imagination of man, and though it cannot exceed that original stock of ideas, furnished by the internal and the external senses, it has unlimited power of mixing, compounding, separating and dividing these ideas, in all the varieties of fiction and vision. It can feign a train of events with all the appearance of reality, ascribe to them a particular time and place, conceive them as existent, and paint them out to itself with every circumstance, that belongs to any historical fact, which it believes with the greatest certainty' – Hume, *Enquiry Concerning Human Understanding*, Section V, ii; Green and Grose, vol. 4, pp. 40–1.

39. For an echo of this, consider E.-F. G. Tol', of the Petrashevskii circle, writing to the Decembrist Baten'kov: 'Self-knowledge without knowledge of nature is illusory knowledge, while knowledge of nature will lead directly to self-knowledge. Man's conception of himself has to grow in proportion to the conquest of nature. In the same proportion grows the conception of God. The higher man's conception of himself, the more he will attempt to conquer nature': G. S. Baten'kov *et al.*: *Pis'ma G. S. Baten'kova I. I. Pushchina i E. G. Tolya*, p. 331.

40. Feuerbach would not wish to deny that such empirical reduction of religious conceptions and images may rob them of a certain charm

associated with undispelled mystery – much as naturalistic explana-
tions of the belief in unicorns or dragons may turn what at first
seemed an exciting image into a prosaic one. In the *Fragments*
collected by Feuerbach to illustrate his philosophical development, he
writes (under the heading *1834–6 – Diary*): 'Religion is the first love,
the love of a lad – the love which thinks it will profane its object by
knowing it. Philosophy, in contrast, is married love, the love of a man
which possesses and uses its object, but which admittedly thereby
destroys all the charm and all the illusions connected with the mystery-
mongering of a first love' (W II, 368).

41. As soon as 'creation' is treated as *real* work, as *making* and not imagin-
ing, the notion of 'creation' '*ex nihilo*' becomes an insoluble paradox.

42. It is perfectly simple, however, and undisturbing to Feuerbach's
general line on religion, to expand Feuerbach's hints in this regard
and bring in the social. Deborin tends to do this in his book on
Feuerbach, a book that follows Plekhanov in endeavouring to bridge,
rather than to emphasize, the gap between Feuerbach and Marxism.
Feuerbach's own view would have been that he was bringing out the
fundamental conception – that of *dependence* – which is manifest in all
fields: politics, family relations, etc. Thus in the *Theogony* he recognizes that 'the feeling of awe in relation to the Gods depends on the
feeling of awe in relation to one's parents' (W IX, 291), but this is
because one's parents are to one *divine*, i.e., are that on which one
recognizes one's nature and being ultimately to depend (W IX, 291–
2). Feuerbach did write, in *Pierre Bayle* (W V 132; GW IV, 27):
'Man's estate, occupation influences his way of thinking, his inner
state, his beliefs much more than man himself realizes', and in his
'The Problem of Immortality from the Standpoint of Anthropology'
(1846), he refers to the proletariat as having positive qualities – the
desire for dignity and education and willingness to work (WI, 185n).

43. Feuerbach's reductive method and his belief in the projection of
feelings have had wider influence than in the criticism of religion.
Marx's materialist conception of history, as I have mentioned,
developed out of the Feuerbachian method and Freud's whole
conception of *projection* is quite Feuerbachian in spirit. The psychological use of the word 'projection' in English originated in George
Eliot's translation of the *Essence of Christianity*. She used it to render
Feuerbach's (Hegelian) terms *Vergegenständlichung* (objectification,
reification) and *Entäusserung* (alienation).

44. Delivered at Düsseldorf in September 1965, reprinted in *Survey* (see
bibliography).

45. On this, see the discussion of the Soviet critique of religion in Eugene
Kamenka, *Soviet Philosophy To-Day*. The recent *advance* in Soviet
work on the philosophy of religion is a *going back* from Lenin to
Feuerbach.

46. Clifford Geertz, 'Religion as a Culture System', in Michael Banton
(ed.), *Anthropological Approaches to the Study of Religion*, p. 4.

47. Geertz, *op. cit.*, pp. 8–9.

48. This view, adumbrated by Kant, received further impetus from the neo-Kantian revival in Germany in the 1860s and its studies in the methodology of science. It forms the fundamental theme, of course, of Vaihinger's *The Philosophy of As-If*.
49. S. Langer, *Philosophy in a New Key*, p. 287, cited by Geertz, *op. cit.*, p. 14.

4. LUDWIG FEUERBACH'S CRITIQUE OF PHILOSOPHY

1. Karl Grün, *Ludwig Feuerbachs Philosophie in seinem Briefwechsel und Nachlass*, p. 387.
2. In 1864, walking around Berlin with Heinrich Benecke, Feuerbach stopped outside the well-known wine bar of Lutter and Wegener and said that, as a young student, he had once sat there with Hegel and had endeavoured to formulate to Hegel the objection that parts of the Hegelian philosophy led in a different direction from that adopted by Hegel himself. (Reported in Heinrich Benecke's 'Recollections of Feuerbach', published in the Berlin *Tägliche Rundschau*, Easter, 1890 issue; cf. Rawidowicz, *Ludwig Feuerbachs Philosophie*, p. 15n.) In a letter to his father in 1824 (W XII, 231), Feuerbach emphasized that Hegel's lectures were much clearer than his writings; they were in fact easy to understand because Hegel paid a great deal of attention to the capacities and knowledge of his hearers.
3. This error, according to Feuerbach (W II, 180), stems from the fact that Fichte begins by presupposing the truth of the Kantian philosophy. While Kant was critical in relation to the old metaphysics, he was not critical in relation to himself – i.e. (one presumes) in relation to his conception of the *ego cogitans* and the *ego agens*.
4. Telesius and Campanella endeavoured to reform the study of physical science as Peter Ramus endeavoured to reform the science of logic: J. D. Morell's *Historical and Critical View of the Speculative Philosophy of Europe in the Nineteenth Century* (1846) indeed begins its discussion of the sources of modern philosophy with these names. See Morell, p. 75.
5. Feuerbach, in this place and elsewhere, stresses that empirical investigation also needs to be guided by a philosophical concern with system, organization, universalization, relevance, the 'essence' of things, etc.

> Of course, the empiricism which does not raise itself or seek to raise itself to the level of philosophical thought is a narrow-minded miserable empiricism; but a philosophy which does not descend to the empirical is equally limited (W II, 207).

> Indeed, while empirical enquiry necessarily leads to philosophy, raises philosophical questions which demand an answer, speculative philosophy, when it does raise questions about nature or passes over to it, does so as a matter of caprice, does so quite arbitrarily (W II, 208).

6. Sidney Hook, *From Hegel to Marx*, p. 221.

7. 'Theology is the belief in ghosts. Ordinary theology keeps its ghosts in the sensual imagination, speculative theology, however, in the non-sensory faculty of abstraction' (W II, 227).

PART III. THE 'PHILOSOPHY OF THE FUTURE'

5. FEUERBACH'S 'TRANSFORMATION OF PHILOSOPHY'

1. This criticism foreshadows in an interesting way criticisms that have been made of Marxism and helps to bring out some of the similarities between the Hegelian and the Marxian system. On the theoretical side the claim often made by Marx's disciples that Marxism represented the ultimate culmination of philosophy, social science and science in general did encourage a 'leap out of history', a sharp dualism between the time-bound, class-bound, 'ideological' sciences of the past and the ultimate knowledge that was Marxism. While it was conceded that Marxism could not arise *before* a certain stage (just as Hegel conceded that *his* philosophy could not arise before a certain stage), it was not conceded that Marxism could in turn be 'outgrown', superseded, revealed to be time-bound and subject to fundamental revision or criticism. Similarly, on the practical side, the Marxian belief in Communism as the culmination of human freedom led to a sharp distinction between the temporal stages of the 'pre-history' of mankind, in which social structures replaced one another, and the fundamentally atemporal 'truly human society' in which structural change was excluded. This is not to say, of course, that Marxists believed that there would be *no* change under Communism or that Marxist theory could not be further developed at all – but it is to say that there was a strong tendency to pull Marxian fundamental structure out of history, to distinguish in quite a sharp, logical way between the pre-Marxian stages of society and the Marxian stage as allegedly 'taking up' and superseding all that had gone before without in turn being taken up and superseded itself.

6. FEUERBACH'S METHOD

1. Friedrich Jodl, *Ludwig Feuerbach*, pp. 1–2.
2. Sidney Hook, *From Hegel to Marx*, p. 223.
3. I cite, however, the translation of this passage given by Hook, *op. cit.*, p. 224. Hook, or his printers, mistakenly gave the name of the recipient as 'C. Reidel'.
4. Karl Grün, *Nachlass*, vol. II, p. 191; also cited in Hook, *op. cit.*, pp. 224–5.
5. Nevertheless, a later naturalist – John Dewey – was also quite unable to recognize that philosophers had to face these problems; in over-reaction to Descartes, he simply excluded epistemology from the true philosophical canon altogether.

7. FEUERBACH'S THEORY OF KNOWLEDGE AND HIS 'MATERIALISM'

1. Cited in Friedrich Jodl, *Ludwig Feuerbach*, p. 25.
2. In the *Basic Propositions* (W II, 269), however, Feuerbach made the perceptive point that philosophers align their conceptions of subject and of object, of knower and of known, If, like Descartes, they take the essence of material things to lie in a concept, substance, they then make that which apprehends concepts (understanding and not sense-perception) the essence of man, the knower.
3. This conflation is helped by Feuerbach's constant playing on the *moral* overtones of the word 'truth' (*Wahrheit*), evident in usages like a 'true (or real) man', a 'true State', a 'true friendship', etc. In English these moral overtones have become much weaker than they are in German or Russian. Feuerbach would not have regarded them as moral, but as drawing a distinction between the *nature* of a thing and accretions or distortions.
4. Dorguth's *Kritik des Idealismus und Materialen zur Grundlegung eines apodiktischen Real-Rationalismus*, which defended a reductive materialism and the view that thought is nothing but brain activity, appeared in 1837. Feuerbach's review of it came out in 1838. At that time, as we shall see, Feuerbach decisively rejected its central propositions, but Bolin and Jodl suggest that even then the book strongly influenced Feuerbach, whose later views came to have a much stronger similarity to Dorguth's. A supplement to Dorguth's critique, published by Dorguth in 1838, first drew Feuerbach's attention to Schopenhauer, whose follower Dorguth was to become (see Bolin and Jodl's editorial note, W II, 131n).
5. I cite, with a slight emendation, the translation in Hook, *op. cit.*, pp. 266–7.
6. Later, in the *Basic Propositions* (W II, 278–9), he was to attack this 'advance' of Kant's by arguing that Kant viciously separated essence from existence by putting existence (mere appearance) in the realm of sense-perception and essence (concepts) into the field of understanding. The result was that things in themselves (*noumena*) can be thought, but do not exist for us. Feuerbach recognized correctly that this 'contradiction' was overcome only in an illusory way in the Philosophy of Identity, which made thought the only reality, but in so far as Feuerbach seemed to be suggesting that the contradiction must be overcome in a real way, it is quite unclear in what way his philosophy does so.
7. This view, deriving from Hegel, was still shared by the older Marx, let alone young Marx. Compare Marx's famous sentence in *Capital*: 'If the appearance of things were identical with their essence, all science would be superfluous.'
8. Hook, *op. cit.*, p. 231n.
9. Plekhanov and his pupil A. M. Deborin, who became in the late 1920s the leading philosophical representative of Soviet dialectical

materialism, were responsible for the fact that the Feuerbachian contribution to epistemology was taken seriously in Russia. It was not, on the whole, taken seriously anywhere else. Lenin clearly departed from it in the direction of a simple Lockean representationism (Lenin's copy-theory of knowledge) and after the official condemnation of Deborin in 1931, the copy-theory or the theory of reflection became official Soviet dogma. On this, and on recent attempts in the Soviet Union to interpret 'reflection' in a more sophisticated way that will avoid the notorious difficulties of Lockean representationism, see T. J. Blakeley, *Soviet Theory of Knowledge, passim*, and the discussion of recent Soviet writing on epistemology in Eugene Kamenka, *Soviet Philosophy To-Day*.

10. Feuerbach here inserted a footnote: 'the reviewer uses the word idealism in a very general sense'; at this stage Feuerbach still called himself an idealist in the special sense of one who believes in the specific and qualitatively independent reality and force of ideas. He used the word idealism in the same sense in the preface to the second edition of the *Essence of Christianity*, to indicate that he believed in *ideals* and *ideas*. But he did not believe that ideas *constituted* reality; he was not an idealist in the normal philosophical sense.

11. Hook, *op. cit.*, pp. 267, 271.

12. As our discussion of Feuerbach's ethics in chapter 9 will show, in an extravagant way Feuerbach was simply putting what was to become one of the main points made by social democrats and welfare workers generally, that 'decent living-conditions' are not only good in themselves but are in general terms conducive to the exercise and formation of what moralists consider 'the virtues' or, alternatively, that the absence of decent living-conditions is generally destructive of them. Taken for its intrinsic features, Feuerbach's medical materialism is far too crude to be any longer interesting (so, indeed, was Moleschott's), but in so far as they both insisted that there was an important relation between body chemistry, emotion and thought, they were right. The point about medical materialism is not to laugh at it, but to see what its findings amount to.

8. FEUERBACH'S CONCEPT OF MAN

1. In the *Essence of Christianity*, Feuerbach explained:

   The obtuse Materialist says: 'Man is distinguished from the brute *only* by consciousness – he is an animal with consciousness superadded; not reflecting, that in a being which awakes to consciousness, there takes place a qualitative change, a differentiation of the entire nature' (EC 3n; W VI, 3n).

2. Marx, 'Towards the Critique of Hegel's *Philosophy of Right:* Introduction', published in the *Deutsch-französische Jahrbücher* in 1844: *Marx-Engels Gesamtausgabe*, Section I, Vol. I–i, pp. 614–15; cf.

Eugene Kamenka, *The Ethical Foundations of Marxism*, p. 30. Feuerbach declined Marx's and Ruge's repeated invitations to contribute to the *Jahrbücher* himself.

3. Marx, 'On the Jewish Question', also published in the *D-f J.: Marx-Engels Gesamtausgabe*, Section I, Vol. I–i, p. 599; Kamenka, *op. cit.*, p. 56.

4. Marx, in the exchange of letters between Bakunin, Ruge and Marx published under the heading 'Correspondence of 1843' in the *D-f J.: Marx-Engels Gesamtausgabe*, Section I, Vol. I–i, p. 561; Kamenka, *op. cit.*, p. 30.

5. See Kamenka, *op. cit.*, pp. 74–81, and Kamenka, *Marxism and Ethics*, pp. 8–30.

6. In the article 'The Communism of the Rheinischer Beobachter' (12 September 1847), *Marx-Engels Gesamtausgabe*, Section I, Vol. 6, p. 278; Kamenka, *op. cit.*, p. 29.

7. 'The British Rule in India', published on 25 June 1853, reprinted in *Marx and Engels on Britain*, pp. 383–4. 'Kanuman' for the monkey-god *Hanuman* appears in the original.

9. FEUERBACH'S ETHICS

1. Marx was thus developing one of Feuerbach's insights when he argued that Robinson Crusoe was a possible and intelligible figure only because he had been a member of a society before he became a castaway: the solitary individual who had never been anything but a solitary individual would not be intelligibly human.

2. J. Schaller, *Darstellung und Kritik der Philosophie L. Feuerbachs* (1847); cf. also A. Kohut, *Ludwig Feuerbach: sein Leben und seine Werke*, pp. 402–3; where Kohut, following Max Heinze's revised edition of Ueberweg's history of nineteenth-century philosophy, represents Feuerbach as pitting 'egoism' against theology. For the view presented by me here, cf. Lange, *History of Materialism*, vol. II, pp. 254–6, though Lange, using the word 'egoism' somewhat conventionally, takes the view that Feuerbach, under the influence of Holbach, relapsed into an inconsistent ethical egoism in his later work.

3. E.g., Sidney Hook, *From Hegel to Marx*, p. 252.

4. EC 245–6; in the third edition of the *Essence*, that given in the Bolin and Jodl edition of the *Collected Works*, it became the twenty-seventh chapter (W VI, 298–325), and underwent slight changes, not significant for our purpose.

5. The early Feuerbach (and presumably still the later) wanted to treat man as a 'loving' being without undermining the concept of man as a rational being. 'The only limitation which is not contradictory to the nature of love', he writes in a footnote (EC 262; W VI, 319), 'is the self-limitation of love by reason, intelligence. The love which despises the stringency, the law, of the intelligence, is theoretically false and practically obnoxious.' Irrational love, according to Feuerbach, is not

real love: or as Feuerbach might have put it, love which cannot afford to know, which requires *illusions* in order to love, is not true or stable love.

6. Feuerbach's discussion is somewhat simplified by the fact that the verbal form of the word 'will' (*Wille*) in German means 'to want' and that there is no natural way in German of distinguishing 'willing' from 'wanting'. Feuerbach has in any case no doubt, that 'the will' can only be understood as a form or modification of drives or desires; he refers with approval to the orthodox doctrine of pre-Kantian philosophy that the will is 'rational desire', i.e., sensuous desire informed by knowledge. The bare sensuous desire, in Feuerbach's view, strives towards a particular object known in sensation only as a particular: 'the will' as rational desire strives towards an object which it recognizes and seeks as a 'concept', as a 'species-thing' (W X, 107). Feuerbach's line here is that the senses give us particulars while reason provides 'concepts' and universality; the will is rational in being determined by concepts and not mere particulars. In that sense, and *only* in that limited sense, can the will be supra-sensual. This whole line of argument will hardly commend itself to philosophers today: the concept of will is not adequately analysed in Feuerbach and the dualism of 'facts' given by sensation and 'concepts' given by the understanding (though still frequently proclaimed by philosophers) is in the end insupportable. But the reader will note that we here find Feuerbach's nominalism persisting, side by side with his realism, into the 1860s.

7. Thus, according to Feuerbach (W X, 115), Kant is right when he says, 'good or evil always denotes a reference to the will and to actions', but wrong when he adds 'and not to the feelings of a person'. It does have such reference, too, not in relation to the person acting, but in relation to the person being acted upon. In deciding what is good and bad we cannot ignore the feeling-state of the sufferer.

> He who destroys inanimate things only in order to prove the freedom of his will is a wanton fellow; but he who allows himself this freedom in relation to things that feel, without finding in their expressions of pain the pangs of conscience of his own drive to happiness, is a villain. The degree of misery therefore determines the degree of wickedness, just as, conversely, the degree of well-being determines the degree of goodness in the doer and the degree of indebtedness in the recipient.

8. The traditional 'duties toward oneself' (e.g., cleanliness); which often conflict with one's inclination at a given moment, Feuerbach regards as an example of the latter situation. These duties are patently 'nothing but rules of conduct for the maintenance or the achievement of bodily and spiritual health originating in the drive for happiness, derived from the experience of their agreement with the weal and nature of man, abstracted from happy, normal healthy men and set up as models to be followed, in case of sickness . . .' (W X, 259).

9. Here we have most interestingly an argument often met with today:

the argument that any non-utilitarian morality can become arbitrary
and despotic, that only utilitarianism provides public criteria for checking the lusts of madness of moral tyrants by building in a reference to
the importance of what others *actually* want.

10 Feuerbach is thus in a position to answer Kant's claim that the difference between the drive for happiness and the moral drive is illustrated
by the difference between feeling self-pity for losing at play and self-
contempt for having cheated at play. Feuerbach argues (W X, 119)
that cheating *is* condemned on the basis of the drive to happiness: I
imagine *my* feelings if *I* had been cheated. The voice of conscience is an
echo of the cry of vengeance of the cheated. Conscience is not the
voice of a supernatural being, but of a human being who avenges.

11. Feuerbach does not go at all into the question whether morality is
concerned with actions (in which case *how* or *why* they are done would
be irrelevant) or with motives (in which case intention and consciousness would be relevant even on his eudaemonist position). To have
considered this question would have made his position more complex
and less immediately persuasive; in fact, he vacillates between the two
alternatives as it suits him.

12. On this basis, Feuerbach now argues that the so-called 'duties toward
oneself' have moral value only in so far as they are recognized as
indirect duties towards my family, my nation, etc. 'One is good only
when one is good to others' (W X, 270).

13. There are, in these propositions, the materials for a Freudian or
neo-Freudian account of morality as linked with the seeking of love
and the avoidance of hate (withdrawal): cf. Ian Suttie, *The Origins of
Love and Hate*.

14. Feuerbach here refers to the just published original (1867) German
edition of volume I of Karl Marx's *Capital* as containing a rich but
gruesome collection of facts illustrating that in English factory
conditions, only the factory-owner can be moral. 'When one lacks the
necessities of life, moral necessity is also wanting' (W X, 267).

15. Feuerbach had already adumbrated this view in the *Theogony* (W IX,
225): 'The laws which the gods give, like those which men make, are
only pious wishes' – which is why they are so often broken.

16. The imputation of free will to the law-breaker, Feuerbach argues
(W X, 141), rests on the sameness of human nature, but ignores the
particular (and determined) character of each man, the particular
circumstances that made this particular man unlike his fellows and a
law-breaker. What I can do, thinks the common man, that the other,
too, can do. 'I, Titus, do not steal, but Caius ... Caius, however, is a man
like me, therefore he can and should not steal, just as I do not.'

17. For a discussion of this view in relation to the young Marx's critique
of law, and to jurisprudence generally, see Eugene Kamenka and
Alice Erh-Soon Tay, *Marxism and the Theory of Law*, chapters II and
III. The later Feuerbach stands half-way between the young Marx and
Bentham, as the two parts of his sentence (one Hegelian, one
Benthamite) indicate.

18. Cf. P. H. Nowell-Smith, *Ethics*, p. 135.
19. Gilbert Ryle, *Dilemmas*, IV, pp. 54–67.
20. Feuerbach's account of such desires is in many respects very muddled. His attempt to derive drives from avoidance rather than seeking is not worked-out and involves a number of logical difficulties; he himself does not adhere to it consistently, as we see in what follows.
21. The qualification 'healthy' is significant. Feuerbach, one suspects, is aware of masochistic drives to self-destruction, abnegation, self-abasement, and somewhat worried about them. He is quite prepared to argue that the suicide and the Buddhist longing for Nirvana (W X, 243) are actuated by the drive for happiness, i.e., are seeking to remove pain and suffering. But what of those who delight in the suffering for its own sake? Here, instead of saying 'that is their pleasure', and thus bringing out that 'pleasure' has a special meaning for him, or instead of saying 'this satisfied some of their drives even if at the expense of others', Feuerbach feels the need to say – 'they are sick'. Behind this, of course, is a theory of the coherence of drives which Feuerbach assumes, but does not examine sufficiently.
22. It is interesting and confirms our point about Feuerbach's rejection of the 'abstract idea' of happiness, that Feuerbach's distinction – only alluded to in passing – is in terms of the *drives* involved and not in terms of the *states of satisfaction*, as it is in J. S. Mill. Feuerbach compares drives and needs, Bentham and Mill compare 'pleasures'.
23. I have attempted to sketch this approach to ethics, based on the work of the late John Anderson, in Kamenka, *The Ethical Foundations of Marxism*, pp. 89–117.
24. See R. M. Hare, *The Language of Morals*, esp. pp. 187f.
25. This line, in a different terminology, was adopted by Urmson in his well-known article, 'On Grading', in A. G. N. Flew (ed.), *Logic and Language (Second Series)*, pp. 159 et seq., esp. p. 184.

POSTSCRIPT

10. IN PLACE OF A CONCLUSION

1. This is not to say that the network of empirical philosophy on the Continent of Europe, which Hitler succeeded in destroying in the late 1930s, should be rebuilt through a study of Feuerbach. Feuerbach's *current* influence on Continental thinkers is primarily in an obscurantist, anti-empirical direction; it is helping to strengthen the false view that 'man' is the central problem of philosophy. German culture needs a thinker like Karl Popper more than it needs a revival of Feuerbach or, for that matter, of Wittgenstein.

BIBLIOGRAPHY

A. FEUERBACH'S WRITINGS, CHRONOLOGICALLY ARRANGED

De ratione, una, universali, infinita [*Of Reason, One, Universal, Infinite*]. Dissertatio inauguralis philosophica Auctore L. A. Feuerbach, phil. Doct. Erlangae 1828. Nuremberg, Stein, 1828.

Gedanken über Tod und Unsterblichkeit, aus den Papieren eines Denkers, nebst Anhang theologisch-satyrischer Xenien, hrsg. von einem seiner Freunde [*Thoughts on Death and Immortality, from the Papers of a Thinker, together with an Appendix of Theological-Satirical Verses,* published by One of his Friends]. Nuremberg. Stein, 1830 (published anonymously).

Geschichte der neueren Philosophie: von Bacon von Verulam bis Benedikt Spinoza [*History of Modern Philosophy: from Bacon of Verulam to Benedict Spinoza*]. Ansbach, Brügel, 1833. Second edition, 1844; (third) revised edition as Volume IV of Feuerbach's *Collected Works,* 1847.

Abälard und Heloise, oder Der Schriftsteller und der Mensch. Eine Reihe humoristisch-philosophischer Aphorismen [*Abelard and Heloise or The Author and the Man. A Series of Humorous-Philosophical Aphorisms*]. Ansbach, Brügel, 1834. Second edition, Leipzig, O. Wigand, 1844.

'Rezension über Karl Rosenkranz, *Hegel.* Sendschreiben an Herrn Dr C. F. Bachmann, Königsberg, 1834' ['Review of Karl Rosenkranz, *Hegel.* Letter to Dr. C. F. Bachmann, Königsberg, 1834']. In *Jahrbücher für wissenschaftliche Kritik,* 1835, Part I, pp. 521ff.

'Kritik der christlichen Rechts – und Staatslehre' ['Critique of the Christian View of State and Law' – a review of F. J. Stahl's *Die Philosophie des Rechts nach geschichtlicher Ansicht,* 1833]. In *Jahrbücher für wissenschaftliche Kritik,* 1835, Part II, pp. 1ff.

'Über Hegels Vorlesungen zur Geschichte der Philosophie' ['On Hegel's Lectures on the History of Philosophy']. In von Henning (ed.), *Jahrbücher für wissenschaftliche Kritik,* 1835, Part II, pp. 369ff.

'Kritik des "Antihegel". Zur Einleitung in das Studium der Philosophie' ['Critique of "Anti-Hegel". An Introduction to the Study of Philosophy']. Ansbach, 1835. Second edition, 1844.

Review of J. Kuhn, *Jakobi und die Philosophie seiner Zeit,* 1834. In *Jahrbücher für wissenschaftliche Kritik,* 1835, pp. 729ff.

'Zwei Schriften über Descartes' ['Two Books on Descartes' – Review of J. E. Erdmann, *Geschichte der neueren Philosophie,* 1. Band, 1. Abt., 1834 and C. F. Hock, *Cartesius und seine Gegner,* 1835]. In *Jahrbücher für wissenschaftliche Kritik,* 1836, Part I, pp. 573ff.

Geschichte der neueren Philosophie. Darstellung, Entwicklung und Kritik der Leibnitz'schen Philosophie [*History of Modern Philosophy. Exposition, Discussion and Criticism of the Leibnizian Philosophy*], Ansbach, Brügel, and Leipzig, Herbig, 1837. Second edition, 1844.

Pierre Bayle, nach seinen für die Geschichte der Philosophie und Menschheit interessantesten Momenten dargestellt und gewürdigt [*Pierre Bayle, Expounded and Honoured in the Light of What is Most Interesting in Him for the History of Philosophy and Humanity*], Ansbach, Brügel, 1838. Second, unchanged, edition, 1844; (third) revised edition as volume VI of Feuerbach's *Collected Works*, 1848.

Review of K. Bayer, *Die Idee der Freiheit und der Begriff des Gedankens*, 1837. In Arnold Ruge and Th. Echtermeyer (eds), *Hallische Jahrbücher für deutsche Wissenschaft und Kunst*, Leipzig, 1838, pp. 46ff.

Review of J. E. Erdmann, *Geschichte der neueren Philosophie*, 1. Band, 2. Abt. In *Jahrbücher für wissenschaftliche Kritik*, 1838, Part I, pp. 534f.

'Zur Kritik des Empirismus' ['Toward the Critique of Empiricism': Review of F. Dorguth, *Kritik des Idealismus und Materialen zur Grundlegung eines apodiktischen Real-Rationalismus*, 1837]. In *Hallische Jahrbücher für deutsche Wissenschaft und Kunst*, 1838, pp. 582ff.

'Zur Kritik der "positiven Philosophie" ' ['Toward the Critique of the "Positive Philosophy" ': Review of J. Sengler, *Über das Wesen und die Bedeutung der spekulativen Philosophie und Theologie in der gegenwärtigen Zeit*, 1837]. In *Hallische Jahrbücher für deutsche Wissenschaft und Kunst*, 1838, pp. 2305ff (published without signature).

'Brief an Riedel' ['Letter to Riedel']. In *Athenäum für Wissenschaft, Kunst und Leben*, Nuremberg, 1839, vol. II.

'Dr Chr. Kapp und seine literarische Leistungen' ['Dr Chr(istian) Kapp and His Literary Achievements']. In *Hallische Jahrbücher für deutsche Wissenschaft und Kunst*, 1839, pp. 2369ff.

'Zur Kritik der Hegelschen Philosophie' ['Contribution to the Critique of Hegelian Philosophy']. In *Hallische Jahrbücher für deutsche Wissenschaft und Kunst*, 1839, pp. 1657ff.

Über Philosophie und Christentum in Beziehung auf den der Hegel'schen Philosophie gemachten Vorwurf der Unchristlichkeit [*On Philosophy and Christianity in Reference to the Accusation Made Against the Hegelian Philosophy, That It is Unchristian*], Mannheim, Hoff, 1839. Part I of this work appeared, under a separate title, in the *Hallische Jahrbücher für deutsche Wissenschaft und Kunst*, 1839, pp. 481f.

'Über das Wunder' ['On Miracles']. In *Athenäum für Wissenschaft, Kunst und Leben*, 1839, vol. II.

Review of Karl Bayer, *Betrachtungen über den Begriff des sittlichen Geistes und über das Wesen der Tugend*, 1839. In *Hallische Jahrbücher für deutsche Wissenschaft und Kunst*, 1840, p. 676, signed only 'von . . . ch'.

'E. C. J. Lützelbergers Schriften zur Bibelkritik' [' E. C. J. Lützelberger's Writings on Biblical Criticism': Review of Lützelberger, *Grundzüge der paulinischen Glaubenslehre*, 1839, and the same author's *Die kirchliche Tradition über den Apostel Johannes und seine Schriften, in ihrer Grundlosigkeit nachgewiesen*]. In *Hallische Jahrbücher für deutsche Wissenschaft und Kunst*, 1840, pp. 1841ff, published anonymously.

'Kritik der christlichen Medizin' ['A Critique of Christian Medicine': Review of J. N. Ringseis, *System der Medizin*]. In *Hallische Jahrbücher für deutsche Wissenschaft und Kunst*, 1841, pp. 521ff, no signature.

Review of J. F. Reiff, *Der Anfang der Philosophie*, 1840. In Arnold Ruge (ed.), *Deutsche Jahrbücher für Wissenschaft und Kunst*, Dresden, 1841, pp. 597ff.

Das Wesen des Christentums [*The Essence of Christianity*], Leipzig, Otto Wigand, 1841. Second, revised edition, Leipzig, 1843; Third, revised edition, Leipzig, 1849 (as volume VII of the *Collected Works*).

'Beleuchtung in den Theologischen Studien und Kritiken (Jg. 1842, 1. Heft) enthaltenen Rezension meiner Schrift: *Das Wesen des Christentums*' ['An Examination of the Review of my Book, *The Essence of Christianity*, contained in the *Theologischen Studien und Kritiken*, 1842, Part I']. In *Deutsche Jahrbücher für Wissenschaft und Kunst*, 1842, pp. 65ff.

'Zur Beurteilung der Schrift: *Das Wesen des Christentums*' ['Toward The Evaluation of the Book: *The Essence of Christianity*']. In *Deutsche Jahrbücher für Wissenschaft und Kunst*, 1842, pp. 153ff.

'Über den Marienkultus' ['Concerning the Cult of Mary': Review of *Die Glorie der heiligen Jungfrau Maria*, a collection of legends and poems on this theme by Eusebius Emmeran, 1841]. In *Deutsche Jahrbücher für Wissenschaft und Kunst*, 1842, pp. 37ff, signed 'Anti-People'.

Grundsätze der Philosophie der Zukunft [*Basic Propositions of the Philosophy of the Future*], Zurich and Winterthur, 1843.

Vorläufige Thesen zur Reform der Philosophie [*Preliminary Theses for the Reform of Philosophy*]. In Arnold Ruge et al., *Anekdota zur neuesten deutschen Philosophie und Publizistik*, Part II, Zurich, 1843, pp. 62ff.

Das Wesen des Glaubens im Sinne Luthers, ein Beitrag zum: 'Wesen des Christentums' [*The Essence of Faith in Luther's Sense, A Supplement to the 'Essence of Christianity'*], Leipzig, O. Wigand, 1844; second edition, Leipzig, 1855.

Das Wesen des Christentums in Beziehung Auf den 'Einzigen und sein Eigentum' [*'The Essence of Christianity' with Reference to 'The Ego and Its Own'*]. In *Wigands Vierteljahrsschrift*, Leipzig, 1845.

Das Wesen der Religion [*The Essence of Religion*]. In *Die Epigonen*, Vol. 5, part 1, Leipzig, 1846.

Sämtliche Werke. Band I: Erläuterungen und Ergänzungen zum Wesen des Christentums [*Collected Works, Volume I: Discussions and Supplementary Material to the 'Essence of Christianity'*], Leipzig, O. Wigand, 1846.

Sämtliche Werke, Band II: Philosophische Kritiken und Grundsätze [*Collected Works, Volume II: Philosophical Critiques and Basic Propositions*], Leipzig, O. Wigand, 1846.

Sämtliche Werke, Band III: Gedanken über Tod und Unsterblichkeit [*Collected Works, Volume III: Thoughts on Death and Immortality*], Leipzig, O. Wigand, 1847.

Sämtliche Werke, Band IV: Geschichte der neueren Philosophie von Bacon von Verulam bis Benedikt Spinoza [*Collected Works, Volume IV: A History of Philosophy from Bacon of Verulam to Benedict Spinoza*], Leipzig, O. Wigand, 1847.

Sämtliche Werke, Band V: Darstellung, Entwicklung und Kritik der Leibnitz'schen Philosophie [*Collected Works, Volume V: An Exposition,*

Development and Criticism of the Leibnizian Philosophy, Leipzig, O. Wigand, 1848.

Sämtliche Werke, Band VI: Pierre Bayle, nach seinen für die Geschichte der Philosophie und Menschheit interessantesten Momenten dargestellt und gewürdigt [Collected Works, Volume VI: Pierre Bayle, Expounded and Honoured in the Light of What is Most Interesting in Him for the History of Philosophy and Humanity], Leipzig, O. Wigand, 1848, 'second revised and expanded edition'.

Entgegnung an R. Haym [Reply to R. Haym]. In *Die Epigonen*, Vol. 5, Leipzig, 1848.

Sämtliche Werke, Band VII: Das Wesen des Christentums [Collected Works, Volume VII: The Essence of Christianity], Leipzig, 1849, 'third revised and expanded edition'.

'Die Naturwissenschaft und Die Revolution' ['Natural Science and the Revolution': Review of Moleschott, *Lehre der Nahrungsmittel*, 1850]. In *Blätter für literarische Unterhaltung*, Leipzig, 1850, pp. 268ff.

Sämtliche Werke, Band VIII: Vorlesungen über das Wesen der Religion, nebst Zusätzen und Anmerkungen [Collected Works, Volume VIII: Lectures on the Essence of Religion, with Notes and Addenda], Leipzig, O. Wigand, 1851.

Sämtliche Werke, Band IX: Theogonie nach den Quellen des classischen, hebräischen und christlichen Altertums [Collected Works, Volume IX: Theogony, According to Sources in Classical, Hebrew and Christian Antiquity], Leipzig, O. Wigand, 1857.

'Dr F. W. Heidenreich'. In *Das Jahrhundert*, Hamburg, 1858, No. 27.

'Spiritualismus und Sensualismus' ['Spiritualism and Sensualism': Review of L. Knapp, *System der Rechtsphilosophie*, 1857]. In *Das Jahrhundert*, 1858, no. 26.

Sämtliche Werke, Band X: Gott, Freiheit und Unsterblichkeit vom Standpunkte der Anthropologie [Collected Works, Volume X: God, Freedom and Immortality from the Standpoint of Anthropology]. Leipzig, O. Wigand, 1866.

After Ludwig Feuerbach's death, some remaining manuscripts and letters were published for the first time in the following:

Grün, Karl: *Ludwig Feuerbachs philosophische Characterentwicklung, Sein Briefwechsel und Nachlass*. Two volumes in one. Leipzig and Heidelberg, C. F. Winter, 1874.

Kapp, August: *Briefwechsel zwischen Ludwig Feuerbach und Christian Kapp*. Leipzig, 1876.

Bolin, Wilhelm and Jodl, Friedrich (eds): *Ludwig Feuerbachs Sämtliche Werke*. Volumes I–X, Stuttgart, Fromann Verlag Günther Holzboog, 1903–11.

Bolin, Wilhelm: *Ausgewählte Briefe von und an Ludwig Feuerbach*. Volumes I and II, Leipzig, 1904.

Herwegh, Marcel and Fleury, Victor: 'Briefwechsel Georg und Emma Herweghs mit Ludwig Feuerbach'. In *Nord und Süd*, 1909, volume 188/9 (Berlin).

Kohut, Adolf: *Ludwig Feuerbach, sein Leben und seine Werke*, Leipzig, F. Eckardt, 1909.

IN ENGLISH

The following English translations of Feuerbach have been published:

The Essence of Christianity, translated from the second German edition by Marian Evans [George Eliot]. London, Chapman's Quarterly Series, vol. 6, 1854, reprinted London, Kegan Paul, 1874, New York, Harper & Row, 1957.

The Essence of Religion, translated [and abridged] by Alexander Loos, New York, A. K. Butts & Co., 1873.

Principles of the Philosophy of the Future, translated and with an introduction by Manfred H. Vogel, Indianapolis, Bobbs-Merrill, 1966.

The Essence of Faith According to Luther, translated by Melvin Cherno, New York, Harper & Row, 1967.

Lectures on the Essence of Religion, translated by Ralph Manheim, New York, Harper & Row, 1967.

B. EDITIONS OF FEUERBACH'S WORK CITED
IN THE TEXT

Feuerbach, Ludwig: *Sämtliche Werke*. Volumes I–XII/XIII (13 volumes in 12), Stuttgart-Bad Canstatt, Fromann Verlag Günther Holzboog, 1960–4. Volumes I to X are a photographic reprint of the Bolin and Jodl edition of Feuerbach's work in 1903–11 (listed above); volume XI contains photographic reprints of Feuerbach's original (1830) version of the *Thoughts on Death and Immortality* and of the Latin original of his inaugural dissertation, together with a table of dates of his life, a biography of Feuerbach's works, and a biography of all publications on Feuerbach in German from 1833 to 1961, arranged by Hans-Martin Sass; volumes XII/XIII are an expanded version of Bolin's edition of Feuerbach's letters (listed above), with Bolin's memoirs and additional letters included by Hans-Martin Sass.

Feuerbach, Ludwig: *Gesammelte Werke*. Projected in 16 volumes, under the editorship of Werner Schuffenhauer, by the Academie-Verlag, Berlin. At the time of writing, Volume 4, *Pierre Bayle*, Berlin, 1967 and Volume 6, *Vorlesungen über das Wesen der Religion*, Berlin, 1967, had been published; three further volumes have appeared since.

Feuerbach, Ludwig: *The Essence of Christianity*, translated from the German by George Eliot [Marian Evans], New York, Harper and Row, 1957 (f.p. London, 1854).

C. OTHER WORKS CITED

Annenkov, P. V.: *Literaturnye vospominaniya*, Moscow, Gospolitizdat, 1960.

Banton, Michael (ed.), *Anthropological Approaches to the Study of Religion*, A.S.A. monograph No. 3, London, Tavistock, 1966.

Baten'kov, G. S. *et al.: Pis`ma G. S. Baten'kova, I. I. Pushchina i E. G. Tolya*, Moscow, 1936.

Blakeley, T. J.: *Soviet Theory of Knowledge*, Dordrecht, Reidel, 1964.

Bolin, Wilhelm: *Ludwig Feuerbach, sein Wirken und seine Zeitgenossen*, Stuttgart, 1891.

Chamberlain, W.: *Heaven Wasn't His Destination*, London, Allen & Unwin, 1941.

Cudworth, Ralph: *The True Intellectual System of the Universe, etc.*, ed. by T. Birch, Vols I–IV, London, Richard Priestley, 1820.

Deborin, A. M.: *Ludvig Feierbakh*, Moscow-Leningrad, Gosizdat, 1929.

Durkheim, Emile: *The Elementary Forms of the Religious Life*, translated by Joseph Ward Swain, London, Allen & Unwin, 1964 (first impression, 1915).

Engels, Friedrich: *Ludwig Feuerbach and the Outcome of Classical German Philosophy*, London, M. Lawrence, 1934.

Evgrafova, V. E. (ed.): *Filosofskie i obshchestvenno-politicheskie proizvedeniya petrashevtsev*, Moscow, Gospolitizdat, 1953.

Flew, A. G. N. (ed.): *Logic and Language (Second Series)*, Oxford, Basil Blackwell, 1953.

Grün, Karl: *Ludwig Feuerbachs philosophische Charakterentwicklung etc.*, see above (p. 179).

Grünhut, Max: *Anselm von Feuerbach und das Problem der strafrechtlichen Zurechnung*, Hamburg, W. Gente, 1922.

Hare, R. M.: *The Language of Morals*, Oxford, Clarendon Press, 1952.

Heller, Erich: *The Disinherited Mind*, London, Penguin Books, 1961.

Hook, Sidney: *From Hegel to Marx: Studies in the Intellectual Development of Karl Marx*, London, Gollancz, 1936; Ann Arbor, University of Michigan Press, 1962 (the reprint contains a new introduction, but keeps the same pagination for the text as the Gollancz edition).

Hume, David: *The Philosophical Works of David Hume*, vols I–IV, edited by T. H. Green and T. H. Grose, London, Longmans, 1875.

Jodl, Friedrich: *Ludwig Feuerbach*, second revised edition, Stuttgart, Fromanns Verlag, 1921.

Kamenka, Eugene: *The Ethical Foundations of Marxism*, London, Routledge & Kegan Paul, New York, Frederick Praeger, 1962.

Kamenka, Eugene: *Marxism and Ethics*, London, Macmillan & Co., 1969.

Kamenka, Eugene: *Soviet Philosophy To-Day*, London and New York, 1971 (forthcoming).

Kamenka, Eugene and Tay, Alice Erh-Soon, *Marxism and the Theory of Law*, London and New York, 1970 (forthcoming).
Kohut, A.: *Ludwig Feuerbach: sein Leben und seine Werke*, Leipzig, F. Eckardt, 1909.
Lange, Friedrich Albert: *The History of Materialism*, London, Routledge & Kegan Paul, 1950.
Langer, Susanne K.: *Philosophy in a New Key*, New York, Mento, 1948.
Lavrov, P. L.: *Filosofiya i sotsiologiya – izbrannye proizvedeniya v dvukh tomakh*, Moscow, Mysl', 1965.
Löwith, Karl: *From Hegel to Nietzsche – The Revolution in Nineteenth Century Thought*, transl. from the German by David E. Green, London, Constable, 1965.
Lovejoy, Arthur O.: *The Great Chain of Being*, New York, Harper, 1960.
Lubac, Henri de, S. J.: *The Drama of Atheist Humanism*, transl. from the French by Edith M. Riley, London, Sheed and Ward, 1949.
Lukács, Georg: *Goethe and His Age*, transl. by Roger Anchor, London, Merlin Press, 1968.
Marcuse, Herbert: *Eros and Civilization – A Philosophical Enquiry into Freud*, London, Routledge & Kegan Paul, 1956.
Marsak, Leonard M. (ed.): *French Philosophers from Descartes to Sartre*, Cleveland, Meridian Books, 1961.
Marx, Karl: *Capital – A Critique of Political Economy*, vols I–III, transl. by Samuel Moore and Edward Aveling, Chicago, Charles H. Kerr & Co., 1912.
Marx-Engels Gesamtausgabe, ed. Marx-Engels Institute, Moscow; Frankfurt, A. M., 1927f, Section I, vols 1–i and 1–ii, 2–7, Section III, vols 1–4.
Marx-Engels *Werke*, vols I–XXXIX, plus index volume and two supplementary volumes (unnumbered), Berlin, Dietz, 1956–68.
Marx and Engels on Britain, Moscow, Foreign Languages Publishing House, 1953.
Morell, J. D.: *An Historical and Critical View of the Speculative Philosophy of Europe in the Nineteenth Century*, vols I and II, London, William Pickering, 1846.
Nowell-Smith, P. H.: *Ethics*, London, Penguin Books, 1954.
Passmore, J. A.: *Philosophical Reasoning*, London, Duckworth, 1961.
Passmore, J. A.: *Ralph Cudworth*, Cambridge U.P., 1951.
Peursen, C. A. van: *Body, Soul, Spirit: A Survey of the Body-Mind Problem*, London, Oxford U.P., 1966.
Radbruch, Gustav: *Paul Johann Anselm Feuerbach – Ein Juristenleben*, Vienna, Julius Springer, 1934.
Rawidowicz, S.: *Ludwig Feuerbachs Philosophie – Ursprung und Schicksal*, Berlin, Reuther und Reichard, 1931; photographic reprint, Berlin, Walter de Gruyter, 1964.
Renan, Ernest: *Études d'histoire religieuse*, second edition, Paris, Lévy frères, 1857; authorized English translation, *Studies in Religious History*, London, Bentley, 1886.
Ryle, Gilbert: *Dilemmas*, Cambridge U.P., 1954.

Schaller, J.: *Darstellung und Kritik der Philosophie L. Feuerbachs*, Leipzig, Geibel, 1847.
Schuffenhauer, Werner: *Feuerbach und der junge Marx*, Berlin, Verlag der Wissenschaften, 1965.
Strauss, David Friedrich: *Ausgewählte Briefe*, Bonn, 1874.
Tsameryan, I. P. *et al.* (eds): *Osnovy nauchnogo ateizma*, Moscow, Gospolitizdat, 1961.
Vaihinger, Hans: *The Philosophy of As-If*, translated by C. K. Ogden, London, Routledge & Kegan Paul, 1949.
Yakovlev, E. P.: *Esteticheskoye chuvstvo i religioznoe perezhivanie*, Moscow, Sovetskii Khudozhnik, 1964.

Articles:

Benecke, Heinrich: 'Errinerungen an Feuerbach', in *Die Tägliche Rundschau*, Berlin, Easter, 1890.
Geertz, Clifford: 'Religion as a Culture System', in Michael Banton (see *supra*), pp. 1–44.
Inkeles, Alex: 'Models in the Analysis of Soviet Society', in (1966) *Survey*, No. 60, p. 3.
Kamenka, Eugene: 'The Baptism of Karl Marx', in *The Hibbert Journal*, vol. LVI (1958), pp. 340–51.
Urmson, J. O.: 'On Grading', in Flew, A.G.N. (see *supra*), pp. 159ff.

Index

For subject headings, the reader should also consult the Table of Contents (p. v). Feuerbach's main works are indexed under the English titles used in the text; mere citations have not been included.

Absolute, the, Absolute Idea, 11, 76, 78
aesthetics, 150, 165–6
after-life, 41
agnosticism, Feuerbach's, 102, 105–6, 109–10
alienation, 114, 165, 167; in philosophy, ix, 7–8, 75, 79–80; in religion, 46–7, 51–5
Althusser, Louis, 151
Anaxagoras, 77
Anderson, John, 175
Annenkov, P. V., 156, 181
anthropotheism, 16, 154
art, 122, 165–6
Avineri, Shlomo, 160

Bachmann, C. F., 26, 104, 176
Bacon, Francis, 77
Baillie, J. B., 155
Bakunin, Michael, 117, 159, 172
Banton, Michael, 167, 181
Barth, Karl, viii, 150, 161
Basic Propositions of the Philosophy of the Future, ix, 26–7, 89–91, 125–8, 153, 170, 178, 180
Baten'kov, G. S., 181
Bauer, Bruno, 14, 163
Bayer, K., 177
Bayle, Pierre, see *Pierre Bayle*
being, category of, 57–8, 74–5, 159–60
Benecke, Heinrich, 168, 183
Bentham, Jeremy, 174
Berdyaev, Nikolai, viii, 151
Berkeley, Bishop, 70
Blakeley, T. J., 171, 181
Boehme, Jacob, 74
Bolin, Wilhelm, x, xiv, 32, 158, 160–1, 170, 179, 181

Brunner, Hans Kasper, 20
Brunner, Nanette, 20, 21
Bruno, Giordano, 77
Brunquell, Johann Salomo, 20
Buber, Martin, viii, 151
Buddhism, 175
Büchner, Ludwig, viii

Cabanis, Pierre-Jean Georges, 106
Campanella, Tommaso, 77, 168
categorical imperative, 136
celibacy, 55
Chamberlain, W., ix, 181
chaos, man's reaction to, 67
Cherno, Melvin, 153, 180
Chernyshevsky, N. G., 150
Chojecki, K. E., 16, 154, 156
Christ, as subjectivity, 49–51, 164
Christianity, 46–51, 153–4, 163–4, 165
classes (estates), 167
Collected Works (1846–66), xiii, 27, 31–2, 178–9
Collected Works (Bolin and Jodl, 1903–11, expanded and reprinted 1960–4), xiv-xv, 180
Collected Works (East German Edition 1968–), xiii-xiv, xv, 180
common experience, 93–6
Condillac, Étienne Bonnot de, 99
conscience, 132
co-operation, in ethics, 134–5, 141–3
Copernicus, 92, 93, 104, 108, 121
Creation, the, 50, 61
Cudworth, Ralph, 164, 181
Cuvier, Frédéric Georges, 94

Darwin, Charles, viii
Daub, Karl, 21, 23
Deborin, A. M., 18, 40, 157, 161, 170, 171, 181
dependence (in religion), 41–2, 56, 162–3
Descartes, René, 9, 23, 71, 77, 83, 85, 121, 135, 169; *cogito* of, 4, 9, 71, 85; dualism of, 70, 84
Deubler, Konrad, 32
Dewey, John, 169
dialectic, in Fichte, 8–9
Diderot, Denis, 3
Dobeneck, Ludwig von, 158
Doctoral dissertation (*de ratione, una, etc.*), xiv, 23–4, 176
Dorguth, F., 103, 104, 106, 107, 170, 177
drives, 175
Dühring, Eugen, 163
Durkheim, Emile, 63, 65, 181
duty, 133–6, 173, 174

ego, 7–11, 72–3, 124, 154
egoism, 126, 127, 172
Egypt, 44, 163
Eliot, George (Marian Evans), vii, xv, 15, 153, 166, 167, 180
emancipation of man, 114–15, 117–19
Emmeran, Eusebius, 178
empiricism, British, Feuerbach's critique of, 104–5, 168
empiricism, Feuerbach's, 25–6, 93–4, 151, 168, 175
Engelhardt, J. G. V., 25
Engels, Friedrich, vii, viii, 38, 156, 157, 160, 171, 181, 182; on Feuerbach, vii, 38
Erdmann, J. E., 26, 77, 158, 159, 176, 177
essence, 160, 166, 170
essence, essentialism in Feuerbach, 96–7
Essence of Christianity, xv, 15, 16, 26, 27, 28, 39–68, 125–8, 161, 162, 166, 167, 178; English translation, vii, ix, xv, 180; French

translation, vii
Essence of Faith in Luther's Sense, The, ix, 39, 153, 164, 178, 180
Essence of Religion, xiii, 27, 39–68, 163, 178, 180
Ethical Fragments, 32
ethics, 100, 124–45, 164–5, 171
Evgrafova, E. V. 154, 156, 181
existence, see *being*
existentialism, viii
Exposition, Discussion and Criticism of the Leibnitzian Philosophy, 25, 156, 161, 176, 178–9

Fabians, 123, 144
faith, 52–3, 126–8
family, the, 167
Faust, 5–6, 153–4
Feder, Johann Georg, 138
fetishism, 126
Feuerbach, Anselm (painter), 20, 157
Feuerbach, (Joseph) Anselm (classical philologist), 20
Feuerbach, (Paul Johann) Anselm von (criminologist), 18, 19, 20, 21, 22, 23, 24, 31, 157, 158
Feuerbach, Bertha, *née* Löw, 25
Feuerbach, Eduard (August), 20, 31
Feuerbach, Ernst Wilhelm, 158
Feuerbach, Friedrich, 20
Feuerbach, Helen (Rebecca Magdalene), 158
Feuerbach, Johann Henrich, 20
Feuerbach, Karl (Wilhelm), 20, 22, 158
Feuerbach, Leonore (Rosina Eleanore), 158
Feuerbach, Ludwig, childhood and student days, 20–4, 158; as university lecturer, 23–5; marriage and Bruckberg, 25–31, 159; at Rechenberg, 31–2; death of, 32; influence and reputation of, vii–x, 15–17, 149–52, 155, 156–7, 160, 170–1
Feuerbach, Sophie Sybille Christine (*née* Krause), 20

Feuerbach, Wilhelmine (née Tröster), 21, 158
Fichte, J. G., 78, 83, 85, 125, 129, 153, 154; philosophy of, 7–13; Feuerbach's critique of, 36, 72–4, 85, 168
Fischer, Kuno, 159
Fleming, William, 153
Fleury, Victor, 179
Flew, A. G. N., 175, 181
Frederick William IV, 83, 115
freedom, 115–21
free will, 174
Freud, Sigmund, viii, 37, 63, 65, 99, 167

Gans, Eduard, 159
Gebhard, Peter von, 157
Geertz, Clifford, 66, 67, 167, 168, 183
God, and his predicates, 55, 57–8; as *ens realissimum*, 48; as ethical predicate, 164–5; as logos, 50; as love, 49–50, 51; as moral perfection, 59; as Reason or Understanding, 48–9; as wholly other, 57–8, 161, as Will, 49
Gönner, 19
Goethe, Johann Wolfgang von, 5–6, 13, 120, 153, 154
grace, 51, 60
Granovskii, T. N., 16, 156
Greece, 44–5, 161, 163
Green, T. H., 165, 166
Grose, T. H., 165, 166
Grün, Karl, xiii, 158, 159, 179
Grünhut, Max, 157, 181

happiness, 130–44; drive to, 130–3, 137–40, 144, 174
Hare, R. M., 145, 175, 181
Harich, Wolfgang, xiii
Hauser, Kaspar, 19
Haym, R., 159, 179
hedonism, 125, 132–3
Hegel, G. W. F., 8, 10–14, 15, 37, 68, 83, 95, 153, 154, 160; and Feuerbach, 16, 18, 21–4, 26,

69–70, 92, 104, 125, 151, 158, 160, 161, 162, 176; Feuerbach's critique of, 69, 74–80, 84–7, 105, 129, 168
Heidegger, Martin, viii, 15
Heidenreich, F. W., 179
Heine, Heinrich, 12, 155
Heinze, Max, 172
Heinzen, Karl, 159
Heller, Erich, 153, 181
Helvétius, Claude-Adrien 24, 99, 125
Hera, 55
Herbart, Johann Friedrich, 37
Herder, Johann Gottfried, 29, 153
Hertz, Frederick, 5
Herwegh, Georg, 28
Herwegh, Marcel, 179
Herzen, Alexander, 16, 156
hieroglyphics, in theory of knowledge, 105–6
History of Modern Philosophy from Bacon of Verulam to Benedikt Spinoza, 24, 26, 158–9, 176, 178
Hitzig, Eduard, 23
Hobbes, Thomas, 121
Hock, C. F., 176
Holbach, Paul-Henri Thiry, Baron d', 24, 125, 130, 172
Hook, Sidney, 15, 79, 93, 105, 112, 156, 162, 169, 181
Hume, David, 3, 5, 70, 134, 165, 166, 181

Idealism, German, 11, 83–4, 154, see also *Kant, Fichte, Schelling, Hegel*; Feuerbach's critique of, 69–80, 160
imagination, 166
immortality, 161
Incarnation, the, 49–50, 53
India, 118–19
industry, vii-viii, 122
infinite, infinity, 61, 76, 86–7, 116; as characteristic of God, 57–9
Inkeles, Alex, 63, 64, 183
Israel, see *Jews, Judaism*

I-Thou, viii, 50, 101–2, 121–2, 125, 134–5, 150–1, 172

Jacobi, F. H., 129
Jaspers, Karl, 15
Jehovah, 45
Jews, Judaism, 45–6, 62–3, 163
Jodl, Friedrich, x, xiv, 92, 158, 179, 181

Kamenka, Eugene, 156, 160, 163, 167, 171, 172, 174, 175, 181–2, 183
Kamienski, H., 154
Kamptz, von (Commission), 22
Kant, Immanuel, 5–7, 9, 10, 11, 12, 37, 70, 92, 95, 153, 168; ethics of, 124, 130, 174; Feuerbach's critique of, 84, 104, 125, 170
Kapp, August, 179
Kapp, Christian, 24, 27, 94, 95, 158–9, 177
Kapp, Emilie, 155
Kapp, Friedrich, 31, 32
Keller, Gottfried, 159
Khanikoff, Jacob von, 32
Kierkegaard, Søren, viii, 150
Knapp, L., 112, 179
knowing, as practical activity, 99
knowledge, problem and theory of, 85–6, 98–107, 169
Kohut, Adolf, 158, 172, 180, 182
Kriege, Hermann, 159
Kuhn, J., 176

La Mettrie, Julien Offray de, 106
Lange, Friedrich Albert, 37, 160, 172, 182
Langer, Susan, 67, 168, 182
language, as social, 122
Lassalle, Ferdinand, viii, 32
Lavrov, Peter L., 38, 156, 160, 182
law (jurisprudence), 136, 174
laws, natural, 140–1
Lectures on the Essence of Religion, ix, xiii, 30, 39–68, 153, 179, 180
Leibniz, Gottfried Wilhelm, 25, 153, 154. See also Exposition, Discussion, etc.

Lenin, V. I., 167, 171
Lewes, George, 15
Locke, John, 70, 171
Löwith, Karl, 151, 153, 154, 182
logic, and reality ('nature'), 70–7; Feuerbach's inadequate treatment of, 37, 95–6
Loos, Alexander, 153, 180
love, 53, 116–17, 121–2, 126–8, 129, 144, 172–3, 174
Lovejoy, Arthur O., 3, 153, 182
Lubac, Henri de, S. J., 155, 182
Lüning, Otto, 31
Lützelberger, E. C. J., 177
Lukács, Georg, 153, 182
Luther, 46, 88, 161, 164, 165
Luther II (Feuerbach as), 150

Malinowski, B., 68
man, and nature, 84–6, 123; as basis of philosophy, 35–7; as basis of religion, 35–6, 39–68; as purely active, 11; as species-being, 119–22; as universal being, 115–20; Deist and Enlightenment view of, 3–4; distinguished from animals, 115–16, 118–19; Feuerbach's concept of, 85–6, 96, 114–23; Kant's view of, 6–7
Manheim, Ralph, 153, 180
Marcuse, Herbert, 3, 11, 153, 155, 182
Marr, Wilhelm, 159
marriage, 55
Marsak, Leonard M., 153, 182
Marx, Heinrich, 21
Marx, Karl, ix, 5, 8, 10, 11–12, 13, 14, 59, 110, 145, 154, 182; and Feuerbach, vii, viii, ix, 18, 37, 83, 90, 97, 115, 118, 121, 122–3, 150, 156–7, 160, 172; on Feuerbach, vii, 16, 27, 117–18
Marxism, 169; and Feuerbach, vii–viii, 156–7, 165–6, 167; on religion, 65, 165–6, 167
masochism, 175
materialism, 36, 99–100, 104–13; 171; in ethics, 124–5

Max Joseph, Crown Prince (later Maximilian I, King of Bavaria), 18, 19, 23
medical materialism, 110–13, 171
medicine, 124, 143
method, Feuerbach's, 36–8, 92–7, 160
Mexico, ancient, 43–4
Mill, J. S., viii, 175
mind, and body, 77, 112; and nature, 70–3, 84–5, 87; in Fichte, 7–10; nature of, 106–9
miracles, 40, 44, 46, 50, 163
models, sociological, 63–5
Moleschott, Jacob, viii, 30, 110, 112, 113, 125, 171, 179
monotheism, 43, 45–7
Montgelas, Maximilian, Graf von, 18
Morell, J. D., 168, 182
mystery (in religion), 61

Napoleon, 13, 19
'Natural Science and the Revolution', 30, 110–13, 179
Nature, and man, 166; as distinguished from man, 74, 109–10; as ultimately unknowable, 109–10
nature gods, 44–5
Nietzsche, Friedrich, viii, 5, 123, 150, 154
Nirvana, 175
nominalism, Feuerbach's, 102, 105
Nowell-Smith, P. H., 137, 175, 182

objectivity, in knowledge, 101–2
Old Testament, 164
On Philosophy and Christianity, 39
ought and is, 140–1

paganism, 163
particularity, particulars (individuality), 75–6, 165
Pascal, Blaise, 14
Passmore, John A., 159, 164, 182
Paulus, H. E. G., 21
Petrashevskii, M.V. (Butashevich-), 155; his circle, 16, 154, 166

Peursen, C. A. van, 162, 182
Philosophical Fragments, 35, 70–1, 167
philosophy, and theology, 36–7; as criticism, 87–8; as practical, 88–9; Feuerbach's conception of, 76–8, 87–91; Feuerbach's critique of, ix, 83-7, 99–100, 123; Feuerbach's transformation of, ix–x, 83–91. See also Idealism
Pierre Bayle, xiii, 25, 161, 163–4, 164–5, 167, 177, 179
Plato, 104, 105, 164
pleasure, 137, 138–9, 175. See also happiness
Plekhanov, G. V., 105, 157, 167, 170
polytheism, 43–5, 163
Pope, Alexander, 3, 6, 153
Popper, Karl R., 175
praxis, vii, 88
prayer, 39–40
Preliminary Theses for the Reform of Philosophy, 15, 26–7, 89–91, 125–6, 178
'principles' (distinguished from 'laws'), 140–1
projection, 167. See also alienation
proletariat, 167
Prometheanism, before Feuerbach, 5–14, 123, 153–4
proof, 85–6
Protestantism, 114
Proudhon, Pierre-Joseph, vii, 154
Providence, 46, 51

Radbruch, Gustav, 157, 182
Ramus, Peter, 168
Rawidowicz, S., 151, 156, 158, 159, 161, 168, 182
realism, Feuerbach's, 102–3
Reason, Age of, 4
reason, as human attribute, 116–17, 121–2
reduction, cognitive, 165
reductionism, 96–7, 112–13, 166–7
Reiff, J. F., 72, 178

religion, and Freudian view of, 63, 65; and politics, 114–15; as a dream, 35–6, 39–40, 50, 59–60; as comforting, 52–3; as feeling, 43–5; as practical, 39, 66–8; Deist and Enlightenment view of, 3–4; distinguished from science and philosophy, 40; Feuerbach's critique of, x, 35–80; Fichte on, 12; Heine on, 12–13; Left Hegelians on, 14; Marxist analysis of, 65; modern anthropological approach to, 65–8
Reinhold, Karl Leonhard, 157
Renan, Ernest, viii, 15, 155, 182
Riazanov, David, 159
Riedel, C., 93, 169, 177
Riley, Edith M., 155
republicanism, Feuerbach's, 114–15
revelation, 54
Revolution, of 1848, and Feuerbach, 28–31
Ringseis, J. N., 177
Robinson Crusoe, 172
Rome, 161, 163, 164
Rosenkranz, Karl, 176
Rousseau, Jean-Jacques, 4, 20
Roy, Joseph, vii
Ruge, Arnold, 27, 28, 29, 117, 159, 172
Ryle, Gilbert, 107, 138, 175, 182

Sacraments, 54
sacrifice, 39
sanctions, 133
Sartre, Jean-Paul, viii, 151
Sass, Hans-Martin, xv, 180
Schaller, J., 126, 172, 182
Scheler, Max, viii, 151
Schelling, Friedrich Wilhelm Joseph von, 7–13, 37, 83, 153, 154; Feuerbach's critique of, 27, 73–4, 78, 170
Schiller, Friedrich, 120
Schleiermacher, Friedrich Daniel Ernst, 23, 41, 161
Schopenhauer, Arthur, 5, 11, 17, 170
Schuffenhauer, Werner, xiii, xv, 159, 183
Schwinge, Professor, 157
science, 77–8, 96, 121–2, 158, 168; as normative, 140–1
self-determination, 11
Sengler, J., 177
senses, 106, 115–16
sense-perception, 98–100
sensualism, Feuerbach's, 98–100
sex, as essential human characteristic, 55; in religion, 51–2, 54–5
social democracy, 123, 144
Sombart, Werner, 163
space and time, 84–5
species-being, 119–22, 127–8, 150; in epistemology, 101–2; in religion, 46–50
Spencer, Herbert, viii
Speshnev, N. A., 16, 154, 156
Spinoza, Benedict (Baruch), 11, 23, 59, 71, 80, 103, 153
Stahl, F. J., 176
Starcke, C. N., x
Stirner, Max, 96, 119, 126
Strauss, David Friedrich, 14, 15, 155, 183
suicide, 129
supernatural, 57–9, 62
Suttie, Ian, 174
systole and diastole, in religion, 62

Tay, Alice Erh-Soon, 174, 182
Telesius, 77, 168
Theogony, xiii, 31, 39–68, 160–1, 163, 167, 179
theology, 35, 79–80, 160, 169; and philosophy (as form of alienation), ix, x, 60, 78–80; distinguished from philosophy, 37; distinguished from religion, 53–4, 60, 164; Feuerbach's disillusionment with, 69
theory of knowledge, 170–1
thought, nature of, 106–9. See also materialism

Thoughts on Death and Immortality, xiv, 24, 25, 26, 161, 176
Tol', E. F. G., 156, 166
Toward the Critique of Hegelian Philosophy, 16, 177
Trinity, the, 63
truth, criterion of, 7–9, 71–2; Feuerbach's theory of, 101–2
Tsameryan, I. P., 162, 183

Ueberweg, Franz, 172
universality, in ethics, 131–5
Urmson, J. O., 175, 183

Vaihinger, Hans, 168, 183
Vaillant, Eduard, vii
Vico, Giambattista, 110, 150
Virgin, the (Mary), 40, 50, 51, 61

Vogel, Manfred H., 153, 180
Vogt, Carl, 29
Voltaire, 4, 153

Wigand, Otto, 28, 29, 31
will, 173; as human attribute, 121–2, 176–7; divine, 168; in ethics, 124–5, 129–31, 173; noumenal, 6, 10, 124–5
wishing, law as, 136, 174; morality as, 136, 145; religion as, 39–42
Wittgenstein, Ludwig, 175

Yakovlev, E. P., 165, 183

Zeus, 45, 55
Zweig, Arnulf, 153